Publisher's Note

FINALLY, HERE IS THE BREAKTHROUGH work that solves the mystery of UFOs and paranormal phenomena. After more than a half-century of investigation, Eric Julien offers a global and scientific solution to one of the greatest challenges known to science. For Julien, the fractal nature of time and its three dimensions led to the emergence of a revolutionary global theory: Absolute Relativity!

Even though this work is of a scientific nature, the general public can easily understand it. The precise explanations in this book will highlight the mistakes of science and will furthermore offer insight into extraterrestrial technology, which the author calls ExtraTemporal. Diagrams are included.

The Science of Extraterrestrials explains anti-gravitation, propulsion of UFOs, alien abductions, formation of crop circles, strange luminous phenomena, poltergeists, ghosts, postmortem survival and time travel. All these phenomena are explained by this single, unique concept. This book will undoubtedly create a philosophical revolution.

The Science of Extraterrestrials
UFOs Explained at Last

ERIC JULIEN

English Translation: Estherella Carstens

alliesbooks.com

The Science of Extraterrestrials
ISBN 1-60177-101-0 (hardcover & dust jacket)

Copyright © Eric Julien, 2006
All rights reserved

First published in French by JMG Editions (France) ©, 2005

First published in English in USA by Allies Publishing, Inc.
Po Box 2187
Fort Oglethorpe
GA 30742

Alliesbooks.com is a trademark of Allies Publishing, Inc.
www.alliesbooks.com is the distributor of The Science of Extraterrestrials

alliesbooks.com

Designed by 1106 Design.

This book is printed by Sheridan Books, Inc. in the United States of America.

Allies Publishing, Inc. has joined the Green Press Initiative in order to save the
nature. www.greenpressinitiative.org

To Eve, Anna, Willyam and Divine

Contents

Introduction

THIS WORK ENDEAVORS TO DISCOVER extraterrestrial technology, explain UFO (unidentified flying objects) phenomena, describe parapsychology, understand anti-gravitation and the missing universal mass, decrypt fundamental forces, combine Einstein's relativity theory and quantum mechanics, unify matter and spirit, decipher the human psyche, capture the nature of dreams, increase our powers and turn our future upside down. All of this can be summarized by a single paradigm: the nature of space and time!

Let us set aside our skepticism and make an effort to forget all our certainties if only to admit that for as long as we read this book, well hidden from critics and sarcasm, absorbed in our pensive solitude, the world is not what we believe it to be. Let us simply accept the presence of non-terrestrial creatures that are different from us. Let us accept that their incredible technologies really do exist. Once you get past the first amazement regarding the explanation of the universal mechanisms described in this book, it will become difficult to doubt the reality of ETs. Extraterrestrials! Such a shock and yet such a logical and inevitable idea. The universe is extraterrestrial!

It is, however, preferable to qualify those we usually call ExtraTerrestrials as ExtraTemporals. This term seems closer to what distinguishes them from us while respecting the widely spread abbreviation ETs. In order to facilitate reading, the abbreviation ETs will be used to designate ExtraTemporals, and ST to define the term Space-Time. This is important to remember, for you will often encounter these terms in the course of this book.

The world of ufology[1] has been wondering about the reality of UFOs for more than fifty years. Testimonies are vast in number but an explanation is missing. Therefore, the phenomenon is repudiated. The following testimony should reconcile the logic of scientific facts, which we deny, with these appearances of great strangeness. The answer proposed here will not fail to challenge many established certainties. The famous American ufologist Professor Joseph Allen Hynek, who was at first very skeptical then wildly in favor of the reality of UFOs, wrote: "When we have the solution of the UFO enigma, I think that it will be revealed to be not just one step more in the advance of science, but a powerful and unexpected quantum leap."

This statement is renowned worldwide! There are dates in history that I believe should not be missed. This book proposes an unexpected solution. Even better, it proposes metaphysics! That is to say physics containing all physics: time has three dimensions! Direction, density and the present. To be more precise, time is three-dimensional, fractal and discrete (discontinuous). This new knowledge bridges the gap between the material and the spiritual world. Therefore, I will hopefully be able to translate the extraordinary genius of the profound laws of nature that leave a congruent portion of reality to the material probabilities.

No doubt you remember the *Matrix* film trilogy in which a small group of men and women succeeded in getting out of the illusory reality of the world. This is exactly what we are going to do, at least in thought. We are going to get out of the matrix for a moment, to understand the universe in which we live.

One cannot explain UFOs and paranormal phenomena with our current means of investigation, nor even with the present interpretation we have of the universe that surrounds us. It comes down to this: none of the criteria for ufology research have been updated. I pay tribute to the scientists of the planet who experience the anxiety of the subject to be resolved every day and who, when they turn around, find no one to whisper the solution. Yet they patiently pursue their research. Together we will discover what they call a new paradigm without which it is perhaps useless to search.

Before leaving our world to grasp the incredible exploits of UFOs, yet so simple once the nature of time has been understood, and the no less disturbing aspect of parapsychology, it would be useful to share with you a question that we need to ask ourselves continuously: to which extent are we prepared to accept the truth?

We assimilate in accordance with our beliefs, our fears and our convictions, even our scientific ones. Ultimately, and that is the most important part, the truth comes only to those who search for it and who make an effort to question themselves over and over again. Without that quest the taste of the truth will not make any sense.

Is not the quest for the absolute all about evolution? There is a link between ETs and this universal quest. Why should we establish such a link? For the simple reason that our need to decipher the mysteries of beings thought to be more advanced than we, the ETs, also applies to them. In other words, the ETs pursue their own quest of what is superior. This is why the upcoming worldwide contact is but one step towards an even greater destination for us. The principle according to which "one is always someone's predator" shows us that there are several degrees of evolution, including among those who are currently beyond our scope of analysis and parameters.

The evolutionary degrees of nature as we presently conceive them are not a view of the mind, but a tangible reality. Whether we study nature from the angle of the composition of its elements, its structure, its reproduction, its creatures or its social structure, the key word is the growth complexity of life. This complexity goes hand in hand with the amount of information processed by a system or a series of systems of which man is a significant example. However, this life form called man should not blind us, even if the functioning of the human brain remains enigmatic and miraculous. This complexity is the reality of a universal need present in all its dimensions. This fundamental complexity is the path of consciousness and freedom. In fact, the greater the freedom, the more expansive consciousness is and conversely. The more we discover, the more we access new means of discovery. History has proven so over and over again. Where does this consciousness and freedom end? What are the limits? Are there any? These are the exact questions the ETs will have to ask themselves. Why should it be any different for them? As long as the mystery remains, any creature will search for and advance towards the absolute!

However, a single word does not encompass its entire meaning. The most astounding fact is that this quest for the absolute justifies in itself the theory of the existence of ETs. Independent of cosmogonies, be they religious or not, once the dogmatic ignorance has been purged, transitional stages preceding the absolute must be "incarnated" by other life forms more complex than our own, more conscious and more liber-ated. A massive dose of blinding is required to make us close our eyes to the potential riches of the universe. Nothing prevents us from imag-ining life forms whose evolutionary stage would be, at best, similar to ours. However, what would be the value of that, since our current tech-nological state does not allow us to meet person to person. Our mod-ern technology barely enables us to reach the terrestrial outskirts.

It is important to remember that Earth hosts fourteen million differ-ent species in all evolutionary stages, including our own. Fourteen mil-lion on Earth alone! We have all heard of the equation of Drake, who formalizes the probabilities of existence of intelligent extraterrestrial life. With dozens of billions of stars, each galaxy is inevitably the cra-dle of abundant life, even if we merely consider the numerous molec-ular traces found in the gaseous galactic clouds. When we speak of ETs we can calculate that each habitable planet might also host several thousands or millions of species. What if there were several billions of habitable planets? Therefore, several millions of billions of species are competing for the qualification of ET. Amongst this astronomical num-ber of species it would be safe to assume that a large number consist of several millions individuals. Earth alone is inhabited by more than six billion people! This opens astonishing perspectives. Let us assume that 10^{30} creatures live relatively close to us in the universe.

Of whom do we speak when we speak of UFOs? We inevitably refer to ETs capable of reaching us geographically and therefore technologi-cally more advanced. Let us imagine that, in this not so distant part of the universe, only one individual out of one billion of one billion is more transformed (conscious) than we are. There would still be one thousand billion above us, which is approximately one hundred times more than there are human beings. We would still have to assume that all human beings are of the same evolutionary level, which I do not believe. The real question we should ask is what a more evolved life form looks like. Does this question regard their material technology, physical form or level of consciousness? It is quite possible that technology and con-sciousness are directly linked in such a way that technology itself is no longer just of a material nature. Let us assume this to be true from now on. As for the Fermi paradox, which asks: "If they exist, then why haven't we seen them?", our answer is that they dematerialize at will.

The exclusion of a third possibility suggests that an object is either material or immaterial. Not both at the same time or neither. Hence the importance of questioning this logicism. An extraterrestrial vessel is an object with the capacity to switch back and forth between the laws of quantum mechanics and the laws of classical mechanics or, in other terms, between the microscopic and the macroscopic. This transfer is possible due to the nature of time, by varying its flow.

Therefore, my approach is to guide us towards understanding a state in which this is possible. In fact, UFO and paranormal phenomena can be so stealthy and imperceptible because they vary the probability of being among us based on an extreme variety of forms, types of manifestations and durations.

Who is our teacher? Who is our creator? Compared to what is the human body the savage? If it were necessary to have our DNA and our range of perception altered in order to live inside an immaterial space vessel on a regular basis, who would be in the position to realize such a transformation? How would we reflect on the goal of ETs? For now our human eyes see only the darkness of the universe. But what about the future? Would our superhuman eyes be able to see something else? Billions of individuals traveling the cosmos and, tomorrow, how many of us? This is the question we should ask ourselves at the end of this book.

We are always and forever someone else's pupil. In all modesty, I would like to share my understanding of these phenomena that divide so many researchers, whether they are mentioned in this book or not, while respecting each person's convictions. A new vision of space and time challenges quite a few certainties that we have learned so far. If the world is indeed an illusion, it matters to know why this is true or not. It is not enough to say it or even to understand it. We need to live it.

You will not be asked to believe or to not believe, but to understand. The time for beliefs is over. The time has come to experience. The results may be extremely spectacular. This work is therefore an attempt to provide an answer to all the arguments and twilight zones that have stopped us from grasping the UFO phenomenon and those who pilot them. In this case the very nature of the conceptual solution of 3D time solves mysterious paranormal events. Science can finally come to terms with the civilization it serves while seeing what the latter has transmitted for thousands of years, i.e., the supernatural. From now on experiments can go public for the veil that clouds our future is finally being lifted. Let us understand that UFOs are not a simple pass-time for mad scientists but our own future! Ever since we became inhabitants of Earth, the status of "inhabitant of the galaxy" was dormant in us. Our wake-up call is probably imminent...

Hundreds of books have been dedicated to the issue of UFOs in the past fifty-plus years. Thousands of secret documents have been declassified. Thousands of photographs, dozens of videos and several thousands of eyewitness accounts have been distributed in news shows, magazines or on the Internet all around the world. In short, a mountain of information has been created, but we still do not have the slightest official, scientific explanation that allows us to understand the behavior of UFOs. We reconcile ourselves to the idea that their concept designers must be terribly advanced, insofar as we accept this extraterrestrial hypothesis. This is the most pertinent aspect possible to the true researcher.

To many of us it is the absence of official scientific explanations for a phenomenon so unique and so strange that prompts a global rejection. However, we have absolute proof! It is at least irrefutable to those who remain objective and use the means and techniques of a criminal investigation. This is definitely a crime against the known laws of physics, or rather lèse-majesté against an anthropocentric fringe of the scientific community that cannot conceive that its theories are incomplete. Since this phenomenon is inexplicable it does not exist, except, of course, in our imagination or for the secret service. Therefore, it remains in the back of our minds. Some people make a real effort to keep this status quo intact.

It is not surprising that this subject brings a smile to the faces of those convinced that this is a hobby of gentle and sympathetic enthusiasts. It is perfectly possible to remain in good spirits while acquiring skills, undoubtedly the highest possible on Earth, necessary to understand the captivating reality of this phenomenon. What would you say if you came face to face with an extraterrestrial right now? Would you still be in good spirits? I wonder…

One question immediately comes to mind. Why did ET visits multiply in the past fifty years? Were they not simply caused by a modern, large-scale, psycho-sociological myth as they would have us believe? Occurring all over Earth? Telling of totally distinct societies and cultures? Why did they only occur in the last fifty years?

The answer is crystal clear. Ever since the first atomic bomb exploded, countless ET creatures have learned that our knowledge is bringing us to the end of an era!

The use of the first nuclear weapon caused an echo of a magnitude of several light years. This test, called Trinity, was carried out in the framework of the Manhattan Project.

Date: 16 July 1945. Location: a few kilometers from Los Alamos[2] in the desert of New Mexico. The first man-made nuclear bomb exploded at half past five. A few weeks later, on 6 August, while Japan had already officially negotiated its surrender, Little Boy hit Hiroshima, followed on 9 August by Fat Man which destroyed Nagasaki. Yet, many scientists[3] who had designed and manufactured this nuclear weapon tried to convince Secretary of War Henry Stimson not to deploy this terrifying weapon. Hundreds of thousands of victims cried out in dismay. This echo still resonates in our conscience. Is it because of the revealing words spoken by Von Neumann,[4] one of the creators of the bomb who favored its use? He laconically stated: "We should not feel responsible for the world we live in!"

So, what should we feel responsible for, then? What can be said about our space ambitions? Would it not be logical if they asked us "what are your nuclear ambitions?" in order to get past the invisible frontier of our stellar development? We know the three effects of such a destructive device: the displacement of air, the heat and the radiation. But we are ignoring the time factor! As we will see, the first atomic explosion created a wave in what we might call the corridors of time! It dispersed well beyond our solar system. This caused a genuine time quake definitely not appreciated by certain ETs. Humanity is in danger and does not know why. Terrible secrets are being hidden from us by a few people in power. The same thing happened with the invisible Manhattan Project. Their actions and bizarre sense of responsibility may lead us down a path to slavery or even worse — to death.

We are at the dawn of a spectacular technological and cultural alliance or of a massive planetary destruction! You will bear witness. We must end the use of nuclear arms immediately. This book will try to show why by providing an essential piece of the puzzle. We feel we need to finish a story before drawing any conclusions. We will see in the following chapters that we were missing some fundamental keys to help us understand UFOs, which are perfectly material one moment, and ghostly and luminous the next, and invisible most of the time! Just like the ones who manipulate us.

Scientists often answer defensively: "I believe only what I can see." This adage is simply not logical when you ask: do you believe in atoms? You do? Can you see them? Do you believe in waves? You do? Can you see them? Do you believe there is a dark side of the moon? Have you seen it? These affirmations are not limited to the aforementioned examples, but are nullified by a million others. Do you have faith in scientists? All the better! But which ones?

We will soon come to see and realize that only our individual experiences exist. We will discover a new model that will profoundly alter our understanding of the universe. This is why widely known testimonies, new discoveries and emerging scientific hypotheses will be used as a basis. Some will say that the intrinsic coherence of the proposed framework for recurrent parameters in tens of thousands of observations is remarkable.

A wise man once said: "Debating only excites indigent minds. You know by experience, or you do not know."

This saying is deliberately rigid because far too often the opposite is fostered by critics, who not only voice their opinion about books they have never read, or read too fast, but who also judge experiences they have never had themselves. Bit by bit we build our truths on the unscrupulous or very sparse appreciation of certain people in the name of an objectivity the deeper meaning of which escapes us. Neutrality does not exist. Even neutrons have their anti-neutrons! Intellectual strabismus never leads to the truth. The mind, and its various limitations, favors the occurrence of inappropriate inferences. Experiencing doubt is necessary and of fundamental importance to our progress. I am in favor of clarified doubt. However, the gap between doubt and judgment is ignorance. Doubt already implies asking yourself questions. This in itself is a sign of intelligence.

Witnesses of unusual phenomena are generally met with insults. It is not so much the fear of the public condemnation of close ones, as long as it is just said in irony, but the personal attacks that render people silent.

Our society is based first and foremost on testimony. It is the number of witnesses, censors or interpreters that forges our beliefs. A candid French comedian said something like: "The fact that so many people are wrong does not mean they are right." We discover who we are by refraining from judgment!

The more we give in to the game of judgment, the more it draws us into aberration, because sooner or later we will come to fear the judgment of others.

A testimony is always strange to someone who has not had any similar experiences. The one who sees is not the one with the handicap. Many people on Earth are contacted by ETs. There is a current in ufology called the lunatic fringe.[5] This movement is probably distrusted most of all, because it is easier to accept the existence of an unusual object than of a superior consciousness, or at least superior in intelligence.

Let me stress the personal nature of my understanding of things. Some of my interpretations of phenomena may only reflect one facet of your own vision. One man cannot possibly encompass an entire encyclopedia and that is exactly why we need one another! Mutual respect and joint research are the essential characteristics of truth.

Because of their rarity, we do not much care about the witnesses of unexplained phenomena and we often totally disrespect these people. Therefore, I dedicate this book to all who have been ostracized, those who have been called crazy and crushed under the steamroller of current beliefs and lies of the state that have persisted for decades. Smiles will be erased as others will illuminate the faces of expanded minds. The latter will be more numerous, but what is extraordinary today will be ordinary tomorrow.

Let us once again look at a summary of an article[6] written by a French ufologist, who lists the following techniques for anti-UFO propaganda. It is an excellent résumé of the means used to keep us in check. So far they have worked quite well. You are cordially invited to continue reading this book, for it is possible you will change your mind. You may no longer have the desire to accept the following precepts.

- Reveling in abstract theoretical arguments in order to avoid having to consider the facts.
- Making believe that the world of science is opposed to the world of beliefs.
- Using the prestige of an authority to disguise the truth.
- Looking down upon the presented evidence by underestimating it.
- Dismissing the unknown as a known fact at the expense of a significant part of a fact.
- Indicating that common sense is the best policy. This is historically false.
- Abusively using the principle of parsimony, or Occam's razor, in spite of recognized scientific contradictions.
- Saying that the testimonies, even if there are numerous, are senseless, whereas scientific experiments are testimonies themselves.
- Affirming that there is no truth to inexistent phenomena, whereas it is scientifically impossible to prove the inexistence of an object.
- Making systematic connections between cases that are dubious and others that are not.
- Asking questions based on truths that are unfounded and come from reducing beliefs.
- Attacking the entourage of an advocate of the paranormal if it is unattackable.
- Attacking a person instead of responding to the relevance of his arguments.

Do not believe that the "debunkers" are not forewarned ufologists. On the contrary, sometimes treason is concealed under a layer of ufological culture and a simulated spiritual opening. The most brilliant debunkers have adjusted so well to their environment that they have managed to lure their "tribe" into a sweet illusion to disorient them more efficiently. This is a simple technique from psychological warfare. All wars pursue goals. This hides an upsetting truth that challenges the political, military, scientific and religious establishment. War strategies always depend on the interests at stake. The larger the number of people involved, the more efficient the tactics. Ill will is hardly ever just the tip of the iceberg of misinformation, which is why it often exists at an unconscious level and manifests in specific, invisible, mental stress. Fighting misinformation requires a strategy that is out of the ordinary, of unprecedented acumen and that is loving to others. The majority of ufologists are not strategists and have no idea of the goals involved.

In general, the scientific community greatly suffers from misinformation and is therefore not interested in ufology. The credo of science with regard to UFOs consists in the elimination of problems that prove irreproducible, ephemeral, intangible and essentially based on testimony. This thing cannot be categorized and does not give any clues as to its future presence. Worse even, it seems to break the laws of physics that have taken us centuries to establish. Since reproducibility is the only criterion used by science, or almost, it is horrified by ufology. Nevertheless, countless disciplines are interested in irreproducible phenomena, but an atmosphere of rejection prevails for reasons of anthropocentrism and propaganda: man has reached the peak of evolution!

It is true that it would be dangerous to forget, for it is capable of leading us to an obscurantism that takes us back to the Middle Ages, which was the source of so many witch hunts. Some scientists still work out theories, not just to justify a salary, or even to get noticed, but for a childishly simple reason: we do not explain everything! In fact, we do not even explain the essentials, starting with quantum mechanics that no one understands, not even those who teach it!

To those who claim they study UFO or paranormal phenomena while forgetting that theories, even strange ones, must also honor the observations of the sensitive world, let me answer that they are dragging their fellow man to a dead end. Science consists only of theories to be validated. Taking a plunge into the utterly astonishing quantum mechanics would greatly open the mind. Even quantum physics teachers affirm that in order to assimilate it, one should not try to understand it, because that is impossible. Ever since ufology came into existence, our peers have tried in vain to scientifically understand how such phenomena could occur. This failure has led to the choice of an opposite movement: the incorporation of the UFO or the paranormal phenomenon into our corpus of understanding. This prompted the creation of groups of skeptics that are just the result of this natural tendency to overlay our modern knowledge on the observations made by thousands of people. Therefore, it is absolutely necessary that the supernatural can be explained by means of traditional diagrams.

Whereas it is quite understandable why the common man is not interested in illustrative diatribes, which would a priori not change anything about his daily life, it is much more astonishing that researchers oppose anti-conformism, no matter how speculative it may seem. There is no complete answer to the question "how does the universe work?". We still do not have a comprehensive explanation. We can tell ourselves that the discussion will sprout several tracks. But some will hastily deny them since this is still a debate. By definition, if we contribute only part of the solution it remains incomplete. The history of ufology is but a series of incomplete solutions that have obviously been set aside because they do not suffice.

The overall principles of absolute relativity presented in this book should bridge the gap that separates supporters and skeptics.

I am a believer. I really believe in intelligence. I believe in the bright lucidity and the aptness of thoughts, remarks and finely expressed judgments of which everyone is capable, because in the end this is what it boils down to: individual consciousness does not form a pact with fame, but with the freedom to be who you are. I believe in the authentic human genius, because the kingdom of ideas is not ruled by a master but by ideals!

This book includes numerous explanatory diagrams of the ideas mentioned in this introduction. A synthetic and, hopefully, inspiring vision of new ideas seemed a more respectful approach than a fastidious formalist development. I have chosen to pay tribute to the busy reader and leave a personal interpretation of such figures up to you. It is preferable to open the door to the generative knowledge of other conceptions, because a discovery that is not shared is like an oasis that cannot expand. It quenches the thirst of only a few. Therefore, the texts and diagrams are complementary without always addressing the same things or addressing them in the same way. My goal is not to provide an exhaustive number of examples, but to introduce new models. It is therefore necessary to read the inherent scientific complexity behind the simplicity of the presentations. I do not pretend to have created academic proof; far from it. In addition, for the purist, these are but speculations and not theories. A theory is the solution of an equation. I formulate the wish that the new paradigm of absolute relativity so impregnates our consciousness that we get past the decisive point of a historical threshold that accumulates the gravest dangers ever known to man.

Finally, our lack of explanation has caused UFOs to become the object of ridicule. I would like to invite the critics of the entire world to review their point of view when they finish this book, because ridicule and, perhaps worse, the betrayal of mankind may very well turn against those who have steered that course. The scientific and religious world will undoubtedly comment on these hypotheses. But how much time do they have left? Let me say right now that these discoveries impose an increasing humility and call upon our human wisdom. Let me also say that the wall of secrets of governmental agencies and major religions will come tumbling down. Be prepared for the most spectacular page in the history of mankind.

Beyond our comprehension of the most mysterious enigma of the past, the future has launched the most important challenge of the heart. Would we be able to accept ETs? Would we be able to be at peace with ourselves so that they would accept us? Let us approach this book with enthusiasm, because it will sustain the intellect, the imagination as well as the heart.

PART

1

TIME FOR REFLECTION

CHAPTER 1

Introduction to the time phenomenon

LET US GET RIGHT TO THE HEART of the matter. Although this chapter only addresses some very elementary principles, I believe that the solution to most enigmas facing humanity can be found in the nature of time. Acknowledging this will shed light on both the mundane and exceptional situations, and will have an extraordinary impact on our approach towards the mysteries of the universe, which will increasingly lose their meaning. Let us assume from now on that the conceptualization of real time is manifold depending on the property we want to express. In view of the difficulty in visualizing this concept, I will use various means to represent it.

A parallel universe is merely a different time line. After all, time is three-dimensional! Space has three dimensions: length, width and height. It is however, less obvious that time also has direction, density and a present! What follows is a very simplified presentation of these three properties. They will be extensively discussed in another chapter.

DIRECTION designates time as everyone pictures it: the trajectory that goes from past to future. Some call it the fourth dimension. The past constitutes our memories as our imagination constitutes the future. The transformation of matter and events describes the apparent time arrow. However, in this case direction has a double arrow, which explains the existence of premonitions.

Keyword: transformation.

DENSITY is the eagerly anticipated encounter with the next great discoveries of fundamental science. What is time density? It is a time flow that influences the state of matter and the perception of which expands or contracts the generally agreed time unit.

Keyword: velocity or rate (of transformation).

PRESENT. Contrary to the generally accepted concept, the present is not a given. Every single moment, time becomes the near past after having been the immediate future, whether you count in nanoseconds or not. The present stands outside classical time. It is linked to the direction and density of time without having the same dimension. The present is intangible, uncreated and is defined by neither past nor future! I will elaborate this concept later on.

Keyword: permanence (the non-transformable).

A priori, it does not seem as if these simplistic definitions will revolutionize our everyday life. However, you will be more likely to perceive the impact of this vision after it is explained.

Let us return to the second term. I will use a simple and convenient image to clarify time density: the hourglass! The flow of sand is determined by the width of the neck through which the sand runs. The convention of our second is the diameter of this neck!

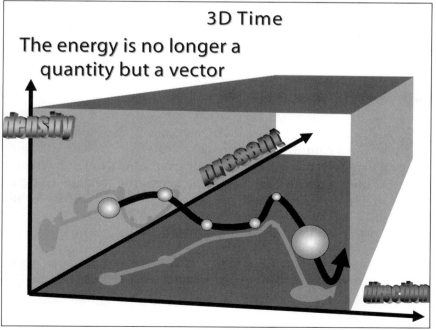

Figure 1

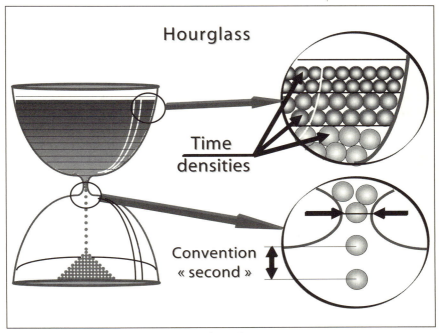

Figure 2

However, it so happens that the hourglass broadens above the neck. Let us gradate the sand in millimeters of time density. The higher we go, the more it broadens and the more grains of sand there are at each gradation. Time density equals the height of the hourglass! It is a sand flow rate. Time density is a relative quantity of time in accordance with the convention used. In the example of the hourglass, all densities come to pass at the same time! This is called fractal time. This notion is essential to the understanding of the universe.

A fractal is a natural or mathematical object that can be divided into parts, each of which is similar to the original object, but at a different scale. Whereas it is easy to visualize a geometric fractal (see figure below), this is more delicate when it comes to time. To be exact, I could call time density discrete time — whole number of values, hence the grains of sand to represent it — ingrained in fractal time (identical reproduction of an object but with increasing or decreasing values). In fact, time is discrete within temporal fractals. I should remind you that a discrete function is opposed to a continuous function in the sense that it is not linear but is made up of different consecutive steps. To grasp this notion of density, just picture an accelerated playback of a budding flower and you will have a better idea of what it is all about.

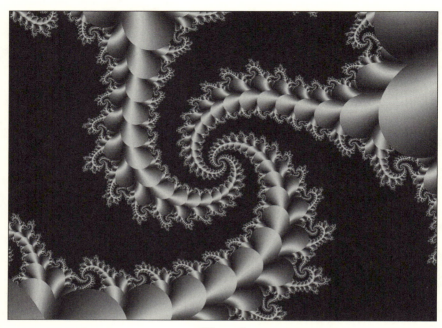

Figure 3

Figure 4

To make a long story short, one could say that a density superior to the convention of our second (a specific fractal) would be a fraction (another fractal), during which just as many things would happen, somewhat similar to the crop circle depicted below.

These actions can be translated into information. We will see next that this notion of information is crucial because it progressively replaces all the other physical magnitudes. In a superior temporal density there is indeed more information. Nevertheless, the mere fragmentation remains basic, because it does not take into account the gradual unification of the universe. It reduces the density of time to an arithmetical problem. However, that is not entirely true.

To give you a better understanding, imagine a building where each floor has its own passage of time. The higher you go in the elevator, the more time passes slowly, but it will be increasingly short for those who live on the first couple of floors. Your physical body is the first floor of our building called "consciousness." In the waking state of our everyday life we are monopolized by the physical ST. Therefore, physical time is our first choice (preferred time) to evolve in the material world.

At the end of the day you go to bed and put your body to a well-deserved rest. In other words, it is motionless. However, time is not.

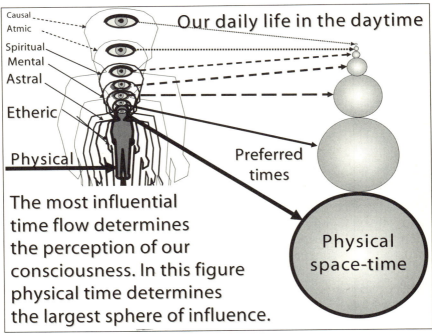

Figure 5

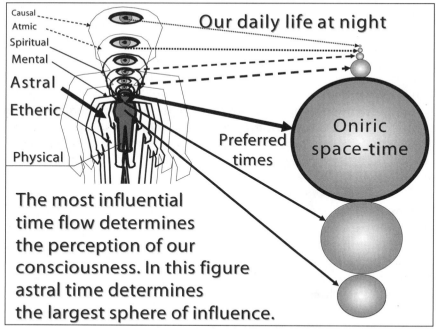

Causal
Atmic
Spiritual
Mental

Astral

Etheric

Physical

Our daily life at night

Preferred times

Oniric space-time

The most influential time flow determines the perception of our consciousness. In this figure astral time determines the largest sphere of influence.

Figure 6

The first hours of sleep are an opportunity to change floors. You enter into the dream state.

The person measuring this paradoxical stage will feel that everything is happening very fast. The consciousness of the person sleeping is two floors up. The person who has not taken the elevator is unaware of this and usually feels this stage has only lasted one or two seconds when looking at the clock of the encephalogram, which sees only a physical body that is on the same floor as he is. However, to the temporary tenant on the second floor many things have happened and several hours may have passed. His experience is what takes preference! This second floor is the realm of dreams.

Let us contemplate the realms of life we currently know: the mineral realm, the plant realm, the animal realm and the human realm. What follows is not a metaphor but a reflection of reality. We must make an effort to struggle out of our observer state. The rate (density) of transformation (direction) of each realm is radically different while all states are identical. From our point of view, plants change much faster than minerals and the same applies to animals and plants. In the same way, humans change much faster than animals thanks to the notion of self-consciousness. It is this rate of relative transformation that lays the foundation for time density.

A real second in the mineral realm reality corresponds to one hour of plant time reality, which represents one month of animal time reality and one year to us, the human observer, in our reality. These quantitative correspondences are, of course, of interest only for demonstration purposes and do not in any way reflect the actual relations. I am arguing, by the way, that density varies between sub-species, and even between families, within each realm. In addition, a fractal relationship is a non-whole number usually located between 1 and 2. I should stress that each category of natural creatures is a temporal fractal whole in itself. Evolution consists for each creature in connecting with multiple fractals in a superior time density of its own structure. As for man, I am arguing that time density varies depending on the evolutionary degree and the circumstances of life, because we are not all in the same boat.

Once we understand that we can achieve increased control of the incoming physical and mental information, our focus will render the

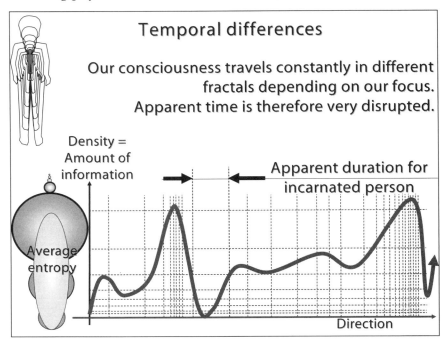

Figure 7

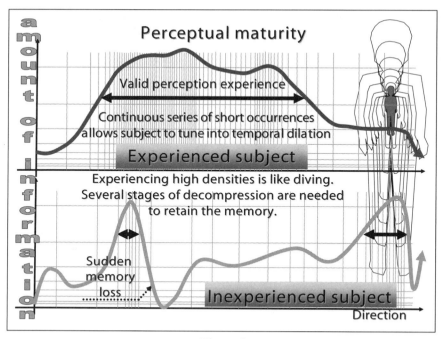

Figure 8

time flow of our experiences considerably more homogeneous and lasting. This is called perceptual maturity. It consists of developing a greater sense of discernment with regard to the nature of what we perceive.

As a result, significant misunderstandings exist between groups of people or between individuals, particularly when it comes to intuition and access to immaterial planes of existence. In part two we will discover in more detail where we can find these spatio-temporal dimensions (an inaccurate and overused term).

Nevertheless, it is important to picture the consequences and principles of fractal time as soon as possible. The various different mental perceptions are experienced at quite different levels according to the evolutionary state and the circumstances known to the individual consciousness.

What can be conceived of these realms is valid for superior time densities, i.e., for ETs. This qualification is therefore based on the active principle of temporal density variation they apply.

Having said that, I would like to make one remark. The description of these density variations is intrinsically related to the materiality, or

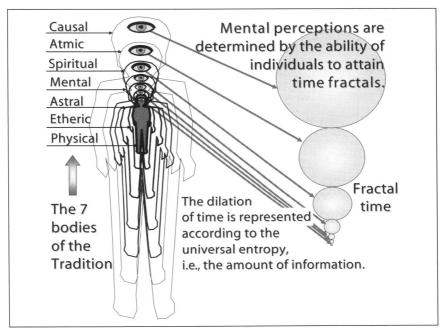

Figure 9

density, of matter. In other words, the more there is temporal density, the less there is material density. Hinting at the famous equation that applies to gravity and electric charge — two powers that we are able to measure without knowing their nature — time density is inversely proportional to the square of material density.

UFOs know how to go back and forth between different temporal densities. They have a so-called "temporal bubble." It surrounds the vessel with a variable density and allows them to produce the most fantastic phenomena.

To inferior realms we are just a hidden movement. We do not exist to plants unless we are the gardener. Therefore, we must learn to notice our own gardeners. As you will understand by now, UFOs travel the great intergalactic spaces effortlessly, because they cover the desired distance in a few of their new seconds by sufficiently changing the time density. This becomes even easier as space is contracting at the same time!

One concluding remark about this aspect: when you think about ETs, it is better to watch the hundredths of a second on your quartz watch than to look at the stars.

Figure 10

A small hint is necessary to prepare you for the developments that follow in the next chapters: the fundamental difference between past and future is the ability to choose. It will thus be easier to identify what the past and future look like depending on the attained level of this ability. In this sense, the past is just the territory of choices already made. The future is that of choices still to be made, while the "ultimate present" (past and future mixed up) is that of contemplation, of the absence of intent, of the "source" where the choice is pointless because everything has already been chosen.

In general you must understand that a millionth of a second (from our physical viewpoint) may contain millions of times more information than three hours (from our physical viewpoint), provided our consciousness is in the right time density to benefit from it. However, our consciousness fluctuates frenetically (when we have little concentration) between several time fractals. The preferred time will be the fractal used by our consciousness under specific circumstances. Since it often changes preferred times throughout the day, it thus accesses an average amount of information, which varies depending on the individuals and their focus of interest. Our evolution is aimed at obtaining more information.

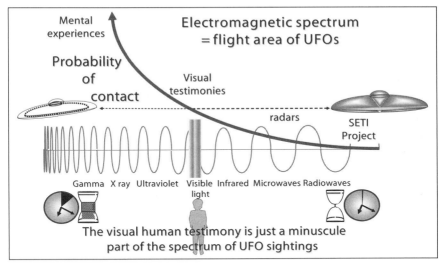

Figure 11

If we are to believe our archetypal realm of imagination, extraterrestrials will reach out to us in classic modalities. The SETI program (the Search for Extra-Terrestrial Intelligence) is in fact not helpful in establishing communication between species. This program aims at capturing electromagnetic signals on a radio frequency range with the help of large parabolas turned towards the sky, i.e., the lowest frequencies! When it comes to ET communication, radio astronomy is what the telegraph is to the Internet of the future. May I remind you that there are twenty-five magnitudes in the range of known frequencies.

The film *Contact* with the extraordinary Jodie Foster, based on a Carl Sagan novel that uses this technique, depicts a rather old-fashioned scenario, particularly since the argument of the language of supposedly universal prime numbers actually fails to convey the essence of a true message: love.

The universal language consists of thought forms, of inner experiences. The exogenous mathematic message is a phantasm of scientists, or of those who place all their trust in the current sciences, a scientism that probably thinks it epitomizes the crème de la crème of human evolution. Whereas mathematics is a universal language, it is unable to translate emotions. The highest probability of contact lies in the mental stage of our evolution, since it touches all aspects of knowledge.

CHAPTER 2

Experiments that raise questions

OF COURSE, THE HISTORY OF UFOLOGY does not begin in 1947. However, on 24 July of that particular year Kenneth Arnold saw nine objects in the sky near Mount Rainier in the state of Washington. This event marked a significant turning point in global history. It stood out for two reasons. First of all, the observer was particularly unique. Kenneth Arnold was a businessman as well as a pilot. While flying his airplane he saw boomerang-shaped objects that would later be known as flying saucers.[7] The second reason was generated by the media. Indeed, the development of press, radio and television underwent enormous growth and the event seemed sufficiently dramatic to be publicized. In fact, the extraterrestrial hypothesis was not even mentioned back then. A third reason can be added. Around the same date, the so-called Roswell crash occurred. Allegedly, a UFO crash-landed in Roswell, New Mexico accidentally. Let me be clear about this. The misinformation episode that took place in 1995 and used the filmed autopsy of a Roswell alien was aimed at discrediting this serious and embarrassing Roswell affair in an elaborate scheme.

Do not forget that Roswell was the first nuclear armament site. The clumsy denial of the UFO crash, by showing a Project Mogul weather balloon as an alleged explanation, concealed the real interests of linking ETs and nuclear weapons at a time when nuclear development programs soared in the framework of a costly and global geopolitical strategy. Endangering such a strategy in the middle of the Cold War was unthinkable. Therefore, a killjoy UFO had to be eliminated from the public debate.

A series of events thus came to trouble the minds just at the end of a horribly destructive war. Nuclear weapons marked the beginning of a new era. However, was this immeasurably lethal weapon related to the incursion of the cosmos as shown on television? Was it sheer coincidence? Far from it. The pressing question on everyone's lips is: did the American government take possession of ET technology?

The scientific development that follows will further your understanding of the multidimensional universe in which we live. I therefore invite you to gradually enter a state of reflection that uses a combination of audacity and surprise. This stage is vital before discovering the explanations about the reality of our world as I understand it, and our place in it. Once certain principles become clear, the solutions will be accessible. Please remember when you read this book that the abbreviation ETs is used to designate ExtraTemporals and that ST stands for space-time.

CHAPTER 3

Ufology: an ambivalent world

I PAY TRIBUTE TO THE REAL UFOLOGISTS who always have the interests of truth and happiness of mankind at heart. They deserve our utmost respect. As in scientific practice, most relations that exist between ufologists reflect their own preconceptions. Exactly where one would expect lively and curious minds, a dust-covered indifference to fundamental questions has crept in. Several thought currents live side by side and many people seem convinced that the truth is inaccessible, whereas, in parallel, science bases its progress on experiences, even if they are imperfect.

Countless debates take place between people of very different cultural and intellectual backgrounds. Renewed public interest has caused the revival of the same questions and the same answers in a deleterious climate of misinformation transmitted by the media, the worst failings of which resurface where you least expect them. Everyone chooses their favorite hypothesis and crosses swords with those advocating opposing theories. The extraterrestrial, psychological, sociological, psychopathological, parapsychological, religious, natural or military hypotheses are some of the most widely accepted. The conspiracy dimension often surfaces in the first and the last, while the real secrets are being kept from us by the misinformation orchestrated by governmental agencies.

Few have accepted the idea that all hypotheses may be valid at the same time. In long-winded casuistry, such an event will be part of one or the other, and sometimes of several at the same time.

Some ufologists have become debunkers, copiers or virtual librarians because they feel powerless. Like everywhere else, ufology is struck by battles of the clans from which leaders emerge. Some spend more time murdering each other than trying to understand. This is one of the reasons why the study of UFOs has not made much progress. Ufology seems to be a private hunt, like intellectual property without a patent. As a consequence, the flying saucer phenomenon transformed from a bubbly torrent to a swamp of bitterness in the past fifty years or so, by continuously using the same investigation methods to no avail. To let the skeptics off the hook, it is not easy to see through the cloud of fiction mixed with the facts of authentic cases. Those who continue to search despite numerous deceptions deserve our respect. We sometimes open our minds to the unknown in vain, or feel betrayed by the untruthful romantic image portrayed by certain minds in search of self-help, taking advantage of the good will of others. This is why my solidarity still lies with the enlightened skeptic. Nevertheless, ufology would benefit from changing tools without changing its vocation by building upon the proven powers of the psyche. The relationship we should have with the ETs requires maturity. While some ponder the UFO phenomenon passively by gathering eyewitness accounts — like ufological stamp collecting — others go about it more actively by communicating with the UFO occupants. This may be the only possible way to proceed. Perhaps we should never have forgotten that "the others" exist in the first place! That is when we understand that the lights at night express themselves, too. They address us every time they show themselves and — if we believe absolute relativity — even more so when they do not show themselves. So what is their message?

CHAPTER 4

The non-debate

WHEN WE SPEAK ABOUT strange circumstances, dozens of questions come to mind and rightfully so. We continuously seek to reconfirm the nature and the reason of our being. Our efforts are focused on controlling our environment to give our actions meaning. The primary reason for the presence of so many critics of the UFO phenomenon is that it is beyond our control! Many skeptics who lack the power of discernment raise and cast doubt on the psychological balance of witnesses to reassure themselves that they are adults whose feet are firmly planted on the ground. Perhaps their feet are not on, but in the ground, preventing them from taking a step forward. It would not be difficult to turn the tables on them. What possesses them to categorically refuse to accept UFOs as ET technology? Which motive, which psychological mechanism prevents them from seeing the imperfections of our intellectual inability? It would be quite interesting to turn this into an elaborate study in order to ascertain the exact influence of their controlling instinct. A well-known adage says that knowledge is power. Let us start by breaching the mysteries of science and assess the nature of the secrets of the powers that be, secrets made up of deliberate sarcasm. The most common response, however, is a natural rejection.

This may seem astounding, but I do not believe in the supernatural! There is only the unexplained natural. This natural is so amazing, so imaginative that we can only see its proscenium.

Let us briefly discuss our common difficulty to perceive reality. UFO and paranormal phenomena are based on scientifically libertarian principles that go beyond the generally known level of freedom. In essence they are fast, intangible and cannot be controlled.

Material proof of these phenomena is very difficult to obtain. It is true that we do not have any direct material evidence for the existence of the smallest components of the matter forming the framework of quantum mechanics. At best, we have some convincing signs. At least that is how many of us will see UFO photographs and videos. Nevertheless, we have been handling this concept with ease. We entered the conceptual world to understand this matter and establish its structural relations a very long time ago. This is also what has led researchers to work out string theories by combining quanta and relativity, thus allowing us to imagine what transpires beyond an inaccessible threshold. In actual fact, this theory does little more than affirm the existence of small vibrations, the most intangible objects, to say the least. The world itself is immaterial.

This assertion only stresses the extent of the hypotheses compared to the certainties, and to what degree the former question the latter. Let me point out that quantum mechanics (for quantities or quanta) is restricted exclusively to the study of measurable phenomena. Unlike classical theories, it does not describe what goes on between measurements.[8] How much do we know about quantum mechanics? We know that the observer is an integral part of the theory! The relativist theory is specifically interested in the relations between magnitudes to explain the functioning of the universe, especially gravitation. Einstein understood that these were dependent on the reference system. How much do we know about general relativity? We know that the gravitational fields are space-time distortions near important masses. Take an observer, add some space-time distortions and immaterialist conceptions are born.

The natural tendency of human reason to content itself with its deductive powers is caused by its self-limiting nature. It deduces its own investigative powers by the same tool that diminishes it: logic. We need to think outside the box of our traditional thought forms and reintroduce new data to go beyond their boundaries. That is what this book is all about. This dilemma explains why skeptics are lucid and avant-garde artists are on the right track. On one side we find an instrument — reason — on the other, a concept — transcendence. Having said that, the two can be united. However, this delicate endeavor is only destined for those who agree to set aside their anthropocentric approach to research. It is impossible to be both judge and participant without falling into the trap of preconceived judgment. As we will see, however, everything can be explained!

Erwin Schrödinger proposed the quantum version of a particle's wave function Ø (r,t), where every moving particle is associated with a bundle of concentrated waves in space, of which the propagation equation is as follows[9]:

$$i\hbar\,(\partial/\partial t)\phi(r,t) = -\,(\hbar^2/2m)\Delta\phi(r,t) + V\,(r)\phi(r,t)$$

where i is the imaginary number, $\sqrt{-1}$, r is the position of the particle, t is time, and Δ is the Laplacian[10] operator. To the right of the = we find kinetic energy (where $\hbar = h/2\pi$, h is Planck's constant) and potential energy. However, what is the meaning of Ø? The physicist Max Born affirmed that the square of the wave function at a given point constitutes the probability to find the particle at this point at the moment in question. The wave functions then become probability waves. The wave function Ø(r, t) is also called amplitude of probability of presence!

A simpler formalism, which considers only a single displacement axis (x), allows us to write the wave function with two variables: t and x, i.e., a time and a position on the disruptive sine curve. This is written as $\psi(t, x)$, or yet f(x-ct) where c is the propagation speed, t is the moment of measurement and x is the wave displacement. The wave function depends only on t and to x via the quantity t-|x|/c. The position of x therefore depends on the propagation speed and the moment of measurement.

Having said that, one of the great principles of quantum mechanics is the Heisenberg uncertainty principle, in which a limitation on accuracy of simultaneous measurement of observables, such as the position and the momentum of a particle, is expressed. It is important to understand that the Heisenberg uncertainty principle in quantum mechanics is based on the assumption that it is impossible to know x if t is not defined. This is like asking two questions at the same time, where the answer to one depends on the answer to the other. However, the definition itself of t or x influences the answer! The propagation rate is an uncertainty in itself, because it will be influenced by the measurement instrument. Furthermore, c depends on a number of iterations in the doubling theory. As a result, the trajectory concept is of no use in quantum mechanics, just as it is impossible to construct a device that determines the position of a particle without changing it. In fact, the underlying principle is the wave-corpuscle duality, but this duality is explained nowhere. In reality, quantum mechanics talks

about probability amplitude, and the existence of coincidence is introduced as a new principle.

Probability functions are an adequate formalism applicable to their
use, but they do not explain anything. They list possibilities depending
on a variable chance of occurrence. In other words, science explains the
nature of things based on a law that does not exist! Chance! Now, what
is left of science if we remove the laws? Pseudo-science! How can
chance be explained? It cannot be explained; we say "it is a coincidence, full stop." That does not seem very scientific. In fact, this is the
essence of science, the lack of an explanation about the origin of things.
Therefore, the key to solving the problem is explaining the nature of
chance and its "density," in other words the place it takes in the occurrence of phenomena. This is where 3D time and absolute relativity
come in!

We are desperately trying to be spectators in this world while existing in it. Therefore, we are actors, whether or not we want to be. Can
we then be comedians breezing through on stage and understand the
scenario of the director? Yes we can! By going within! In my opinion,
this is the only way to the ultimate understanding of the world. Once
quantum mechanics and the relativity theory have been interlinked
and understood (which is what I propose here), once all technologies
have come to fruition, once the material answers have been provided…
what do we do? We will have assimilated the fact that intent is a fundamental given of the order of the universe! The only major interest of
this contribution is to ask ourselves this question with more acuity.
Throughout history man never stopped observing his environment in
order to get closer to the truth. But what has he observed, and with
what has he observed it? The instrument! This is exactly the point.

Those who relentlessly doubt superior realities rely on instruments without ever questioning them. "Doubt your doubts," the wise
man said. However, this is where they are wrong. They do not see
their logic or their doubts through. After all, the real skeptic, the only
one who deserves this noble name, cannot derive any benefits from
this query. Instruments distort reality! This is the exact dilemma of
quantum mechanics: the object, the measuring instrument and the
observer are closely connected. Therefore, let us rid ourselves of the
categorical affirmations of scientific proof. I will show you that scientific proof is a belief! Ever since Kuhn's *Structure of Scientific Revolu-
tions,* we know that such proof and even logic is flimsy because of

their historical context. In my opinion, a scientific web surfer expressed an objective vision of science:

"Saying that science is the true nature of reality does not only seem to represent an unawareness of the application of science in the real world, but also means going beyond the scientific domain itself. Scientific methods constitute a discipline that approaches reality by balancing theory and empiricism. It seems to be the most profitable discipline at the level of the understanding of the universe if we define this understanding as being the influence we are able to have on our environment. Meanwhile, in spite of its atheistic methodology, the presence of self-criticism in science ensures that it never claims to hold the Truth."

—Khayman

CHAPTER 5

Our blind spots

THIS REMARKABLE EXAMPLE is far from being an isolated one. Hundreds of scientists and philosophers sincerely share this vision. Science itself goes through an identity crisis because of its very own hypothetical speculations and instrumental empiricism. It is important to understand that the eye cannot see reality! Science and its history have been, and still are, fundamentally bound to discover reality. However, science and its history are viscerally dependent on visual observations. The eye is the most complex organ after the brain and contains the largest number of nervous fibers. The brain has gradually conformed to the information it receives from the other senses. However, it is the eye that is by far our most important source of information about the world around us. The other senses are often the poor parents of the matrix master, confirming what he sees or bowing down before him if their information is different. They are the vassals of the "lord of perception"! The proof lies in the fact that ultimately, all scientific instruments translate physical magnitudes through a filter: the visual information of the instrumental readout.

Just as curtailed information transmitted by the media becomes true and then prevalent after being repeated to the public a thousand times, space is misinformation that man has kept in existence ever since the dawn of science. The same filter applies: the eye!

Think about it! It is a genuine Pavlov reflex. Only what is visually verifiable is true! This is so persistent that we need sketches to understand how the universe works. I am also resorting to this useful but quite incomplete technique. However, if a picture is worth a thousand words, a contact is worth a thousand pictures! My insistence on approaching our intrinsic problem, on speaking about our blind spots, on how much this handicap is the height of the height, is no epistolary frivolity but academic truth. We invariably return to spatial, thus visual and encoded information almost unrelated to the source information. If what is ordinarily and readily accessible to us is misrepresented, then what can be said about what it is not: the other ranges of the electromagnetic spectrum!

Let me be clear! We see the sinusoid of the wave, but we do not know what it means, just like the dichotomy I just mentioned. Information is not the medium of information! A feeling is not a wave. Moreover, the boundaries, varying between radio waves and gamma frequencies allocated to the universal electromagnetic spectrum, are not at all real and only correspond to those preferred by our theories. After the visual domination we are currently dominated by the instrument. We gradually started questioning what our eyes translated of the exterior world. Measurements became a preeminent scientific act, and the standard for measurements an act of faith!

A famous statement attributed to St. Thomas sums up the situation brilliantly: "I believe only what I can see." Far from being anecdotal, this sentence created entire generations of rationalists. It laid the foundations for our classical mathematics based on the certainty that the universe is fundamentally spatial (we see only what has mass) and has temporal incongruity. This phrase entered the collective subconscious mind with such conviction that it is virtually impossible to get rid of it. Today, a growing divide separates scientific research from uncommon facts, in other words, unexplained situations. We have even reached the point of "affirming that paranormal" phenomena exist next to normality, the norm, the standard, i.e., they do not fit in the domain of reality decreed by some. Being a prisoner of space is being a prisoner of the norm. Not only disingenuous scientists argue that science describes reality. We have always being running away from reality by making the unconscious choice to favor the preeminence of visual information.

As a consequence, the belief that space prevails was born, because that is what we observed. Scholars hastily reduced time to an additional dimension of space, because mass, the spatial contours, literally jumps out at us and no one dares to refute it since it is part of our mental structure! All our research efforts are based on an "incontestable" and therefore "uncontested" postulate. However, this mathematical convention (time as the fourth dimension of space) is not real. The convention has gradually become a belief. Official science is based on a belief; therefore, science is a belief.

CHAPTER 6

Progress means a better perception of reality

REFERRING TO OUR PAST ACHIEVEMENTS slows down progress. Of course, we know how to fly space shuttles and generate nuclear electricity, but that is already in the past. However, we persist in hanging on to the classic inertial model. Curiously, the theory of special relativity is already one hundred years old. It is said that the balance tipped one century ago. In fact, light speed is in the hot seat. Approaching it leads to relativistic physics. Einstein made two assumptions. The first was that gravitational and inertial mass are equal. The second was that light speed c is constant regardless of the chosen benchmark. To this day, neither one can be verified incontestably for an extremely simple reason. We have never measured a phenomenon. In addition, neither the measuring device itself, nor any of the observers has ever exceeded this speed by even one percent! For instance, the best aircraft can only achieve a difference of one millionth of a second between their clock and ours. Our best spacecraft reach only one ten thousandth of c and show only a difference of one thousandth of a second. Of course, the difficulty is that the instrument follows the distortions of its new Galilean benchmark. We measure particles, i.e., entities presumed corpuscular, on the outside! They are part of a specific spatio-temporal frame of reference: the measuring instrument! It is a bit like judging the performance of an airplane at high altitude when it is about to land. Here, the instrument (the runway) is a wave function that significantly perturbs the wave function of the particle. The resultant has nothing to do with the intrinsic reality of the particle.

This subtlety is eclipsed by the affirmation according to which light speed c is a constraint, because mass would then be infinite and require infinite energy to be reached. However, this does not take into account the idea that inertial mass can no longer exist if part of this speed is approached! The problem is how. Do not mix up mass and — the corollary by which it is measured — gravitation, or energy! Inert mass is an axiom and thus refutable. What remains is gravity mass that is itself directly linked to acceleration. What is acceleration if not a change of spatio-temporal reference frame? If E is energy in the general equation $E=Mc^2$, then M is in reality the inertia. The inertia is what slows down the acceleration so long as it is correlated with the inert mass, which remains to be proven because, as we have just seen, mass can change states to respectable portions of c providing that the mass is redefined.

It is great to hear that teleportation experiments with photons and even with quantum states of atoms have been successful, because they support a thesis suggesting that light speed is not a constant, in which case the current concept of special relativity may be challenged. There are not many theories that can explain this teleportation phenomenon. We speak of entanglement but we cannot explain it. There are not many theories either that can combine the relativist theory with quantum mechanics. However, 3D time can and, in a larger framework, so can absolute relativity, as we will see.

We cannot simply address these concepts without first doing the groundwork. The upcoming generation of witnesses will know much more than students of the paranormal since they will start using the powers they are becoming aware of. Teachers are gradually changing sides. Witnesses now write themselves what their interviewers misrepresented in the past.

The information manifests itself by its energy capable of traveling through space-times. We "trap" the information by allowing time to derive the observation. The measurement is taking a photo of a phenomenon at moment t, whereas in reality only the properties of a specific ST are measured, ours, because we believe in its universality. For now, this moment still remains pretty much unchallenged. By playing a domino game made of equations, a physical magnitude is supposed to characterize a state based on a measurement (the readout of a measurement) that has nothing to do with what is described. Of course, if countless observations verify a model, why put them aside and lose time challenging the equation? If a phenomenon contradicts the equation it simply does not exist! The reason is simple: the equation has become reality in the scientific subconscious mind!

However, there is an experiential area where equations do not a priori render us subservient and that escapes the canonical approach of determinism: quantum mechanics. It endeavors to reduce physical magnitudes and the smallest parts of matter to quantities. This distinguishes it from the relativity theory that aims at establishing relations between physical magnitudes (comparison of two Galilean references).

The predilection area of general relativity is the infinitely big because in the interstellar vacuum it is possible to observe the distortion of the trajectory of photons generated by high-mass stars. However, the infinitely big is inaccessible by definition. Our instruments cannot attest to the size of the universe with absolute certainty.

Let us follow this reasoning through. Considering the velocity of light, the light of the stars we see comes from the past. The sky does not reflect our present reality but a previous situation. However, imagine stars so distant that they cannot be detected by any of our current measuring instruments, either because their intrinsic luminosity is too weak — when they are hidden by stellar dust or other celestial objects — or because their light will not reach us for another few billion years. What then is the Big Bang? The Big Bang is defined by the real size of the universe. If we cannot measure it, then how can we claim that its mass is defined and, as a consequence, that we can use it to deduce the thermodynamic and gravitational forces at work? What if the Big Bang is the exact antithesis of future observations? If the biggest scientific mistake in history is to make us acknowledge the existence of a primordial God as the church sees it, then where did the theory with the same name come from?

On the other hand, quantum mechanics is invariably interested in the infinitely small. It forces us to always take the structuring of matter one step further in order to answer the question: what is matter made of? Before tackling this question I will give you the general principles of the standard model of which the experimental results are promising. Nevertheless, the technical terms hide concepts that are far from being materialist. Therefore, we must fathom the interpretation of these concepts, which physicists have never been able to do.

There are two forms of particles: messenger particles, also called gauge fields, and particles of "matter." In reality, the latter do not consist of matter at all. These matter particles can be divided into two families: quarks and leptons. The vast majority of particles are quarks (which is the case for the atomic nucleus). There are two types of combinations: the hadrons that are composed of three quarks and the

mesons that only contain two. Messenger particles mediate interaction between particles. There is however, possible and impossible interaction. The four interactions are as follows:
- gravitation
- electromagnetism
- strong nuclear interaction
- weak nuclear interaction.

Therefore, there are four families of messenger particles:
- gravitons (theoretical particle never detected)
- photons
- gluons
- bosons.

I am slightly simplifying because there are sub-parts within these interactions. Based on these two particle categories (messenger and "matter"), diffusion matrices have been developed describing the possible combinations between them. The essential property of these diffusion matrices is that they describe probability amplitudes suggesting that a certain result will be produced (position, motion quantity, etc.). The larger the number of particles included in the game, the higher the uncertainty factor.

INTERACTIONS

Interactions are exchanges of messenger particules (photons, bosons, gluons). These interactions take place between particles of specific matter. Gravitons have not yet been found in gravitational interaction.

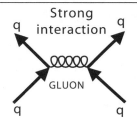

These simplified representations are called Feynman diagrams.

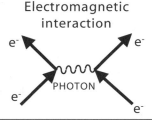

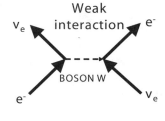

Figure 12

Physicists use the perturbation theory. They use an expression in terms of a power series in a small physical parameter:

$$\alpha = e^2 \,/\, 4\pi\hbar c \approx 1/137$$

The objective is therefore to count every way to go from an initial state to a fixed definite state and to associate a physical quantity with each of these combinations, at each level of the power. The Feynman diagrams are a synthetic vision of these combinations where particles may instantaneously appear and disappear.

The rate of time expressed as transformation velocity of the cause towards the effect proposed by professor N. A. Kozyrev and subsequently by L. S. Shikhobalov, which will be elaborated later in this book, is defined by the formula:

$$v = c \,/\, 137$$

where $1/137$ is the fine structure constant and c is the velocity of light. Similar equations proposed by S. M. Poliakov describe the inner structure of energy for any photon that consists of 137 discrete parts. Understanding the structure of photons opens the door to a time structure description and time control.

According to the theory of time rate control (TRC), there are various ways to control the velocity of photons up to the zero velocity photon state. We will elaborate on the light speed constraint later. Let me state here that in terms of crossing intersidereal space, c may very well be an impassable limit…on our macroscopic scale. Ufology skeptics have every reason to oppose this light speed argument. Unfortunately, they do so because they have a narrow-minded vision of the nature of space travel realized by ETs. To this day we have been thinking inside out when it comes to UFOs. They do not try to exceed this speed c, but reduce it, from our point of view, to a minimum! Physicists know that this is quite possible because the most recent experiments slowed down velocity c to 1.5 m/s! Some argue that they even stopped time completely. To do so, the traveling system (vessel + occupants) must "descend" to the infinitely small or, to be more precise, use a property of time, its fractal nature, that imitates the states described by quantum mechanics.

In the absence of any Brownian motion of the particles, i.e., at absolute zero ($-273.25°$ C), the speed of light is null. Be advised, I am not talking about light speed in a vacuum, but in a material structure (see part II). In this state special quantum states appear naturally: so-called Bose-Einstein condensates. UFOs generate such condensates via superconductor circuits. As a consequence, space contracts completely. It is not the vessel that travels, it is space that varies. The stars come closer. This is possible thanks to the variation of fractal time. This discrete value 1/137 is exactly what constitutes the different fractal states of time.

The physical world is therefore made of quarks and leptons. Quarks (6) are, among others, the components of atomic nuclei, whereas leptons (6) consist of electrons, neutrinos, muons and other Tau particles. Although physicists have counted nearly two hundred particles, they can basically be divided into these two elementary families that include the other particles. The following table sums up the situation.

I chose not to represent particles as marbles, but as wave fractions, which is closer to reality. It is remarkable that particles become "heavier" as they grow more unstable. Instability pertains to lifespan in this respect. In the schedule below, I put the mass between quotation marks because I am arguing that in quantum mechanics, mass is only the reflection of a spatio-temporal fractal differential. We will see that

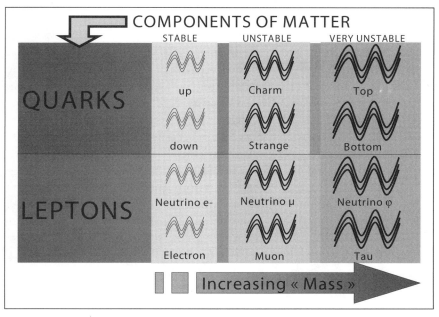

Figure 13

energy is a temporal scale difference. Mass is not what it seems to be because to define it, we deduce it from Einstein's equation $E=Mc^2$. In the experimental reality of the infinitely small we always measure energy. The equation should therefore be redefined.

The most important question is indeed why the world that surrounds us is made of the least heavy components. Physicists would answer that the heaviest particles disintegrate into the least heavy elementary particles! This answer is, of course, not an answer at all. Why is the sum of masses of generated particles always lower than the mass of the original particle, which explains the stability of the atom?

When a quark or a lepton transforms (a muon into an electron, for instance), it is said that it transforms into another flavor. In the standard model, every change of flavor content is caused by weak interaction. The messenger particle (or gauge field) of this interaction is the boson (W+, W– or Z^0).

The stability of everyday matter therefore stems from temporal instability! One of the principles of quantum mechanics is the following: the shorter the lifespan of a particle, the more energy it contains. Similarly, short distances are synonymous with high energies. The logical question is therefore: what is this disintegration that produced these transformations towards greater stability? The answer from absolute relativity: it is a transfer of information from one temporal fractal to another in a lower temporal density.

I should add that these two particle families (quarks and leptons) possess some properties that can be quite annoying in materialist thinking. Leptons, in particular electrons, manifest themselves as clouds of presence. We do not know their exact position, to the point of wondering if they really do exist, because we can only see the effects. Quarks, which always come in pairs or threes, have a very peculiar property, so-called "asymptotic freedom." The closer they are, the more their motion is free. We do not know where they are either. Once again, we only see some effects. Therefore, the less there is space, the more there is freedom.

Thus, the answer to the question "what is matter?" is in fact another question: since matter does not exist, what is reality? Our measuring instruments were replaced by models long ago, because their visual limits were reached with regard to the smallness of what we claim to see. At best, the eye can only see objects a thousand times larger than a high performance microscope. The best optical microscopes can see up to 10^{-6} meter (micrometer). Atoms are 10^{-10} m large (a thousand times smaller), protons are 10^{-15} m large (one million times smaller) and electrons and quarks are 10^{-18} m large. The latter are therefore one thousand billion times smaller than our eyes can see.

So imagine what the Planck length[11] represents the smallest theoretical physical scale approximately the size of 10^{-35} m. It is one hundred billion billion billion times smaller than what we can see. Can we still say: "I believe only what I can see?". Even quarks, the smallest elementary particles, are still one hundred million billion times larger than the Planck scale. If a quark is as big as a soccer field, a neutron is the size of Earth and the first electron, which is also as big as a soccer field, would be larger than the sun. Despite this huge magnification, the Planck length would still be invisible.

Infinitely small, infinitely big? We are still influenced by the visual! We are still influenced by the three-dimensionality of space that we believe to be reality. However, what does infinitely long mean? What is infinitely short? What is the present? What if we used only time variations to understand the universe from now on? Fundamentally, that is what this book invites you to do. Planck time[12], supposedly the shortest time interval in existence, is a mathematic deduction of the Planck length. By dividing the Planck length by light speed c we obtain the value of Planck time. Once again, to grasp its extreme smallness, something as elusive as a flash of lightning in a stormy sky lasts one hundred billion billion billion billion (one and thirty-seven zeros) times longer than this infinitesimal length of time. The instruction time of the world's fastest computers is barely one hundred times shorter than a flash of lightning. Even the switching time of a transistor (one picosecond, 10^{-13} second) is an eternity compared to Planck time. While our mind is quite capable of imagining space differences by relating back the proportions to our scale, it is impossible for us to picture time differences, because our human life is a pretty poor standard. If Planck time represents one second on our watch, the flash of lightning of a thunderstorm lasts — brace yourself — one thousand billion billion billion centuries.[13] Surely many events may occur in this eternal interval, which is incommensurably longer than the presumed age of the universe. Worlds may appear and disappear billions of times. Life and death would inevitably seem simultaneous. Is this not what happens in our dreams?

It is not so much the idea that space does not have a reality that blinds us, but the idea that space describes the world. The world is defined by exchange. An exchange consists in the motion followed by information sent from an emitter to a receiver…when they are different! This motion is segmented into iterative quantities, hence the integral function.

Therefore, quantum mechanics measures quantities, quantum states especially characterized by energy, spin and mass. This is the definition of state functions designed to formalize a model so that phenomena are reproducible — the magic word of scientific acknowledgment in its present form — up to one percent exact. However, unlike classical mechanics, this uncertainty factor is significant. We therefore speak of indeterminist and probabilistic physics. It is important to understand the nature of this indeterminism.

Do not forget that Planck laid down a simple principle: electromagnetic radiation is emitted or absorbed by packets (quanta). The quantum of energy is thus defined by:

$$E = h.f$$

where f is the radiation frequency and h is Planck's constant.[14] It is crucial not to confuse a quantum with a particle.

Conservation of energy, also known as the first law of thermodynamics, is much less rigid than we believe. In the framework of the expanding universe, astrophysicists acknowledge a loss of energy because the frequency is changed by this expanding space, reducing the number of cycles per conventional time unit. There is therefore no mortal sin in making this law fly into pieces. On the other hand, the kinetic energy of a particle equals:

$$E = \tfrac{1}{2} \times m \times v^2$$

where m is its mass and v is its velocity. In the standard cosmological model, mass is sustained and a correlative loss of energy is observed as the particle recedes into expanding space! Therefore, in the infinitely small we can accept that energy increases without the correlative increase of mass by "playing" on the frequency and ultimately, that we succeed in grasping the nature of time that is in the denominator. A frequency is a number of cycles per time unit. By acknowledging that this temporal unit does not reflect the reality of time flow, but underestimates it in the framework of fractal time, we then obtain larger energies at the wave scale that are imperceptible on our scale, i.e., that of our unit "second." It is in fact an underestimation in the infinitely small and an overestimation in the infinitely big. I will get back to this later after describing fractal time.

The true meaning of quantum mechanics may escape us completely unless we accept that the measurement depends upon the instrument ne observer. The most amazing is that the result is produced at the moment of observation. It does not exist before! In other words, no microscopic phenomenon exists intrinsically outside the observation! This seems difficult to digest, for we are used to thinking that the world keeps on turning even without us. Quantum decoherence is based on this simple hypothesis. It means that non-observed phenomena do not exist or even that there may be other phenomena than the ones we have to measure. This has important consequences: matter can quite simply disappear in the atomic or subatomic state without leaving visible traces in our so-called material world, except for a structuring effect on the macroscopic scale at the moment of interaction. Matter exists only because "it is used"!

The whole of quantum mechanics is built on a simple principle: state functions assign "discrete" states (discontinuous) to the particles. This is the very definition of quantum states. Has anyone ever explained these discontinuities? No! What happens between two quantum states that induce spatial changes at the same time? No one knows! This is where sometimes instantaneous dematerialization of matter takes place. We then understand in a flash of genius that matter exists only because time goes by slowly!

When we compare this apparent mystery with our temporary inability to see beyond 10^{-15} seconds converted into wavelengths, it is easy to deduce that matter becomes invisible. Imagine for an instant that we live in a stroboscopic world of which the intervals of material non-existence are so short that it is impossible to see them. Everything will seem continuous to us. And this is in fact the case. It is the principle of film and its twenty-four images per second. Now imagine that these stroboscopic intervals of immateriality increase considerably to the point of perceiving a tangible rift between two situations. We then speak of paranormal phenomena because we do not understand what links these two events. Thus is matter. It is important to understand what happens between two quantum states or events. The undulating nature of matter preserves the memory of its properties because the state of a particle is defined by a frequency, while entanglement causes the particles to form aggregates. We will see further on how the coherence of atomic structures is kept intact even in a dematerialized state. Dematerialization is nothing other than a passage from one spatial scale to an even smaller one. It is interesting to note that light, the frequency of which lies between 4 and 7.5 10^{14} Hz, is at the outer limit of what we can currently see of the infinitely small. However, I am pressing on rather boldly with my reflections that lead towards absolute relativity.

The eye cannot see reality! Now imagine that we are a society without sight or touch. How would we interpret the world? How would we see the universe? Could we still say: "this is bigger than that"? Absolutely not! So many questions with the same answer: time would have three dimensions to us!

The principle of exchange between emitter and receiver would be just as valid, but the amount of exchanged information would be our measuring standard. This amount would depend on the flow of time, its viscosity and its dilation. Every sequence of information would be in itself a temporal density of reality. Like our proprioceptive sensitivity that allows us to feel the effects of Earth gravity, this blind civilization would acquire chronoceptive sensitivity!

Thus the energy is not in itself a quantity but the translation of a temporal density change translated by mathematicians in a vector, or even a quantity of motion applied to time. Reality is made of systems, i.e., of wholes that have internal coherence and that can relate to other identical, smaller or larger wholes. These are called fractals. The consequence of all this is that paranormal phenomena are the manifestation of incursions of higher temporal densities in ours. In other words, parapsychological phenomena are pockets of one ST within another. That is why these phenomena happen so fast or, rather, they are instantaneous and incomprehensible from our point of view. It is also why quantum mechanics is so inaccessible: it is paranormal. There is a transformation but we do not perceive its sequences. That is what makes it so rare. Fortean phenomena[15] are the juncture of relativist phenomena and quantum phenomena in our space-time continuum. UFO phenomena are the technically mastered paranormal; parapsychological phenomena are the mentally manifested paranormal.

CHAPTER 7

Scientific culture or the cause of errors

MEN OF SCIENCE MAY FEEL that these considerations are of little interest to everyday research. Let us dwell on the world of science for a moment. Do not let the following affect your good mood, because the collective interest requires that the "scientific wall of Berlin" also comes tumbling down. Ultimately, the land that lies behind this wall is not so different from what we find in companies or politics: power struggles, protection of personal status and prerogatives, people holding back information, confidentiality pledges and intrigue. This picture is certainly a bit negative, but we are all still human. Nothing is sterile in this low world, not even in laboratories.

We often speak of the pioneers of scientific history. They were few by definition. So why does our culture make an abstraction of all those who were crushed by the train of progress because they held on to their ephemeral certainties? Is it because we hate losers? Let us have mercy on future losers. They become losers only because we lack compassion for the mistakes of others. Let us not be the ones to cast the first stone, for who has not abused his authority, at any level, to impose certain views? Let us be forgiving and simply invite our scientists to acknowledge that the perks of their social position are legitimate as they stand united and become dedicated to serving mankind, rather than science, which would be self-justification. Nevertheless, I have the utmost respect for the hours, months and years of dedicated research conducted by these brilliant men and women.

I observed that there were always two major types of actions from which all others ensue: justifications and questions; to justify ourselves… or to question ourselves. All the rest proceeds from and depends on these two attitudes!

More than one hundred thousand UFO eyewitness accounts have been counted to this day. Based on the laws of statistics, it is safe to assume that many millions have seen UFOs without even remembering it, unless they keep their story to themselves. It is estimated that almost seventy percent of the population think ET civilizations are likely to exist. Even most astrophysicists are convinced that there is life in the cosmos. More than twenty molecules constituting the foundations of life have been surveyed in interstellar gases. Provided there is or ever was life on Mars[16] and this can be demonstrated conclusively, this rate may even go up to ninety percent. Credibility is just a matter of propaganda.

The next logical question deals with the laws of physics; the Caudine Forks that have trapped so many ufologists. If UFOs exist in matter, how can they defy the laws that are the foundation of material existence? That is simple. Our discoveries are incomplete! This will be obvious to those who manage to take a step back and study the history of science teaching us that every turning point in time was characterized by acclaimed knowledge. I will express the dilemma as follows: every law is part of a higher law.

Just as traffic laws are laid down in the constitution, the laws of thermodynamics are part of a larger legal whole. That is the problem with UFOs: do we need to link different worlds by their planetary position or by their nature? This is where the shoe pinches: the nature of things!

CHAPTER 8

Time versus materialism

LET US MAKE OUR FIRST INCURSION in the ET world. What is the nature of time? This subject may at first strike us as complex because we experience it with a brain that seems to have deactivated the part designated to understand it. To us time is flat, whereas it should be seen in 3D. In the beginning, this may require some exhausting gymnastics like continuously switching focus between an object close by and an object at a great distance.

When we speak of the past and the future we must first ask: the past or the future of what? We see everything around us on the same plane. We instinctively create a logic based on this illusion: everything is in one and the same whole called "time." This state of fact exists because we identify ourselves with our body, a piece of matter just like many others.

Usually films on time travel show a view of a city where time is fast-forwarded. Everything moves very fast, but when we look more closely we notice that some things do not move as fast as others. Unfortunately, such films do not show thoughts, emotions or reflections. Suppose we could materialize and film them in fast motion; they would obviously be invisible due to their extreme speed. Remember the hypervelocity stroboscope. You are probably beginning to understand where (i.e., when) the ETs are. In a way, we are ETs to plants. However, we remain utterly materialist!

This does not mean that our scale of values solely tends towards the lure of profits or that our explanations are falsely rationalist. We are materialists when we accept the point of view of the "matrix," i.e., this causality that depends on time. Just as we believe that time is one and the same universal bath, being materialist means that everything we see is associated with the same material whole. Our unconscious mind makes a shortcut by conflating things of a different nature. The contact with matter dominates our senses! Matter does exist, but we should picture it as a whole of circulating information. As the amount of information grows, matter becomes increasingly subtle and complex, increasingly malleable and changeable, and increasingly fast and furtive. The exchange is life! It is this circulation that creates time that goes by, temporal density and its viscosity. We humans live many different passing times. Several stroboscopes of different rates are superimposed within us.

Like other creatures here and elsewhere, we are made of several passing times! From our skeleton to our highest thoughts, countless passing times exist in the same being. All creatures do not have the same number of such times, or the same time rates. This explains so many perceptual differences, so many misunderstandings, jealousies and fears! And yet, there are so many passing times within us, so many identities! Why fight when we can choose our identity? Seen from this new point of view, the past or future of what are we talking about?

Many want to recreate a phenomenon outside its context. This natural tendency is caused by the fact that we cannot stop our awkward imitations of nature. This mimicry often has to deal with numerous errors of interpretation. Our collective memory rejects the mistakes and only stores the success stories. Does not wisdom command us to study our aberrations? Most of them are caused because we believe that the laws of physics have been established once and for all. There is a big difference between being subject to a law of physics and obeying it. This difference is called adaptation.

It is not because we lack imagination that something cannot exist. Our intellect can use reason to establish the links between possible causes and apparent effects. We can find correlations with numerous other testimonies. For now, we have not yet found an "official" technical solution for UFOs. This book aims at lifting the veil on the common point we were missing. At best, we found unknown causes for known effects. Eyewitness accounts and confirmed physical effects were our breviaries. However, we now know the causes, as we will see in the following part. Witnesses will thus regain their dignity, for even ufology lost faith in them.

A web surfer brilliantly wrote with regard to witnesses: "here is a postulate for us to consider: someone will not lie if he does not have personal or pathological reasons to do so. Our knowledge of neuro-physiology, neurobiology and sociobiology must be updated so we can learn how to validate human testimonies. Someone whose neuronal outline differs too much from the one he is offered will reject it, often violently and regardless of the nature of the evidence…so one single question remains: how much truth can we take?" This verbal violence often translates in lawsuits against the witness. Many censors fall into this fear trap because of what Jean-Pierre Petit[17] called the 'immunolog-ical reflex'. Similar to relations between bacteria and cells in nature, social groups reject ideological aggressions (new ideas) that may lead to change. This highly unstable homeostasis resembles a protection of the social group. Curiously, since 1973 the poll of the American survey research institute Gallup observed a priori no significant differences between those who have and who have not seen UFOs "in terms of profession, religion, political attitudes and educational level."[18]

Considering the intrinsic frailty of our scientific research methods, compared to the scope and complexity of reality, and of testimonies, what is left? Statistics! In my opinion, statistics inspire us most to ask questions. A phenomenon is true up to a certain percentage of values. This "small" percentage goes up as other variables are introduced in the "mechanics" of a phenomenon. It is the core of the science of com-plexity. The life of the simplest in its most complex state. What do we really know about the final levels? Would they not equal the parame-ters of cosmic consciousness? We see that complexity increases just like the freedom to do and evolve. In other words, the more freedom a crea-ture possesses, the less it is confined and the more the "small" percent-age of uncertainty goes up.

Far from stating the obvious, it so happens that the synchronicity of phenomena is directly related to the "intent" discussed earlier — as demonstrated in experiments[19] — because the prevalence of the intent grows just like the scientific uncertainty. This detour via the basics should clarify a great deal of information.

3D Time solves the dilemma of the probabilistic nature of events. Coincidence is essentially a spatio-temporal scale problem in the framework of absolute relativity, i.e., "the more there is space, the less there is time, and conversely." Coincidence is the translation of the place of time in phenomenology. Time dominates the microscopic world. In the macroscopic world space is the authority. The chair we sit on remains stable and keeps us from having a painful encounter with the floor because the influence of chance is very weak on our macro-scopic scale. It is even weaker on the galactic scale. That is why stars have extremely stable relative positions. We will readdress this essential notion of statistic mechanics, because it is absolutely necessary that science explains the causal nature of probabilities. They are actually the best advocate of 3D time. However, accepting this also brings us much closer to UFO and paranormal phenomena.

In the trench war between skeptics and protagonists, both parties want to convince each other of their personal truth. This war is pointless because an observer has legitimate reasons to describe his own vision and understanding. His reality is true in the framework of his own observations. If two individuals experience very different passing times, it is clear that the person less prepared will remain skeptical about the existence of passing times that he is not endowed with, or rather, that he is unaware of. Logic dictates that individuals with the ability to perceive phenomena and who are in hypervelocity passing times are extremely rare in a macroscopic physical world where the dominant passing time is much weaker. Indeed, authentic mediums are hard to find. The clan of skeptics uses statistics to disprove important cases by keeping them out of the standard deviations. In other words, the way in which statistics are often applied is a genuine tautology, the worst mental disorder! They say without realizing it: "since the world is physical, time must also be physical." The source of the paranormal (fractal time) generates exceptional cases itself. Observation is science, but there are countless types of observation! Including the inappropriately termed "sixth sense." The rift is always caused by a new reference system. The old system is about to be replaced.

CHAPTER 9

The instruments that shape us

WE SUBCONSCIOUSLY TRUST INSTRUMENTS to externalize our intuitions, although they reduce our range of observation (those renowned faster passing times). We often try to categorize it in an admissible framework, which, however, cuts it off from valuable information. All the more so because there is much more of it. Admissible means "temporarily acceptable." This natural tendency is caused by a lack of self-confidence, a personal flaw raising doubts about the experience of others and their testimonies. Of course, some testimonies are false or imaginary, but those are a minority. Once again, statistics speak if we make them speak correctly. It is unreasonable to think that testimonies cannot be used as a reliable instrument, particularly when correlations can be established. The vast majority of people are perfectly able to describe as objectively as possible what they have seen, heard or felt without necessarily understanding it.

People are of good faith and are really just conservative, no matter what other terms we use. It is time to rise above the contingencies of some micro-cosmos. The true difficulty lies in the fact that each human being has a different level of perception and is therefore more or less reliable. It all boils down to ascertaining which witnesses has the highest level of perceptual maturity. Who is capable of making that assessment?

Let us reflect on the evolutionary nature of beings. It may not seem so, but psychism is at the very core of UFO and ET problems, while also addressing the material side of their manifestations. How much do we now about psychism? That it is the origin of disturbances, even of illnesses unsuitably called "mental" disorders. This is how the human mind has been represented since the dawn of modern psychology: we are more or less perverse or perverted. At best, we are balanced when we attend to the things of this material world. How did we arrive at this belief? The original axioms were false! What is psychism? It is the universe of thought forms. They come as pictures, feelings or ideas. Our life consists of numerous thought forms that we only have little control of. We have moved away from what is felt — the most complete form of observation — and from the signified — the highest cognitive state of the observer.

Research methods have been developed further by observing nature and understanding the mechanisms at work. We have focused our efforts on the mathematic and linguistic formalization of our research. In this process, we have grown accustomed to crystallizing the reproduction of nature outside of us and even sublimating it in order to have an even firmer grip. The distance between the subject and the object is the foundation of rationality and, in general, of secular society. However, quantum mechanics, hugely undervalued by our contemporaries, has rejected this principle of alienation, cutting off the head of the so-called Cartesian mind. We should not forget that.

This is how aerospace, nuclear or genetic technologies are born. We have always considered the material universe to be different from rational beings, incidentally leaving an immense void inside. We have created pathologies by giving them names. The latest invention is the fantasy-prone personality, justifying the perception of an immaterial reality by a "light" hallucination, i.e., a subtle form of creativity midway between observational "normality" and mental delirium. In fact this is the chicken or the egg story. Is the observation of a phenomenon in an altered state of consciousness a mechanism triggered by the person, or an underlying and primordial reality manifesting a personality increasingly capable of grasping this reality? The vast majority of psychologists and even neuropsychiatrists use scientific terms under the guise of being an explanation and as a cover. However, they never explain where and when the pictures, sounds and sensations are that they qualify as imaginary. What makes an electric signal equivalent to complex information? The only real basic question is: what is the perception of something that does not exist? Or the non-perception of something that does not exist? Be lenient and do not make fun of the answers of contemporary human science.

The answer invariably depends on the intrinsic nature of space and time on which we invariably base our observations, whatever they are. In fact, without space-time it is impossible to see anything. The correct definition of space and time thus provides the basis for an incalculable number of revolutionary consequences about the truth of facts.

Psychiatry has become the self-justification of the materialist imbalance. In other words, mental disturbances are nothing other than seeing the powerlessness of this depression triggered by external stress. This ambition of the material world, in the sense of fluid mechanics, has led to a lack of understanding of our inherent human mechanisms. In reality, not only have we slowly but surely strayed from our true nature, we have also entered the one-way street called skepticism!

What have we lost? The signified, the feelings and direct contact!

Immaterial thought forms are creations born from the formation of either the original universe or its creatures. They are more or less crystallized in the cosmos, up to material density, depending on the energy and focus maintained over time dedicated to concretizing them. However, every creation is a reality in itself, regardless of the material or immaterial form. To really understand this mechanism, we must personally commit ourselves to comprehending and practicing thought forms. For now, we are like undisciplined children who muddle through and perhaps master only a mind that is oversized compared to other abilities. There are, however, creatures whose powers of creation have developed to the highest level. It is therefore an illusion to see only the manifestation of our own thoughts in parapsychological phenomena. Most of the so-called supernatural cases are produced by invisible entities, but the intense emotions of a child, whose thoughts have not been formatted by the materialist depression of adults, may be enough to generate such phenomena.

What is a thought form? It is information or an information structure (just like a molecule) that contains the energy its creator has been able to put into it. This energy is often of emotional origins, but other energy forms exist also. Let me give an example. What is an apple? A five-letter word, a symbol of downfall of paradise lost, a piece of fruit? An apple is a densified thought form in which we can find the following information: it is round, beautiful, with an appendix coming out of a cavity and a shiny and spotty texture. It is usually red, has a sweet taste and its flesh is both soft and crunchy. It smells of spring…and it offers itself without condition. All of this applies at the same time! You will agree with me that simply saying "apple" is a lot faster! It is faster but also less true! We are beginning to see a glimpse of the true power of poetry in the authentic sense of the word: giving us back what is true, where the information is direct and unmasked, full of recovered emotion, without the mediation of dictionaries, without the mediation of words that describe other words. That is, however, the path we have chosen: describing increasingly unreal things taken out of their context of spatio-temporal oneness. So-called objectivity!

If reality cannot be described it is not because we lack the words, but because we can do without them! Scientists know — that is why they are a priori scientists — that the test of experience is the source of discoveries. Indeed, nothing exists outside the experience! Being a pragmatist does not mean being a materialist, but being able to experiment…and create the means to do so. A mystic is the greatest pragmatist of all. Nothing else matters to him than the personal experience of transcendental knowledge. If he is enlightened he will know! He has had experiences others do not know anything about. They discuss them, but he remains quiet. Except perhaps about how and under which conditions he got there in order to share with realistic and active souls the fruits of his personal experiences. He knows they will discover other aspects of reality, because each person has a specific role to play and lessons to learn.

In this sense, equations are like the words and syntax of sentences. They come close to reality, but they never quite grasp it. So do not search for the truth in contemporary formalist science. By definition, it cannot possibly give it to you. Do you doubt that? Scientists say so themselves. We will verify that. Moreover, if there are so many ways to describe reality, even in mathematics, it is because a description always omits the information contributed by the experience.

Supported by this new understanding of how to access and understand the truth, we can dismiss everything around us and subsequently re-establish contact, including with feelings like brotherhood or love. Human psychism in its present state is a kind of shapeless and misrepresented mash. It explains why our dreams are utterly disorganized, fickle and without interest. Guess how we see them? As unreal! In a way that is true. They do not have any power or harmonious structure, or intention to be controlled. It is essentially what separates us from the technological and mental level of ETs. It is our Achilles' heel that may be exploited by ill-intentioned ETs. It is also the path of apprenticeship benevolent ETs would like us to take.

Without intention or focused intent there is nothing. Most of our mental experiences, such as our dreams, are rich in the stimuli of life that are the core of our badly expressed desires or our deepest fears. Thus, we endure our own and other people's thought forms. We lack the mental discipline of ETs because we do not choose the information we receive. It comes in erratically in heteroclite packets. Have you ever wondered how many thoughts we have each day? Thousands. Which of those do you really control? The ones you have consciously projected? In other words, we look at things without focus, both on the outside and the inside. There exists no better focus than in relaxation. As a consequence, we can emit what is strictly useful to reach our goal. Imagine that a computer opens all its files at the same time when you only want one. It will be impossible to carry out your task because the RAM (Random Access Memory) is full. It is not surprising that extrasensory perception occurs when we relax our mind, because letting go is the ideal form of reception. Nothing else is received at the same time. Nonetheless, you should learn to protect yourself against potential viruses and hackers. That is the real work of future psychiatrists, for there are numerous parasites.

In our centenary education we have completely passed over the valuable knowledge of how to master thought forms. This is so true that we have difficulty accepting the idea that material crystallization is possible in this way. Creation comes from the power, i.e., the energy, and from the focus of the plan. The combination of power and focus is called visualization. The expression that power is in numbers applies to us humans because our single mind is undisciplined (we use only ten to twenty percent of our full brain capacity). However, focus is by far the ability we lack most. Visualization means the "imaginative" — not imaginary — expression of everything our senses can access. Since it does not include higher aspects, the term visualization is in fact inappropriate. This "plus" is called transcendence, i.e., what transcends the possible description made by our mind of a piece of knowledge. Therefore, reality is transcendental, beyond the descriptive.

We intuitively understand that every person is a potential creator. This requires a long apprenticeship. A superior nature of beings comes from transcendence acquired by continuous visualization with a pure intent and, if possible, expurgated from ego that clouds the lucidity of what is true. The power of creation generates most of our dreams. Numerous ETs have mastered the art of visualization. Some of them have come halfway by contenting themselves with control, allowing them to navigate their vessel and contact humans (or other creatures) according to modalities that may seem deceitful to us. Like us, they prefer to dominate rather than share. Since we are both deaf and blind, their superiority is, however, already a fact. Our handicaps are a source of fear when we become aware of this superiority in the nature of beings.

Others, who choose to encourage our evolution, have access to transcendence, the nature of the divinity within us and that, sooner or later, we will be part of with indescribable joy! It is important to accept that this nature is within us instead of handing over our potential to religious or scientific representatives. The more we accept intermediaries, the more original words or knowledge will be distorted. Why not go to the source directly? Let us stop hiding. This requires only a minimum of effort. What kind of effort do we choose in order to justify or question ourselves? In other words, perceptual maturity depends first and foremost on the dynamics of conscious efforts towards more inner sincerity and truth.

As promising as an explanation may be, it does not describe the intent of people, as they are always responsible for their own future, which I feel may be dim before the "great leap." By persisting in the acceptance of the yoke of beliefs we allow them to control us. The news says more about its own nature than about the events it reports about. Ignorance begets war!

Can the opposite — knowledge — bring peace? We often confuse science and knowledge for the simple reason that we decree our present research methods as universal. They are useful but incomplete. An enlightened mind will easily understand and accept that knowledge has changed over time and after many centuries. Unlike Popperian cosmology, what is universal and persistent is our error in judgment: we borrow our academic references from the past to create the future! That is why only those who succeed in leaving the limbo of common conventions are able to help their fellow beings move forward. Being outside the convention is being beside the norm, it is being "paranormal"! Degrees, titles and prizes do not change that situation. Their only objective is to freeze in time our temporary ability to "solve" specific problems. Where do we get this typical idea that the sanction of a degree lasts forever? Every important man made mistakes at some point in his life, even after receiving the recognition of his peers. Einstein is not the exception to this rule. In the beginning, he had the approval of many of his colleagues, but he is now being subjected to scrutiny after becoming a modern standard!

CHAPTER 10

Science or stage?

USUALLY WE ACCEPT WITHOUT QUESTION that the universe is the stage of other life forms that do not necessarily visit us, as long as — we tell ourselves — they are just harmless single-cell organisms like scientific magazines show us. If life begins in the cosmos, as many are beginning to see, it would be best if it were dispatched by asteroidal mail parcel. Even if such a celestial body is capable of destroying all life in a collision with Earth, it is still much less dangerous for our ego than the cosmic sowing of a highly advanced civilization. Yes, but how is it established? I refer you to the power of creation of the aforementioned thought forms. Be that as it may, Darwin and his fellow believers still have not solved the enigma of the missing link.

One doubt therefore remains. The percentage of confirmed cases of observations keeps the ET cause alive (do they need us to exist?) despite elaborate disinformation episodes. That is why the number of ufological Internet sites in the world is so impressive. The wisest among them remain vigilant for the same reason that prompted me to write this book! I dedicate "the biggest discovery of all times" to them. It is time to regain the hope of a future free from obscurantism, bathing in the light of tomorrow's science.

Let us get back to the unexplained phenomena by arming ourselves with the most fundamental scientific method: observation. Always keep in mind that those who try to include the UFO phenomenon in the scientific field are facing a great difficulty: they are not themselves observers. Scientists are limited to using testimonies that vary significantly in their level of understanding of and confusion about the phenomenon. Heisenberg taught us that the observed object is dependent on the observer, which slightly complicates matters assuming that UFOs are, as we will see, ships with the ability to switch between the microscopic (quantum mechanics) and the macroscopic (classical mechanics).

We can play with detailed ufological information to our heart's content and quote every comment apropos of testimonies, but that will not get us any closer to the commonly accepted reality. Many only and still have a one-sided vision of the UFO phenomenon, whereas we need a more comprehensive vision! This vision is both scientific and spiritual (as in the nature of spirit). Both cases have to do with awareness.

We will see how extraordinary phenomena, called "paranormal," are discredited and misjudged, whereas they deserve our attention. This will definitely be the price to pay for changing our everyday life, not only from a technological point of view, but in the true sense of life.

The awareness we have of ourselves is the sum of our education, our beliefs and the picture others send back to us. We are both an individual and a collective being. We exist in our own thoughts and in the thoughts of others. Depending on how much we are influenced, we think a little less freely, except when we regularly and frequently retreat in our "private space" to reflect and meditate. Our information civilization plunges us in what is probably the worst test of influence ever known to man, slowly but surely distancing us from our ability to apply these introspections. To the point that it becomes suspect to promote such mental efforts towards more freedom. Media information is an absolute necessity, or at least, that is what they want us to believe.

If information is an opportunity to move forward in the knowledge that we have of ourselves and of the world that surrounds us, it still needs to be relevant. We compartmentalize the essence of the pedagogic function into school education, increasingly considering it as something it was never originally intended for. This effect is even reinforced by the fact that it is rarely state of the art. We thus create our future handicaps. Knowledge becomes a matter of specialists, who should not be glorified based on the priorities and the value scale instilled into our minds by the consumption and drama society.

This specialization of knowledge, together with the collective indifference that has replaced knowledge, favored the appearance of castes of hierarchized science drawing its power from controlling the budgets rather than from actual understanding. It is clear that the costs of science are soaring due to the increasingly elaborate experiments. These costs inevitably urge us to choose our discoveries. Often what we have not yet discovered is what we have not yet financed. "It does not exist" because the cash registers are empty. This financial power attributes a specific status to its beneficiaries, that of the "official" voice of science. In a reflex of cold-bloodedness, we give more moral credit to scientific institutions, even though they are stages of power struggles, than to the genius of mankind. As a consequence, interdisciplinary encounters are rare. They exist like the separate subsidiaries of a financial holding. In essence, fundamental physics should be "contagious." The partitioning, if only phraseological and whether it is horizontal or vertical, does not promote the self-realization of research. It is remarkable that genuine science is practiced by junior scientists — the vast majority of discoveries, theoretical or otherwise, are made by the youngest — whereas science is predominantly organized by senior scientists who, once past a certain age, are no longer able to produce knowledge. Of course and fortunately there are still exceptions to that rule. Nevertheless, this urges us to make a triage of scientific articles written by these organizers who were educated years ago, i.e., based on normalized and compartmentalized referents. Saying scientific articles is saying "official knowledge" and even official theories.

This is how the great theories of the twentieth century became success stories. It is true that their predictive powers, particularly with regard to general relativity and quantum mechanics, are very big and meet the criterion of reproducibility in countless areas. This criterion has even become a barrier beyond which hardly any science exists. This deficiency is the status attributed to the soft sciences (human sciences, etc.). If history, still considered a science, is the exception to this criterion — since past events only occurred once — it is because we lean on tangible, material traces, providing of course that the instruments of pure science (still controversial in some situations) attest to the temporal origin of artifacts (radiocarbon dating, photoluminescence, etc.). Cosmology, supported by the greatly publicized theory of the Big Bang, gathers experimental data that many feel cannot be reproduced by man because they represent the universe itself. Therefore, a cosmological view of the universe decrees what is right or not, measured against the contribution of the important theories mentioned above.

A panoramic view of science could therefore give us the illusion that we know a great deal about it, enough to solve various problems, even to the point that some astrophysicists authorize themselves to invade cosmogony with the instruments of cosmology. However, in scientific research the word research should lead to more modesty and more work.

When Newton established his Principia in the eighteenth century, he caused a revolution, just like Copernicus did in his time. Copernicus proved that Earth was not the center of the universe (geocentrism) because it revolves around the sun. What seems a nameless banality to us resembled an earthquake back then. In the same way, Newton described celestial mechanics by proving the law of universal gravitation. The public gradually understood this principle and it became widely accepted a few years later. This process is called "common sense."

Subsequently, Einstein patiently and continuously redefined the knowledge acquired after Newton by establishing his theory of special relativity and general relativity. Once again, common sense recovered from the surprise. Even if our daily life does not seem fundamentally changed by these theories, we see tangible reflections in technologies, such as secure navigation of airplanes, satellite television and on-board atomic clocks, which could be qualified as "relativist" ensuring the coordination of information exchanges between the Earth and the sky.

I am still presenting just a few of the most publicized people to illustrate the subject. However, we should not forget Laplace, Lorentz, Mawell, Bohr, Heisenberg, De Broglie, Dirac, Pauli, Wheeler, Feynman and so many others (sorry for all the great minds, from fundamental physics or otherwise, that I did not mention); hundreds in the past and the present that contributed and still contribute to improving the description of our reality each day without ever succeeding completely. They were nonetheless at the origins of what defines us as a civilization.

Today we are on the brink of a "catastrophe" called a new paradigm. The stage is being prepared for a new act. As in the days of Einstein, this is taking place in deafening silence, in the most general indifference. That is why we are not making any progress. What led Einstein to propose his theories is simply what inspires every theoretical scientist on Earth: present theories do not even begin to explain it all! We are in fact at an impasse because these seemingly successful theories contradict themselves. Therefore, the novelty is that this nascent paradigm (that of this book) no longer just belongs to physicists but to all of science!

CHAPTER 11

Tomorrow is another day

MANY OF US FEEL THAT VAGUE and risky speculations do not seem to be of any help in handling our daily business. I am making this remark because we are maintaining this panoramic view of science without subjecting it to scrutiny. We often confuse science with techno-science. If science is to give us the instruments for greater comfort, a higher quality of life and greater happiness, it must also show us the place we take in the universe and better forms of interaction between living beings. It is important to start defining the universe correctly so we know what the word "place" and even "living" means. Perhaps then will this happiness be more authentic and less ephemeral than what is generated by the consumption and drama society. The fall of Rome became unavoidable when bread and games had taken precedence over democracy.

We know our past, or at least we think we know it. We know what our present looks like. We use it to deduce our future by defining where the present ends. Our experience does not seem to be of use to us. In the past fifty years, we may have experienced the most radical changes that have ever taken place in the history of mankind. However, the fact that we are immersed in our society means that we do not see the upcoming confusion, for it will come.

Modern science is not characterized by a smooth and continuous practice. On the contrary, it advances in often violent and radical leaps and transitions. So we understand that our daily life is bound to disappear shortly. The transformations experienced by the oldest generations will be experienced as even more spectacular by the youngest. Is this compatible with the scientific inertia I mentioned earlier? Yes, because the breaker wave is too powerful. Every pore of mankind oozes knowledge, both in and outside of "official" science. This movement is entropic because the Internet has changed the hand we have been dealt. Publications are often boycotted by scientists who use archive sites built on the World Wide Web to leave behind their contributions.

It is in this context of effervescence, of profound redefinition, of accelerated erosion of certainties that so-called paranormal phenomena find their true significance. They mess up our lives because schemes have been kept in existence. After being a parlor game in the eighteenth and nineteenth century, after being thrown into the gutter in the twentieth century that promoted excessive materialism, paranormal phenomena are rising from the depths of amateur parapsychology[20] to call out to the honest scientific. The paranormal can become normal only if we change the norm!

A scientist asks: "what will I be able to do with these eyewitness accounts and these situations? They do not fit in my theory." That is not completely true. There are theories, but they have not received any acclaim. The prejudice is strong. We associate the smell of suffering that surrounds the supernatural with the irrationalism of rebellious scientists and not with strict and open-minded objectivity. It is true that the conditions of scientific research do not promote the interest in parapsychology. A friend once told me something very important: "setting conditions is of prime importance." Imagine that each of us assumes the power over himself, what would become of our highly hierarchized society? A transition is needed, even if it is a fast one. The great difficulty is to make the actors of science understand that although their theories can be used to explain some observations, they do not apply to a considerable number of other phenomena. The perihelion advance of Mercury was inexplicable with Newtonian gravitation and the laws of Kepler. The details and exceptions troubled the rigid minds. It was time to change paradigms. The world had to yield and embrace the unexpected. The then unknown factor was twenty-six years old and his name was Albert Einstein! Today history repeats itself.

The paranormal is what Mercury represented in astronomy more than a century ago: an exception! Remember the two Pioneer probes that are well on their way out of our solar system by now? They seem to be in the grip of a mysterious force that is holding them back. They refuse to obey our gravitational equations. How embarrassing and disrespectful! The answer lies in 3D time. Science is then bound to change its point of view. Scientists actually admit it. Sir John Maddox, editor emeritus of the pre-eminent science magazine *Nature,* confessed in a recent interview[21] that: "we enter the third millennium in a state of ignorance! What stands out is that there is no field of modern science that is free from glaring ignorance, even contradiction. In the light of past experience, it would be crazy to suggest that a professed 'theory of everything' can be formulated in terms of our modern physics. Breaking through the mystery of the origin of the universe requires the advent to a new physics, a physics regulated by as yet unimaginable principles. In my opinion, that is the crucial point…The person who discovers a new way of describing time and space will be the next Einstein."

CHAPTER 12

Science without consciousness is the ruin of the soul

AT FIRST SIGHT this expression appeals to the morals, or rather to the ethics. We immediately picture the atomic bomb as the product of a science that some have developed against our common interests, against humanity. This one-liner also reflects an aspect of bioethics. Human cloning seems a science without consciousness, ignoring the place reserved for the soul. However, the dilemma of ethics is common to all basic moral contradictions.

In fact, this truism is so much more. It is a key! It is the key to understanding what the universe is made of. I do not know if the great thinker Rabelais had the following vision in mind when he expressed this fundamental truth, but we can conclude only that his saying is spot on.

Consciousness is science — i.e., knowledge — that goes with. With what? With consciousness! Whatever the profundity of the view it pertains to, it is an auto-similarity of itself. This view could be called "fractal consciousness." In other words, science is about consciousness!

I am not talking about good and evil, but about every aspect of consciousness: perceptions, desires, intentions and ethics, of which the highest level is called love, or, to use a more scientific expression, unity consciousness. Therefore, science is the knowledge of consciousness. Modern science studies all modalities that lead to the understanding of consciousness, but without going directly to the goal that it should have set for itself from the very beginning. The fact that this saying is still applicable today actually shows the shortcomings of science.

Paranormal phenomena, such as UFOs, are an excellent pretext as well as a stimulus for a global reinterpretation of the scientific truth.

Explaining these phenomena means destroying everything that is not adjusted to a holistic understanding of the universe and ourselves. A short list of dogmas we would have to "dismantle" includes the Big Bang, light speed, the current quantum theory, special and general relativity, the functioning of the brain, dreams, free will, identity and God. As for the first of these examples, Jayant V. Narlikar, an astrophysicist from India, wrote a very surprising article entitled "Belief in the Big Bang is an act of faith" in a highly acclaimed scientific journal.[22] You are not dreaming. This is science!

A correct definition of the norm is still required if we wish to change something in the formulation of reality, to which we are trying to add paranormal phenomena.

CHAPTER 13

Seeing is not foreseeing

WHAT WE KNOW A PRIORI IS what our senses show us of experiences. Nothing could be further from the truth! Our senses limit us to a very small part of reality. The spectrum of what is visible is very small on the scale of electromagnetic waves. No more than a few grains of sand on the beach of frequencies. Based on this spectrum, of this thimble of sand, our brain uses our eyes to receive input about the vast majority of information that comes to us from the physical world. In any case, this is how we function. Hence the expression "I believe only what I can see." In a way, the ones who use this expression are the obscurantists of the modern world, like the clergy from the Middle Ages.

This expression is so successful because we give much more credit to vision than to other senses, as we have already...seen. Aside from the fact that this expression is in itself contradictory to what we already know about scientific reality, we unconsciously superimpose it with the notion of reproducibility. We tell ourselves "if someone has seen it and if what he says is true, I will see it too." History screams the inconsistency of this approach at us. After all, history is irreversible. Still we hold on to it. Millions of occurrences have taken place since the dawn of time that will never happen again. We set forth untenable conditions to what reality must be, which is nothing like a clock. On the contrary, reality is in motion. One could even say that man has invented reproducibility to provide a better basis for predictability. In truth, the only reproducibility that nature has planned is embodied by cycles, which have the annoying tendency not to cooperate with the direction of ordinary linear causality, as we will see in the analysis of the nature of time.

Predictability is not a flaw as such. After all, foreseeing is controlling our future. It is adapting to the circumstances to come. It is avoiding sufferance and catastrophes. It is even showing divinity when we understand the meaning of synchronicity and true prayer. However, it is also an anomaly of our mind that tends to submit others to its laws. Man-made science therefore never stopped controlling free will, or even reducing it nothing. It is what the mechanist vision of the world expressed without explicitly saying so. Moreover, without explicitly admitting it, we are seduced by the enormous potential powers generated by paranormal phenomena and ETs, i.e., the ability to reproduce the supernatural to control nature. The question that remains is if, in view of the extraordinary powers at work, this is not precisely how nature punishes us for our tendency to subdue others. In other words, will intent supplant reason in the course of our evolution?

The expression "I believe only what I can see" forces the universe into our mold instead of vice versa. In the past, pre-Copernican geocentrism struck the minds with a "mental viscosity" that we joke about today. Mankind "saw" the sun moving in the sky and "believed" that it revolved around the Earth, remaining the center of the universe. We should stop laughing, because this is how "official" science, practiced or imposed by officials, welcomes paranormal phenomena and UFOs. We are still the center of the universe from a certain point of view, that of identity, that which we call chronocentrism. Indeed, after the central vision in space (geocentrism), we have to shatter the belief of a central vision in time (chronocentrism). This belief is famous for the constant and unconditional use of the physical magnitude called hertz, which is a number of cycles per unit of conventional time. It consists in relating back every manifestation to our physical time. We "see" frequencies on our oscilloscope and we "believe" that the world turns in function of a human time unit. As you can see, modern science is, in a more subtle way, like past religions. Nothing more, nothing less.

This mental viscosity of a new kind is the heart of our contemporary society. It is proud of its work, like all civilizations that were contemporary in their own time. It has good reasons to be proud but it has hundreds of times more human beings at its disposal to do the work, which puts its work into perspective, both the good and the bad. In fact, it sees only what it believes.

CHAPTER 14

Representation and Reality

THERE IS A GREAT DEAL of circumstantial evidence to support the presence of ETs around us. It must, however, be examined with care because our understanding of reality is flawed. The correct question is why this evidence is circumstantial.

What follows requires more than an effort to understand, rather a tour de force of our intellect to leave behind our preconceptions. Therefore, it is possible that some of us will not immediately understand what this is all about. I am suggesting that mathematical language is like dictionary language: a representation of the idea, of the concept. However, the concept must be correct. All of science is based on three essential aspects: the concept we want to comprehend (relativity, for instance), the representations that describe it (equations) and the means to verify it (measuring instruments). Whereas the triptych concept-representation-means poses hardly any difficulties (and we will find out why) when it comes to easily accessible facts — both from an intellectual and a material point of view — non-trivial facts are a whole different story.

Whereas the concept may not adequately describe reality, in the framework of the concept, the representations do not necessarily have to be clear. The fact determines the concept and recognizes its relevance or the absence thereof. The evidence of a fact then depends on the means of verification that can be used to affirm the recognized reality, used by our civilization to create progress. In fact, the functioning of the measuring instrument itself depends on the representations (equations) that have helped to establish it. I am not saying that the equations are flawed, but rather incomplete, either because the facts were incorrectly interpreted, or because there is no distinctive frame of reference. Sometimes even the problem itself has to do with accuracy. That is why physicists apply perturbative calculus and try to assess the effect of a physical quantity in a certain result. This evidence also depends on the verification conditions. The confirmation of a hypothesis depends largely on the protocols chosen for the test, and even these protocols are being questioned.

The great difficulty is that representations must not be substituted for concepts and that means of verification must not be substituted for representations. These deviations, these substitutions, are called interpretations. Every scientist who expresses himself thus delivers testimony of his own interpretation. I sometimes regret that certain philosophers disregard the frailty of scientific truth and allow themselves to be deluded by a certain form of autocracy. This is quite an obstacle because it actually leads to an impasse, as Maddox emphasized.

Many scientists cannot resist the temptation to satisfy themselves with the outlandish formalism of representations, at the risk of presenting them as reality in guarded terms, thus keeping the entire discussion out of the circle of initiates of this formalism. In essence we must consistently insist on the importance of these concepts to break away from the mountain of interpretations that take us further away from reality, from the pure experience. It is important to understand that this is not about pointless and lengthy talks, on the contrary, it is about attacking the evil that eats away at us — the distortion of the truth to be more precise — first by mistake, then out of interest.

Let us return to the debate and apprehend a little more this dichotomy between representation and reality, by staying in the universe of academics for a moment. They are to literature what mathematicians are to physics. They define words, groups of words and their grammatical relations that will hopefully bring meaning and enrich our mind. By dissecting the characteristics of an object, by categorizing them, by creating relations between their components, we move away from reality, we divide it, we explain part of it. Therefore, unless we actually bite into an apple — which is the experience itself — this is a thought form of which we, depending on our abilities, succeed in visualizing all or part of its characteristics, at the same time or separately (an important differentiation in consequences). What then is the real difference between the object-apple (reality) and the apple-object (representation)? The electric signals of the brain? The ones it produces or the ones it receives? We should be well aware of the fact that it is impossible to know with absolute certainty the path taken by electric information. Does it go from the muscle to the brain, or vice versa? At light speed, it will take a corporeal electric signal one three hundred millionth of a second to traverse one meter of nerve fiber (electric resistance disregarded). It is simply impossible to measure this duration for at least two reasons. The first is that there is no such thing as an adapted measuring instrument. The second is that it is impossible to exactly isolate the electric signal in question in the brain. That is why the animated is different from the inert. In addition, the fact that our waking consciousness is apparently oblivious to an event that happens to our body does not mean that part of us does not already know of its occurrence in advance, or may even create it! The logical shortcut of the information route is in itself a tautology[23] of causality. This is an example where the epistemology applicable to fundamental physics has to find a response in the physical-chemical interpretation of the functioning of the brain.

Where do we draw the line between imagination and electric image? What is imagination? Is it the realm of the unreal or the real of someplace else? Unless there is no reality in the time of a variable stroboscope? So many questions that the progress of the cognitive sciences has pretended to ignore. After all, what is at stake is not the least of the wagers of our understanding: what is the experience of reality? If we want to know whether or not UFOs are real, then let us start by defining reality! Just like the words of this book are trying to make us see things differently, apple is a word. But the reference-object (another word) is not one of them. In the same way, the equation is a representation. But the object-concept is not one of them, even though the concept itself can be questioned, but this will be addressed in the next part. Thus, the distinction between "signified" and "signifier" must be permanent in our mind to avoid that it literally falls right through the nonsense. We now know that what we call a particle in quantum mechanics is neither exactly a punctual body, nor exactly a wave. It is neither! This is a violation of a logical principle: the exclusion of a third possibility. The particle shows only corpuscular or wave patterns of behavior. When you imitate someone, do you actually become that person? That is why it is important to remember that in an equation this is what happens if...

In fact, this debate refers to the objective and the subjective. Hence the rational and the irrational. Which one describes reality best? Both at the same time? Are they then compatible? How and to what extent?

That is what we will try to discover. What is at stake is enormous, because what is hidden behind this anodyne question, considered by many to be unproductive, is quite simply the truth. Our society is based on our perception of the truth, be it scientific, moral or religious. All scientific debates, whether they are public or limited to select circles, implicitly reduce scientific facts to the rational truth. This truth is based on a particular form of reasoning: it is the measuring instrument that ensures recognition.

Let us take a brief look at time to illustrate the trap we must avoid. How do we usually envision time? There are two types of time: measurable time and psychological time.

Measurable time is objective! It is a universal convention! In other words, it is a fixed interval between two phenomena: before/after. Science uses seconds that have multiples and subdivisions. This time is recognized by our intellect! It is quite useful in the organization of numerous things and equations. These are called the hard sciences.

There is a distinction between duration-time and date-time. Everyone knows that duration is the difference between two dates. In the same way, one can pinpoint the date by using constant durations. Hence the existence of time mechanisms such as watches and clocks. The modern version of these two types of time consists of the time unit and the time scale. Thus, the duration-time called second has become the standard, whereas the clock counts the conventional time units to define the time scale. A modern time scale must check four qualities[24]:

1. Durability: a time scale must be able to continue to date all future events.
2. Accessibility — universality: a time scale must be accessible to all potential users.
3. Stability: the duration of the unit of a time scale must be constant over time.
4. Precision: the duration of the unit of a time scale must be equal to the definition of the unit.

Through these definitions we immediately observe the source of the tautology. Imposing the universality of the time scale reduces our ability to understand phenomena that are exceptionally sensitive to temporal fluctuations. In the same way, stability gives time the reproducible nature of its flow. Therefore, a choice has been made in favor of these attributes that deprive time of its intrinsic qualities. This shows us that time scales and units are purely conventional. Based on these arbitrary conventions human intelligence intends to solve the mysteries of the universe.

Psychological time is subjective! Sometimes, an experience seems to have lasted one minute in one situation and ten in another, etc. The time measured will determine by convention the average time and establish admissible proportions in our consciousness; e.g., eighty percent of our life is gauged by the standard of psychological time. Curiously, we are capable of waking up at exactly six o'clock if we really put our mind to it. This concurrence is designated by the term internal clock. No one has ever seen it, but everyone accepts it. Psychological time is called subjective because it seems imaginary! Yet have we ever wondered how it is possible that something so widely accepted as the imaginary did not exist as such? These are called the soft sciences.

It is therefore customary to distinguish between objective time, which is measured, from subjective time, which is perceived. Which one truly constitutes reality? A priori, measurable time appears to be a good candidate, but on second thought it is based on notion, on a convention: seconds.

An atomic clock merely determines the most extensive conventional definition of seconds, not their reality. Here the instrument only serves to illustrate what intellect has not deduced, but a priori induced. Nevertheless, regardless of how exact and stable the latter may be, it is

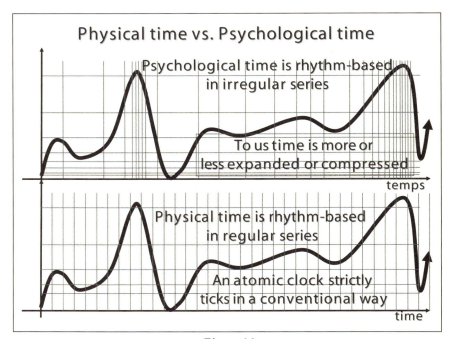

Figure 14

perfectly subjective, while it is a given that it is in no sense a product of reality. If this were the case, we would not need cesium 133 because of its intrinsic properties in atomic clocks. The radiation of microwaves, the frequency of which is adjusted to induce the chosen atomic transition, takes place in the Ramsay chamber that constitutes part of this clock. In addition, a bombardment of photons enters to cool off and thus to slow the flow of cesium 133 particles in order to regulate the true clock, which is made up of a quartz crystal that drives the microwave generator. This quartz crystal supports the process. So time is by definition linked to a constant (transition of the hyperfine level) and a frequency that is permanently adjusted to conform with the arbitrary convention man applies to locate himself in time. Seconds are the product of a human, non-conditional postulate. In fact the purpose is subjective because artificial, and thus unnatural. A contrario, the supernatural is natural, i.e., not artificial, or even beyond the mental.

On the other hand, psychological time originated from a perception that seems subjective in every sense, but that is direct information, without a go-between, like the signified object being the apple is to our senses. This object-apple and this object-time are in fact pristine information, by any interpretation. They are quite simply reality, even if this reality relies on the perceiver. We understand that the term subjective must be restricted to the meaning of the word personal (consciousness) instead of the meaning of imaginary (non-existence). Therefore, reality is personal, as is truth. On the other hand, interpreting the latter is not equal to the truth. Interpretations have occasionally led to impasses.

According to Etienne Klein,[25] subjective time "elaborates a type of coexistence amidst the present, the immediate past and the imminent future. It unites what physical time continually separates, it retains what the latter carries away, includes what it excludes, preserves what it eliminates…Strictly speaking there would be no melody without this alliance in the heart of consciousness. By focusing on all their schematic representations, physicists may have forgotten some of the fundamental properties of time. The monotonous time of physicists, made up of independent, identical and repeated ticks, might well be but a very poor idealization of our lifetime and obviously more tedious than an algebraic variable."

We quickly see that reality is simply how it is being perceived, without a detour, without a go-between, without excuses. Psychological time is objective time, because it is the true object-time. It varies, because the consciousness that perceives time is informed of when it is, just as we are informed of where we are. We could summarize the situation by saying that the subjective irrational is formed by information about reality, whereas the objective rational is formed by "interpretations" of information about reality that have actually been generated by the alienation decreed by the rationalism of the Enlightenment. We should understand that the purpose of research of this objective rationality is to reproduce what we are trying to break through and control. As by chance, this technician-scientist exactly affirms that the proof lies in this reproducibility. This circular reasoning, stating that proof comes from reproduction, invariably conceals the rigid sense of domination of creatures towards their environment by means of a unilateral decree (interpretative convention) that sustains this "superiority" instead of harmonious living. The evidence is used as an intrinsic justification of our superiority in the cosmos. It is called anthropocentrism. Man is right because. He says so now and has always said so. The fact that the nature of evidence changes with time seems merely a detail.

We might add that cyclical time is nature's clock. It expresses itself in millions of different cycles. These cycles are not just part of the cosmos, but of all natural regimes and conditions. Even when they are perfectly concrete, they are still a principle indication of fractal time and of the violation of linear causality! Let us make a minor digression and linger on a minute detail of the magnitude of 10^{-34}.

Astrology uses cycles. Needless to say that Planck's constant h equals 6.6×10^{-34} joules/second. Subsequently, a wave of a length of 10^{34} meters (ten million billions of billions of kilometers) is linked to a macroscopic object with a movement quantity of 1 kg x m/s. We do not feel the effects of this wave while the object is on Earth. This wavelength is too big to observe undulatory phenomena, even on our macroscopic scale. We therefore describe phenomena with the only classical clockwork we have. Celestial bodies are a different story. Nearby or distant planets have a direct scientific impact on the behavior of objects and creatures on Earth (and elsewhere). Considering the energy they give off (movement quantity of billions of meter-tons per second) and the harmonics associated with them, these planets (and stars) really affect us depending on their relative position. These positions engender phases, phase oppositions, etc. So astrology is a genuine science...unless all science is false.

On the other hand, the interpretation of the effects of these waves is a more subtle matter. We will see that it is related to the fractal network of causal relations with high temporal densities (taking into account the energy of the propagated frequencies), where the symbol, being the causal structure, is a cause in itself (explained later). Therefore it is not a matter of precession that will modify the symbolic structure located in the high energies. Symbols are the software of the mind just like algorithms are the software of a computer. Once again, those who do not have the fastest time-going-by at their disposal will not understand this truth. It is therefore useless to try to convince those immersed in physical time. Establishing the exact symbolic definitions (and their effects) calls for an extremely long apprenticeship as it constantly requires going back and forth between the observation of human behavior (after having categorized it more or less) and the position of the planets to deduce their occurrences.

The substance itself of the scientific act, i.e., the observation, thus requires a long period of time. Unlike numerous modern disciplines, astrology proves multimillenary. Its statistic principles (although quite empirical) are therefore probably the world's most recognized basis. Quantum mechanics is not any better with its probabilistic nature. The difficulty of the exercise consists in fact in integrating the increasing share of free will as man evolves in consciousness, and thus his capacity to make increasingly numerous and diversified choices. Astrologists may therefore benefit from integrating the causal parameter sets addressed further on. We should not forget that by changing the paradigm, we also modify the old schematic representations of our increasingly enlightened behavior, leaving behind causes that can no longer affect us.

What hampers scientific formalism is that reality in its entirety depends on the individual rather than on unalterable laws outside the individual. What causes the separation is that reality is defined by consciousness! This is the battle led by the materialists who feel that man is subject to the laws in question. Again, the distinction we have made before between signified and signifier comes to the rescue. How do we define man? What is it inside man — since he and he alone considers the object studied — that compels him to obey the laws or that frees him from them?

The matter is not just philosophical, unless it is redefined, but regards the realization of science with a consciousness. It is clear that the goal of the scientist, as mentioned above, is not to describe all of reality, because that would be impossible, but to come as close to it as possible. However, science clearly has double standards. It displays humility before the evidence question where the philosopher is concerned and still allows itself to use this same evidence as a means to deny reality. This reality does not seem to enter the scope of research and knowledge, particularly with regard to researchers of the paranormal. Epistemology is to science what ethics are to human relations. Scientists have a perfect memory of the epistemological precautions: "Yes, I know these concepts very well," they often answer. Indeed they do. In practice however, they are far from applying the rules they know exist. That is why the debates are often fruitless, because what matters are the actions taken and the spirit in which the experiment takes place.

It is wrong to personify science to condemn it more, just as it is wrong to personify religion. There are scientists and there are devotees. What we fight most of all is the dogmatic interpretation that they both have of their occupation of faith. If we clearly understand what religious faith is, we see less what scientific faith is all about. It pertains to representations, i.e., equations such as the icons of our priests. At least the latter have the courage to openly speak about faith, unlike certain scientists who take offence.

Nevertheless, the history of science shows us that there are different ways to demonstrate the same thing, more or less by chance. It also shows the capacity of a mathematic device to broaden the scope of its applications and thus of the profound meaning of the concept it proposes. Let me illustrate this comment. In 1965 the Nobel Prize in physics was awarded to Julian Schwinger, Shin-Itiro Tomonaga and Richard Feynman for their work in quantum electro-dynamics. All three used a different formalist approach to say more or less the same thing, or almost (the three formulations were compared by Freeman Dyson, to Feynman's good fortune, because his work was misunderstood). Whereas the first two stayed within a very conventional and complex framework, the third distinguished himself by simplifying diagrams that have become standard today. But what is tomorrow's standard?

There may be a middle term between two a priori opposite positions, between rationality and irrationality: the frame of reference! If a rule is true in one whole, the laws of classical physics for instance, it may no longer be true in another. Think of the laws of the mind. We could also speak of the principle of the excluded third possibility. In other words, why fight when we are not even talking about the same issue?

CHAPTER 15

Free at last?

IN KANT'S *CRITIQUE OF PURE REASON*, he presented his antinomies, one of which is related to the structure of truth. Freedom constitutes the thesis; determinism (natural causality) is the antithesis. The paradox of absolute truth is caused by the fact that "each act is always both the effect of a cause according to a certain degree of determinism and the cause of an effect according to causality through freedom. Paradoxically, every act is therefore both free and determined."[26]

Let me state the dilemma as clearly as possible. Which extreme solutions are within our reach?

If causality through freedom does not exist, our choices do not make any concrete ripples in the universal pond. The results do not correspond to our expectations due to this lack of causality. Choosing is unnecessary, because it does not produce an adequate result. Daily life clearly shows proof to the contrary. Strict determinism, caused by "lawful" causality, strips free will of its validity because every choice is as such the impersonal result of a series of causes that led to this apparent choice. In other words, our choice was predetermined. An Oriental proverb says that freedom does not exist, only the act of freeing ourselves! However, of what should we free ourselves? I believe in variable causality. If determinism was indeed a universal law, quantum mechanics and its probabilistic nature simply would not exist. It is this research method that endeavors to grasp the nature of the world.

Freedom means leaving the deterministic path by gradually breaking free from what we believe determines our choices: ego! Ego is part of a range of possible behaviors that we apologetically qualify as psychological, preventing us from developing the knowledge offered by esoteric traditions for lack of space. However, did we not say that thoughts have the power to create? Consciousness has the power to create when it possesses knowledge. We can create based only on what we know; in the opposite case, someone else creates for us...or inspires us. If causality is variable, it is so in the very nature of the cause. We are going from a deterministic physical causality to a libertarian metaphysical causality. This metaphysical, thus invisible and intangible, causality poses a problem for the materialists who have chosen...materialism. It would be wrong to think that there are two separate worlds of matter and mind. This logic of excluding a third possibility blinds us so completely that it is difficult for us to see intermediate stages between pure determinism and freedom. These antagonisms are subject to the spatio-temporal scale and absolute relativity (the more there is space, the less there is time, and vice versa).

What — besides our consciousness — can lift this paradox between deterministic causality and causality through freedom? In fact, we give more weight to determinism in case our consciousness is less developed, or more weight to freedom when, on the contrary, the consciousness of the act (and the laws set in motion) is of a high level. As a consequence, something is not true or false, but depends on our degree of consciousness. Experience shows that mental abilities are inevitably the corollary of consciousness. We should distinguish between our understanding of the individual and the understanding of our consciousness. It is actually for this reason that when we change the perception of our individuality, our mental abilities first of all affect our body (placebo and other effects). This correspondence between the physical and the mental body is caused by the variable entanglement that binds them. Other mental levels, also linked to the phenomenon of entanglement, generate interaction with our surroundings. By consistently seeing everything as relative to our level of consciousness, we may need to reconsider the role of consciousness in the reality of things. The modus operandi of causality should therefore be revised. The problem is that causality establishes the proof...

CHAPTER 16

The proof or the inferno of error

BEFORE ADDRESSING THE MATTER OF PROOF, I should define the context in which it should be discussed. The basic problem of paranormal phenomena such as UFOs, but even more of science in general, lies in the "jungle" we call our mind: we want proof! Many wish wholeheartedly to prove the existence of paranormal phenomena, including UFOs, but we still need the right instruments to establish this proof. We use equations. However, do equations describe reality? According to the Chambers dictionary, proof is "something which proves or establishes the truth of anything." The editorial of a once-only edition[27] dedicated to scientific proof paints an objective picture:

"For a long time, we used to see scientific proof as the paragon of the way in which truth was established. Today this picture seems singularly eroded….Has scientific proof lost its merits? This issue proves it has not…provided we strip this expression of its outdated content! [I will address the concept of the signified later].

"Whether they are part of the action or science historians, our authors hardly seem to focus their concerns on the research of truth or falsity….Once the power of intimidation of scientific proof eliminated and the diversity and vulnerability restored, will it regain the general favor?"

This shows the relativity of the quasi sanction of proof that becomes "officially" vulnerable. A scientific result may exist only because we expected it, since the biases of the formulation made the theory ad hoc. Postulates are sometimes proven with the same postulates. That is the definition of a tautology.

This tells us that scientific proof is an ambivalent notion, but can we do without it? We owe most of humanity's progress to the commitment of scientists to formalizing and deducing the laws of nature by constantly going back and forth between their thoughts and the facts they observe. Epistemologists know that our instruments of reason must be adjusted: logicism, formalism and intuitionism do not have any universal scope.

Thus, the traditional proof of the existence of a phenomenon does not lie in the phenomenon itself, particularly if it is unique (e.g., the unique SN1987A supernova in the large Magellanic cloud; was it a case of double standards?), but in the way we conceive it. In other words, proof is a fragmented approach towards the reality of an event that does not diminish the latter. Proof and phenomena are two separate categories because the modalities of one category are not always followed by the other. Hence the complementary importance of eyewitness accounts. Unfortunately, these are the mere prism of incarnated consciousness and therefore limited. The problem is that we expect to see events occurring in the framework of what we already know. Everything that does not fit the description causes a problem. This is why theoretical science created a repertoire of models, different for each discipline, that can be validated or not by the facts. Of course, one menu (a theory) does not constitute an entire cuisine (reality). These models are considered seriously only if they have some predictive power from which man can draw a reproduction potential. Prediction and reproducibility are the paragons of the hard sciences, i.e., disciplines related to matter and its wave derivatives. Explaining and understanding are not enough when the means to produce or verify a phenomenon remain inaccessible. This is often what happens in cosmology and quantum mechanics.

The French magazine *La Recherche* therefore suggests that "proof is eventually reduced, not to the beauty of an explanation or a model, not to common sense that evolves over time, but to the production and verification of a fact." Implicitly, this restriction holds us back because it implies that the necessary means are available to meet these conditions. Producing equals, in fact, reproducing. Verifying equals seeing it in tangible form. If we make innuendos all the time, we do not understand things in the same way anymore. In other words, even the formulation of the research of proof is threatened, because the means are material!

However, whereas the model goes well beyond this material requirement, it cannot be proven by using the current canonical approach of scientific experimentation, which brings us right back to the perceptual maturity mentioned above. Contemporary science thus does not reflect the reality of the facts but part thereof. In other words, it is unable to ascertain the truth or falsity of the paranormal. It would be nice if skeptics simply admitted that. Ego has built a barrier between disputing a fact and expressing its inability to understand it. Since it is scientifically impossible to prove the non-existence of something, this dilemma persists. The irrational status of the string theory is the best example of this boundary. However odd it may seem, the concept of proof does not exist in astrophysics! If we wanted to apply this to the definition provided by *La Recherche* (producing and verifying a fact), we would need the power to create a star, a galaxy or a Big Bang and we would have to verify all the events constituting the hypotheses of a model, from birth to death. In other words, our theories about the reality of the events of space are an uninterrupted series of assumptions based on continuous space-time variables. However, the Frenchman Nottale, for instance, has been trying to share his vision of scale relativity in cosmology for almost twenty years now.

In general, scientists usually fuss about a specific aspect of a model to avoid this problem, with rather limited results, if I may say so. If this aspect is verified, i.e., reproduced several times on our scale, the model gains better predictability. Nevertheless, verification is but one indication of a more comprehensive outline. It is possible that this indication is not part of the proposed model, but we would still have to propose another one, like this book does. The history of general relativity is a typical example. For a long time, the indication of the perihelion advance of Mercury was its only foundation, followed by the disputed observation of the gravitational lensing effects during the eclipse of 1919 and, finally, the discovery of cosmic microwave background radiation conclusively proven fifty years later!

We clearly see that our acceptance of the existence of ETs is based only on indirect or circumstantial proof — considering the countless manifestations of advanced physics. To definitively eliminate the doubt and obtain direct proof, we could quite simply ask the ETs to show themselves collectively, for personal proof is testimony by definition. They may agree to do so if enough of us ask them. However, as we have seen that proof is another way to express total control over nature, it is not certain that the scientific community will make that request.

Aside from the fact that the competition did not come up with anything better, general relativity became important because of the publicity it received! If Einstein had not doubled his efforts to promote his theory, the history of mankind might have turned out differently. This significant example is far from being an exception. It is a rule. The media are trying very hard to turn this into a law. Today this applies to the Big Bang theory. In the same way, the superstrings of the allegedly unitary M (Mother) theory do not even seem to exist. One of the most important promoters of superstrings, Nima Arkani-Hamed, said: "it is certain that all we do is consider a concept as mathematical. Up until now, it has just proven a wonderful dream." It is easy to understand that this law — the power of promotion — is not the truth, just like the Keynesian economic model is not the truth, but an excuse used by the rich who sustain it. This model promotes the principle of scarcity of a good or service; hence the existence of "regulating" mechanisms anticipating and even creating this scarcity. If we changed this scarcity into abundance, the model would immediately disintegrate. We need to acknowledge that scientific rigor is banished more often than it should. As I quoted before, "the fact that so many people are wrong does not mean they are right." Indeed, credit and discredit are often the products of propaganda. "Against experience, what good are all the reasons?" asked Jessica Riskin in *La Recherche*. Perhaps to understand the conditions of the experience before drawing preformatted conclusions. It is reassuring to read from this Stanford history professor that "general truths are founded in particular facts, not because of the facts' places in general theories, but on the contrary, because of their irreducible particularity. The facts are factual since they are not dependent on theories. Therefore, they do not require expertise and are accessible to anyone with common sense." At the risk of this common sense being disturbed, I should add. A fact, permanent or otherwise, suggests the presence of eyewitness accounts, collective or otherwise. This covers the entire matter of the supernatural.

There are numerous examples in the history of science suggesting that proof is fragile. This vulnerability is inherent in the complexity of reality, of its approximations, its exceptions and above all of the conditions in which the facts take place. We can therefore just as easily translate this discipline of the analysis of proof and apply it to telepathy, clairvoyance, remote viewing, poltergeists, precognition and telekinesis, which would gain official recognition if a minimum of intellectual honesty remained in the minds of rebellious scientists.

The purpose of proof may not be as transparent as it seems. There are countless examples in the history of science where the person producing a fact is not asked to prove its existence, but on the contrary, its non-existence. Neurogenesis, for example, is a caricature in this respect. An established critic and acclaimed expert persisted in his dogmatic views and argued that it was impossible to reproduce neurons as they diminish in number indefinitely, whereas proof had actually been established to the contrary. The problem originated with the measuring instrument used and Elizabeth Gould's young, innovative team. Fifteen years earlier, this researcher had already rejected the works of Michael Kaplan on the same topic. Kaplan described every condescending enmity and the resistance he experienced from fellow researchers (including Gould) pushing him to leave the field. This is not an isolated example. Hundreds of others pave the winding road of knowledge. In general, the purpose of proof depends on the amount of indexed data. In the case of paranormal phenomena and UFOs, the mass of data is undoubtedly significant. Of course, we are only considering the fifteen percent[28] of observations that cannot be explained in a traditional manner. Normally, this would suggest that the data as such constitutes solid proof of the reality of phenomena that may not be explained yet, but the axioms of which are dawning on the horizon. If we had to categorize the proof studied by advanced science based on its solidity, depending on the number of occurrences, then UFOs would probably be one of the world's most substantiated phenomena. However, by validating this fifteen percent, a considerable number of cases (among the other eighty-five percent) is ignored that may also be explained in the traditional way, but are still left out when the proof is established using classical explanation methods. We allow ourselves to believe that this is true, which is the opposite of the scientific method. Once again, Occam's razor, the principle according to which the simplest explanation is always the best, presents only one side of the story.

To end this discussion of proof, the special edition of *La Recherche* once again comes to the rescue. Historians describe proof as a dynamic object and definitely not as a guillotine that separates true from false. The following principles of establishing proof have been described by historians[29]:

1   Arbitrariness caused by the moment of the experience affects the meaning of proof.
2   Numerous cultural interpretation criteria remain implicit and cannot be proven by the scientist involved.
3   The confirmed validity of proof varies constantly and evolves depending on the doubts that arise over time.
4   The effectiveness of proof is forged through personal experience with what is read or heard, assimilated and verbalized in the individual's own words.

5. Proof is negotiated by those who take part in the personal assimilation of the experience. History is constantly rewritten.

Science historians therefore argue: "Thinking that proof is absolute, a permanent given, would be historically false. Is there any statement that was not refuted one day?"

This shows us the frailty of "scientific proof" that only has status in a specific context, that of temporarily accepted laws. Let us start using our calculators for purposes that go well beyond "advanced physics," which may only be a few years old but will be considered prehistoric in the coming decades.

It may be useful to add that the views of science historians are not shared by scientists who cannot be judge and jury at the same time. The assimilation of what we read or hear therefore takes place prior to the establishment of proof. The vast majority of skeptics do not follow that approach. They merely retain their status of believers. Better even, negotiating the proof requires at least two individuals. The irrational does not come from the one we believe, but from the one who shows off the arguments of the proof he failed to understand, as we have just seen. Unfortunately, ufology fans and skeptics often stick to their positions. We often witness dialogues between the deaf. It is what others do with the proof provided that counts in the acknowledgment of the supernatural. However, can contempt be considered proof? Proof of what?

Finally, we have seen that genuine certainty, another word for the designation of proof, comes only from experience. When it comes to paranormal phenomena, is there another approach than by experience in order to obtain the authority required to debate it? In other terms, if the witness is able to search for explanations, does not that make him the highest authority to speak about the experience? Do not the five points mentioned above defined by historians to establish the foundations of proof in fact describe consciousness?

CHAPTER 17

The market of theories

IN THE JUNGLE OF MODELS, regardless of the discipline studied, it is difficult to be prepared for everything. There are indeed countless theories, varying from formalism, adhered to by so many scientists, to personal interpretations supported by small groups of scientists and, more simply, different conceptions or proposals. There are even theories within theories.

The example of the Big Bang, also a speculation, is significant. There are no fewer than some one hundred versions of inflation[30] theories about the first second of an alleged explosion of the universe alone (in fact a dilation of space), which is but one possibility to describe the beginning of the Big Bang; another mere assumption.

Quantum mechanics is in the same boat. Without speaking of the string theory that has no fewer than five[31] thought currents, the quantum theory is split into no fewer than nine that are a cross with strange notions, such as materialism, idealism, non-local hidden variables, space, time and the oneness of the universe.[32] There are numerous other, less-known options that just have not received enough media publicity attention.

Whether we speak of the post-Darwin evolution, biology, chemistry, ecology, geophysics, but also of social sciences — in fact all disciplines — there is not a single research field that has not been the stage of academic and sometimes quite unbecoming confrontations. Is there anyone without a personal theory?

The insights of louts regarding televised science or of the written press are an illusion. It seems indeed that consensus prevails. However, reality is quite different. So many theories and we do not have a clue as to what to do with them. Choice; the worst embarrassment.

"Official" science is therefore on a self-imposed mission to cut back the branches. However, what do we know of the fruits they could bear? We could envision positive things and tell ourselves that the harvest of sometimes antinomian proposals is the manifestation of a springlike vitality among scientists who eventually manage to reach agreement on the great unalterable principles. On the other hand, we could also see this effervescence as a sign of the neverending fight to impose our views, at the risk of changing the balance of research ethics via commit-tees of mediating referees.[33] Are we in an assembly of wise men or in an arena of gladiators fighting for their lives? It would be nice if those who favor a psycho-sociological explanation of ufology made a psy-chological study of the members of these committees on which they actually rely to refute the existence of serious ufology research. How-ever, perhaps they would then become both judge and jury. Perhaps they would use research instruments that are actually avoided by absolute relativity.

Wise men or gladiators? Probably both at the same time, depending on the height that each is willing to take. However, which place is occu-pied by the truth in all this? Just like the truth is not meant to be spo-ken all the time, every truth is not meant to be found. How many research proposals have been rejected simply because the theme they broached was not in line with the dogmatic framework of prevailing theories? Is the love of truth the birthright of our society, considering how it is used by voters on election day and, most of all, by the media when it comes to information? Most citizens wrongly think that the truth (signified) prevails. Many are not interested in knowing the truth, but in the opinion of others. The truth often frightens us when it opposes the beliefs that validate our choices. We use the signifier (the word truth) to "mold" the signified instead of expressing it. The progress made by science should not be measured in terms of pub-lished articles, but of rejected articles, because those are the mark of a true researcher. Finally, it is rare to find genuine researchers of the truth who really see beyond appearances and are fully dedicated to that cause. The lack of time, the solicitations and the pressure of all kinds prevail too often over our enthusiasm.

Can we still add other proposals to this ambivalent and vaguely outlined universe of knowledge consisting of shrewd manipulations? Of course. It is even a necessity; a vital one at that!

Can new proposals still be part of the framework of modern physics? A new theory should obligatorily get off the beaten path, which has been so frequently traveled that it has become barren land. There is therefore an absolute need for radical innovation since the labyrinth of knowledge lacks any form of conceptual homogeneity. What is lacking is flexibility, the seed of every contemporary approach. What is lacking is the magistrate who re-establishes peace between disciplines: time!

CHAPTER 18

Time, an answer to space

A STRANGE THOUGHT MOVEMENT appeared in the corridors of fundamental research in the early twentieth century. As we added knowledge to our libraries, we also started adding space dimensions to our universe, particularly when Klein and Kaluza appeared, the fathers of the fourth spatial dimension. The idea of adding overlaps of space to what we cannot explain is the successful syndrome of the prevailing materialism, because our eyes decided that matter takes up space. We therefore continue to see the world through our eyes in the conceptions that we can work with. The parallel worlds of the string theory are typical of this intention to see the effects "some-where," which our eyes could possibly conceive. The promoters of superstrings argue that we do not feel the effects of these dimensions because they are too small. In fact, that is because they do not exist. Small-scale experiments of Newtonian gravity (one tenth of a millimeter) were conducted to estimate the presence of hidden dimensions. Newton is always right on this small scale. On the other hand, we clearly feel the effects of temporal dimensions via psychological time! After the dogma of finite light speed, after the dogma of a ST with three space dimensions and one time dimension, we have come to a standstill in our search for space "elsewhere." That is because our dictionary can only say "some-where" and not "some-when."

By insisting on dividing the whole into ever smaller parts we eventually dissect the bigger whole. We collect spaces as if they were objects. Materialism obliges us to reserve a thing for every place and a place for every thing. This propensity also comes from our difficulty to imagine time to be other than linear, going from the past to the future

97

with us — but who are we? — in a specific place: the present. Convince yourself and draw a straight line (a notion of space) placing past, present and future on it. Almost everything we do is related back to a spatial representation in the name of unchangeable, sacrosanct causality. Even pedagogy needs to draw reality. Thus, the "design" of the universe has become the "drawing" of the world by force of habit. I am not surprised that we lost sight of the first and gave preference to the second. Logic and its principle of excluding a third possibility made us believe in a logical flow between cause and effect, without even considering any other principles. Hence the idea that every flow has an upstream and a downstream (another notion of space). How do we get out of this space matrix? How do we get out of this clearly deterministic causality? Does free will, of which we are so proud, really exist? Can the scientific and philosophical issue of determinism and its opposite indeterminism be solved in a mutually non-exclusive way? Is the universe governed by one or the other? Or must a third principle be included so that thesis and antithesis find their synthesis? I think so. We will see that 3D time is the secret ingredient in this symmetry.

By arguing the absolute opposite of this multiplying logic of spaces, I think — and the facts will convince you — that only time dimensions can be multiplied. We have to build a new frame of reference consisting of multiple floors, where space will actually have fewer dimensions instead of more. It is time that will be gaining relief. However, instead of turning STs into conceptual virtualities, we will make them come alive, capable of forcing nature to behave itself in a certain way. In other words, an ST is not a simple box or an ordinary container, but a fluid that we can mold like a potter shapes his clay on a potter's wheel. The shape of this modeling clay will subsequently be multi-purpose (in fact omni-purpose). What is time?

Roland Lehouc,[34] astrophysicist in the astrophysics department of the Atomic Energy Authority CEA,[35] described it as follows: "Time could seem one-dimensional without it being so really, a little as we lose our sight of relief by closing an eye...For instance [note: if time was three-dimensional], energy would no longer be just a number, but a vector indicating the temporal direction of movement....If two observers who are moving according to different temporal directions meet, they will inevitably separate to follow the irrespective temporal trajectory, incapable of staying together. From the point of view of an observer, the other one would appear and then disappear immediately" [note: as UFOs or ghosts do]. I should add for the sake of completeness that this

CEA researcher still reminds us that the stability of atoms opposes this three-dimensional conception. He therefore rejects the idea that time could be fractal (a property of one of the three dimensions, that of its density). This particularity would explain precisely this in fact quite relative stability, which the traditional conception of time does not! That is a breakthrough for official science.

CHAPTER 19

To unite or to separate?

THIS A PRIORI INTANGIBLE NOTION of time is the keystone of all of the following developments. The difficulty of the scientific exercise consists of dissociating from the fact in order to analyze it. In other words, the ideal point of view for a scientist is that of a discrete and impartial observer. The canonical approach of science, based on the experience outside oneself, is therefore the mascot of research professionals and the essential reason for the rise of materialism.

If the research object is outside of us, then the formal approval is validated by separating the observer from the object observed. This is what lays the foundation for objectivity as it has been understood since the Age of Enlightenment. This separation is not just useful in research. It is indispensable, for it establishes the legitimacy of the researcher! In other words, truth requires separation. However, it seems that mystics have always seen reality as a unity. We are beginning to understand that the intelligence of materialist science is a rather pale copy of the science of the future: holistic science.

This notion of separation is what underlies the "hard" or "pure" sciences. We can avoid the subject or pay lip service to the influence of the observer on quantum mechanics experiments, but we continue to pretend it does not exist when we use the representations (equations) of mathematical formalism. A physicist (specialized in missile manufacturing) who sat next to me at lunch one day told me about the gap between reality, concept and representation: "it is not perfect, but it is the only way we know how. In addition, experiments often prove us right." Indeed, we have not found a better way yet.

It is true…they are right because they "make" it so in the framework of the formalism they invented; an increasingly complicated formalism aimed at using an increasing number of instruments by controlling a maximum number of parameters, sterilizing laboratories and ridding them of the chaos of life, i.e., stripping reality of what is real! In quantum mechanics more than thirty parameters must be neutralized! Maybe the universe is really very complex after all. It is, but for different reasons than the belief in the universality of formalism. As we have seen, the difficulty is that the discrete notions of determinism and reproducibility hide behind the research of formalization. To shed new light on the categorical statement made by debunkers, for whom "the paranormal solely results from a willingness to believe in supernatural phenomena," we could very well ask them why they believe taking the real out of reality makes it non-existent (the neutralization of parameters).

First of all, either science clearly defines its own activities by drawing a dividing line between determinism and indeterminism, which would immediately usher in its downfall (leaving behind a society of engineers), or it agrees to abandon the idea of objectivity and separation, of which formalism is an expression. Only then can another science emerge. This new science, a hybrid between determinism and indeterminism, between constraint and freedoms, must appreciate the variable degrees of freedom and of non-separation. The new science must give up its current status in favor of awareness. Philosophy and science still have a long way to go before they meet up, but eventually they will meet. That moment is approaching fast. It may even happen before you finish this book.

We immediately see a seeming contradiction: freedom and unity versus constraint and separation. Can we be both free and united? Can we be constrained and separated at the same time? We will see that all of this is conceivable in the light of a new vision of time.

While time is a common place for many of us, there are hardly any specialists in the matter. There is no universal definition of time. As Etienne Klein put it — a great time specialist who believes that physics abuses its power by speaking of what is real whereas it only has access to phenomena: "we are an inexorable part of time." No observer, even if he is a scientist, can step out of time to evaluate this highly debated philosophical and scientific issue, as is space for that matter. In special cases, the observer (scientist) and the object observed (time) are not only inseparable, but the first completely depends on the second. Countless quasi truths are affirmed resolutely and never even justified. Are we condemned to remain both judge and jury? To live the permanent illusion of our beliefs? Even the question contains several biases.

Who are we? Are we not our multiple selves? Are we all identical? Who should "judge"? What should be judged? Who is the "jury" we are talking about? It is obvious that dissecting a question the rationalist way brings up other questions. Quantum mechanics as well as special and general relativity taught us to beware of common sense, which is rarely just the temporary state of what is generally accepted. Common sense is not synonymous with truth, far from it.

Do we use the right words to discuss time? Some say that time is what happens when nothing happens — as the CEA scientist suggested — that it is the most convenient means nature found to stop everything from happening at once. I think the truth is quite different. We will see that everything converges to form a trustworthy representation of 3D time. In absolute relativity, an extension of 3D time, time does not exist when nothing happens. However, it always exists when something does happen. We still need to know how to perceive this "something."

This immediately becomes an ambitious endeavor. We are not just connecting important theories, but reconnecting matter and mind that only seem separate because we do not perceive the temporal dimension. Matter and mind are separated by the "conventional time" we carry on our wrist as if we have been shackled. Another objective is to explain paranormal phenomena and the behavior of UFOs. Schopenhauer argued that "the amazement of scientists is characterized as extraordinary, while the amazement of philosophers is characterized as ordinary." Ordinary reality is in fact extraordinary: all is one! You will see.

CHAPTER 20

Reality put to the test

SPEAKING OF THE CONJUNCTION of the three aspects of science — theory, simulation and experiment — Jean-Marc Lévy-Leblond, lecturer at the University of Nice, said: "physicists do not even begin to cover what we want to know about reality, because specifying reality implies a considerable limitation of the scope of this reality, not in the least by the instruments adapted to our visual range....We are about to witness a change in the nature of scientific knowledge"[36]. This author of popular science books testified: "reality is a mental construct rather than a whole of objects." A mental construct? In other words, we are talking about consciousness!

For Emmanuel Marode, director of research at CNRS[37] (note: emphasis added by the author), "simulation is based on the *idea* that reproducibility is a characteristic of reality [note: this is in itself a very restrictive and self-justifying axiom!]. In other words, we explain our observations by *inventing* entities with properties. We then *visualize* their behavior in the reality we try to reproduce in equations. We subsequently *try* to solve these equations and find stable solutions. Unfortunately, there are numerous cases where this is not true! The obtained solutions behave randomly and differ greatly if we make even the slightest change to the initial data." This testimony tells us that reproducibility has its limitations. We indeed need to reflect on the scale of approximation in which we work and the probability amplitudes of the diffusion matrices. The divergences (the appearance of infinities in equations) still cause a problem (except in 3D time). The truth therefore lies in the internal coherence of the theory.

When it comes to reality, Klein's testimony brings up very relevant trick questions: "how real is the reality proposed by physics when the

Nobel Prize is awarded to an experiment with superfluid helium-3 that only requires a temperature of a few milli-Kelvin, whereas astrophysicists tell us that such a temperature does not exist in the universe? How real was this reality when the top quark was discovered, whereas there are not any left in the universe?" An embarrassing comment perhaps but we are discovering the non-existent! Does that not ring a bell?

In essence, the universe is as we create it. We can create conditions that allow us to obtain any result. In general, it is hardly known that most of the "exotic" effects of quantum mechanics have been created artificially by selecting the conditions of an experiment. These conditions are renewed by choice after "chance" has affected the results that were not in line with the experimenter's expectations. He therefore feels the need to know more about it, thinking that he could use that knowledge to his advantage. Hence the appearance of a longing. In general, if we feel the need to invent something, we will make it happen! The universe is necessity inspired by longing. If necessity is a law, it is because desire is a law!

Mathematics strayed from physics and developed an arsenal that is utterly useless in physics, Klein observed. It became complex to the point of being inefficient. On the other hand, path integrals,[38] for example, are not mathematically tractable (problems related to action S when its value is sensitive to the scale of Planck's constant) and they are used by physics in Feynman diagrams and diffusion matrices every day. What about the Banach-Tarski paradox based on the axiom of choice, as opposed to the axiom of measurability? A peculiar choice to "prefer" either determinism or indeterminism!

For mathematicians, mathematics is too beautiful not to exist, time experts tell themselves. However, is the painting of an artist too beautiful to see it as just an expression of his imagination? Is this a case of double standards? Is not mathematics merely one possible form of longing disguised as necessity? We have clearly invented virtual entities on which the standard model of quantum mechanics is based! How many constants or coefficients are we forced to add to the equations to arrive at an accurate description of reality? What is the deeper meaning of the "divine" referees? Do these questions not mean that mathematics consists of purely imaginary numbers,[39] just like dreams fill a need created by an underlying desire? Dreams are effective because they clear some of the emotional load that an individual has been unable to express in words. It is true that emotions cannot be expressed in an equation, but does that mean they are non-existent?

CHAPTER 21

Mathematician or Creator of the universe?

ETIENNE KLEIN GAVE A PARTICULARLY enlightening lecture on the efficiency of mathematics. He presented two ways to decipher this intriguing efficiency, expressing what the entire scientific community already acknowledges:

- "either this language is thought to be the language of nature and those who study and wish to understand nature must evidently master it,

- or on the contrary, this language is thought to be the language of man and the facts of nature must therefore inevitably be translated into that language if we are to understand them."

Many, particularly Plato, Aristotle and Kant, but also those who look closely at the proliferation of instruments and utterly invented concepts, believe that the first solution is wrong. As for the latter, we assume that mathematics is the only human language capable of describing the world. In my opinion, that is the biggest error of contemporary science. Ubu said: "So here I am, King in this country!". Is that convincing enough? It is true that the Coué method has its merits. Feynman felt that "we practice mathematical physics for lack of a better way."

In the article "Zur Elektrodynamik bewegte Körper,"[40] published in 1905 describing special relativity through the bias of clock coordination,[41] Einstein used a style that was met with astonishment. Peter Galison observed[42]: "it does not really look like an ordinary article on physics. There are hardly any footnotes, very few equations, it does not mention new experimental results, but uses a great deal of banter to describe simple physical processes that do not seem anywhere near the boundaries of science." I take this demonstrative stance on the matter instead of using opaquely complex phraseology.

Finally, let me say that mathematics is effective as there is a large variety of constants relative to various transformations.[43] Dirac said that the presence of a large number of constants is often an indication of the profundity of a theory. This polytechnic professor defined the matter well: "the presence of constants associated with some transformations is always seen as an indication of the existence of an 'element of reality,' of something that possesses a relative independence, just as we succeed in acknowledging the 'reality' of an object in normal perception, by seeing how it behaves when we change our relative position to it."

However, what is an element of reality, he asked. "Being able to speak of a reality requires that something subsists or persists in temporal flux or in changed points of view or observation instruments. A first criterion of reality is therefore the existence of constants under specific transformations." To conclusively prove the existence of something we must look at an object from every angle. "However, reality," he added, "is also what appears to be endowed with a certain unity, a certain internal coherence." We are very far from pure and solid materialism. We can say, for instance, that astrology possesses a certain internal coherence.

We become aware of a specific reality when we perceive a relation between the parts and the whole,. Therefore, persistence and coherence constitute the foundations of reality, mathematical or otherwise, but unstable particles do not necessarily prove the accuracy of these criteria. In technical terms, this is called general covariance, i.e., the invariance of physical laws that take the same mathematical form regardless of their expression in a reference frame: the Galilean transformation in classical mechanics and the transformations of the Poincaré group in special relativity. This covariance describes a physical reality instead of an effect caused by a specifically chosen point of view. To identify this element of reality, it must still be linked to a more general concept, while guaranteeing its singularity. This is where science fails in its theoretical foundations. Conceptual links and singular identification are two indispensable requirements in establishing an element of reality.

The indisputable, astonishing and quite real effectiveness of evolved mathematics in particle physics and cosmology is connected to this intuitive property of a language rich in constants, the scientist suggested. These rich and constant structures are nothing other than generalized symmetries. It is the code of conduct I propose in the next part arguing that "the more there is time, the less there is space, and vice versa."[44] Klein, respected by the scientific community for his reflections on time, has written a large number of scientific books and articles focusing on the nature of temporality. In this chapter, I was inspired by one of his lectures. Let us be grateful for his brilliant mind.

CHAPTER 22

Let us take time to think about it

"PHYSICAL TIME IS VITAL to the formalized understanding of reality. It is however, just a concept of operation without a precise definition. We even ask ourselves if it exists as a conceptual state. Indeed, the past is gone, the future is not yet and as for the present, it ceases to exist when it is ready to begin," he stated. In other words, Klein asked if anything can exist if it only exists of nonexistence. "It only proves refuted," Marcel Conche wrote. The problem is that if we cannot a priori imagine the existence of time, we cannot imagine its inexistence either, because every experience, human or otherwise, seems to follow this abstraction. This actually serves science because causality, the corollary of linear time, is the justification of its contributions! Let us see if it is as solid as we think.

We know that psychological time possesses a variable fluidity and that its consistency is quite relative. We have seen that psychological time comes from within. In fact, it varies with age and is determined by the intensity of events. Even temporal isolation experiments on individuals have not been able to elucidate the matter. Therefore, our reflex response is to focus on what is called "physical" time.

Klein put it beautifully. "It seems impossible to derive the time of the world from the time of the soul." Would the seeming aporia between the punctual instant (before/after) and the living present (immediate past/immediate future) condemn us to incompatibility, i.e. to the principle of excluding a third possibility? Is the thickness of time a chimera? Nothing is less certain! Time is energy in the broadest sense of the word and vice versa (personal conception). In fact, unstable, ephemeral and intangible time is a nuisance to scientists, who subconsciously want to eliminate it from their equations. They try to find connections that avoid the variations. However, the Frenchman asked, are flow, sequences, duration and irreversibility uninfluenced by matter-form relations? As a matter of fact, time can be found in all physical equations, in one form or another. As Klein put it: "physics claims the unchangeable and the constant. However, in practice, it bumps into time." When it comes to temporal flow, classical physics and special relativity offer different answers. Duration suggests a beginning and an end seducing cosmologists to hold on to the Big Bang theory. "Irreversibility seems to be the actual temporality of time rather than one of its traits." May I add that it is even the source of the most persistent tautology there is. Is time really irreversible? Does the past always precede the future?

The continuity of time imposes itself upon our mind because its hiatuses do not seem to exist. This allows us to establish dates and use dating instruments. Parameter t seems only to have one adjustable dimension. This tells us that time has weak topology. It can be expressed in two ways, lines or circles. The latter method was abandoned by physicists because it does not observe the principle of causality, as the cause cannot come after its effect.[45] They cannot cut the branch they are sitting on. We now understand that the utter flaw of science — the dogma of causality and therefore of equations — prevents it from clearly perceiving the nature of reality and of paranormal phenomena in particular. Pretending to reproduce such a so-called supernatural phenomenon (by deterministic causality) therefore boils down to pure and simple ignorance! In short, skeptics ask the rain to fall only into a glass. In our mind we make the universe logical in agreement with our own logic! That is the definition of anthropocentrism. Scientists thus adhered to the idea of an irremediable, well-structured sequence. Nevertheless, the principle of least action, used by Feynman for quantum electrodynamics, reveals deep holes: "we have lost the idea of causality, according to which the particle feels the force and moves under its influence. Instead, the particle magnificently explores all the curves, all the possibilities, and decides which way to go by choosing the one where our presence is minimal." So is the world a system or the unfolding of a story? On the one hand, the philosopher Parmenides argued that the reality of the world is one being (the Way of Truth): an unchanging, indestructible whole; on the other, the philosopher Heraclitus believed that change is real and stability illusory. For him everything is "in flux." Does physics describe permanence or metamorphosis? Maybe it eventually just describes a variation, a probability of…choice! The researcher from Jouy-en-Josas asked a good question: "is the time of thermodynamics the same as that of mechanics or of cosmology?"…or of the mind, we might add. I can say that neither the matter of irreversibility of time, nor the status of the alleged asymmetrical structure of subjective time have been solved by physics. The famous time arrow, the principle on which all of science rests, could very well only exist in our consciousness…or our imagination! The matrix is not that far anymore…

We should keep in the back of our mind that this development aims to show the nature of paranormal phenomena.

CHAPTER 23

Time for theories

To Newton, time goes by consistently and is universal and absolute. The principles of his mechanics were based on this claim. The calculus of trajectories, time being the external parameter of the dynamics, thus determines positions from one moment to the next. Curiously, the temporal dissymmetry does not show up in the fundamental law of dynamics. It remains invariant because we can use the same equation to calculate, at random, a position in the past and in the future. This is called symmetric evolution. It is how nature could undo its doings. Klein emphasized that "therefore, in the ideal case, where there is no friction, Newtonian phenomena are reversible. Newton's time is scrupulously neutral. It neither creates, nor destroys. It only keeps track of the passage of time and sets markers for trajectories." According to Newton, all instants are equivalent.

Special relativity, the theory of ST, affirms that time and space are entirely physical phenomena. They are not virtual containers. However, time, although quite different from the Newtonian conception, does not have the three-dimensional stature of space. Since Galileo, time has not only become a quantified magnitude, it has been decreed a fundamental parameter. So during the fall of an object, the acquired speed is proportional to the duration of the fall. This proportionality has induced a bias that is particularly difficult to undo: it is said that a phenomenon changes over time rather than that the passage of time changes during a phenomenon. It seems that exterior time — advancing continuously and isometrically rather than observer time — advances more or less quickly than that of the falling object, or vice versa. In other words, in the spatial frame of reference that is identical to all and unquestioned, objects move according to the same time scale. It seems indeed counterintuitive to tell ourselves a priori that time changes during a transformation of state. After all, how can time itself change? This is what 3D time proposes, and particularly absolute relativity that, by definition, builds a new temporal topology.

The following diagrams illustrate how time unfolds with 3D time from a physical viewpoint. We know that in nature all is vibration. In addition, Einstein taught us that time is not absolute but relative to an inertial frame of reference. The novelty of 3D time is that nothing exists outside phenomena. Time is actually conveyed by the phenomena and from a larger point of view by the structured wholes! This seems a simple approach, but is in fact a revolution of scientific conceptual structures. As everything is vibration, time can only be found in waves.

In reality it is time that creates waves! A wave is a traveling disruption. The wave energy comes from the kinetic energy transmitted by the disruption to the matter the wave traverses. Each section of matter is the seat of a "force" that goes up or down and tends to stretch it at the moment of the "surge." This explains the saying that waves transport energy. It is important to understand what the elongations

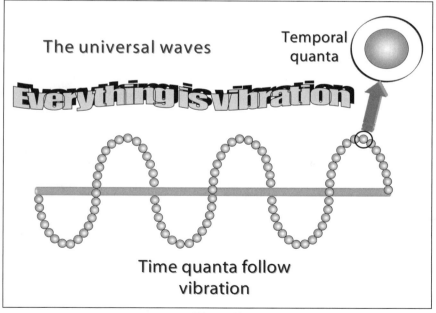

Figure 15

and compressions correspond with. This is clearly described by a natural "object" called longitudinal waves! These consist of compressed waves followed by stretched waves as in helicoidal springs. In other words, a sinusoid is a succession of much smaller longitudinal waves that move up and in the center of the primary wave. These longitudinal waves behave in a quantum manner. They form a sequence of bundles represented in the diagrams by circles.

Waves change in several ways. Eager to develop a concept, man developed the arbitrary and conventional time of the standard "second." By doing so we completely suppressed the idea that time could be variable (variable quantum time). We lost sight of the fundamental idea of inspired thinkers that all is one. However, first a giant leap, greater than man's first step on the moon[46] was needed to bridge the gap between admitting the unity and feeling it.

To grasp the immediate impact of this new vision, one need only spread out time quanta on a linear axis. We see that by attaching them to one another we obtain a totally different duration of the metrological orthodoxy generally called physical time.

We can therefore compare waves with time spirals. The peculiarity of these spirals is that the number of temporal quanta varies during

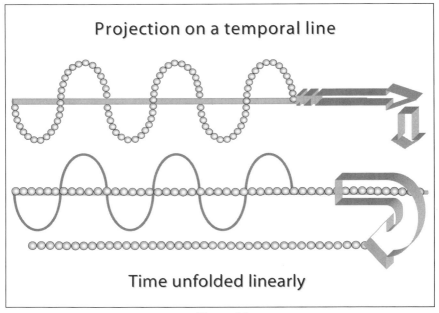

Figure 16

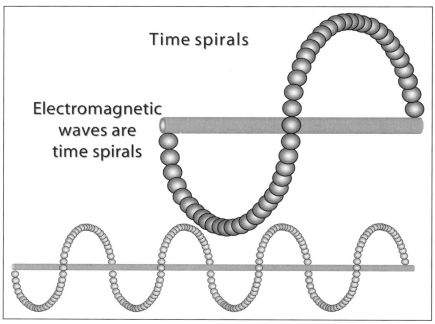

Figure 17

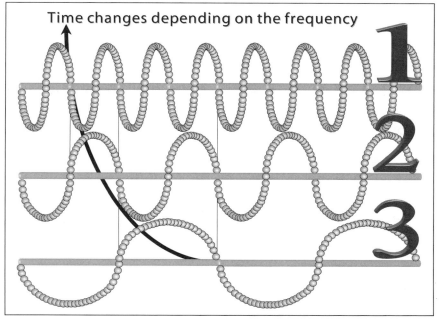

Figure 18

our classic time passage, in particular when nearing amplitude maxima. We should keep in mind that this classic passage of time (as shown by our watch) does not exist. A frequency is a number of cycles per time unit. If this time unit is just a projection of the human mind, everything we think up in order to understand reality will be fundamentally biased. This error prevents us from conceiving that, as the diagram below shows, time quanta are very close to one another and are even superimposed on top or underneath the curves.

One of the directly observable aspects is that quantum time changes depending on the frequency. The closer the time spirals, the greater quantum time will be.

Similarly, the amplitude of the wave changes significantly this quantum time, in particular the sections of superimposed quanta, at the top or the bottom of the curves.

By correctly spreading out these variations we observe a remarkable singularity. Temporal portals appear! These portals convey the concentration of quantum time, in other words the superposition of time quanta. We will see that this superposition is in fact an effect of spatio-temporal diffraction caused by the holographic nature of the universe. The universal hologram hides the primordial unity of the world.

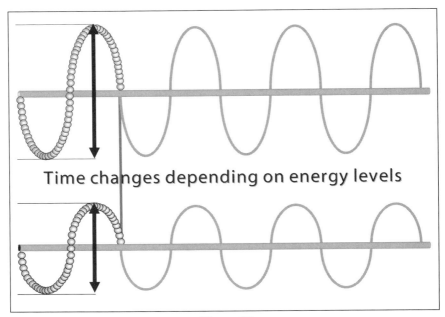

Figure 19

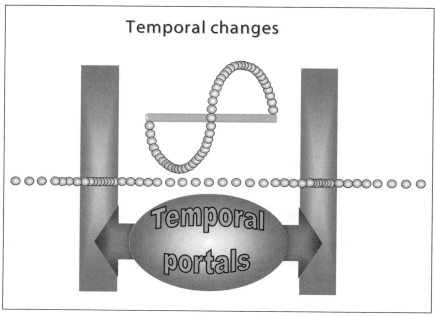

Figure 20

This could prove to be a crucial figure in our analysis. It illustrates the existence of a manifestation and disappearance frequency in these temporal portals that affect the behavior of a large number of particles in the framework of probability amplitudes in quantum mechanics. Let me remind you that these amplitudes grow larger like the forces (scale leap) of the calculus of disruptions. This diagram also affects the results of interferometry in Young's double-slit experiment, where areas of wave concentration appear at the interference point of two photons. Above all, it seems clear that entropy, a synonym for temporal irreversibility, is caused by the fact that the temporal quanta are separated by two temporal portals with, however, an intermediate boundary where the quanta are neither superimposed (temporal portals), nor separated. In other words, the entropy is also cyclical if we observe this sinusoid from a much slower passage of time, which we can do with the help of a temporal convention (seconds). We can summarize this comment by the following figure.

In absolute relativity causality thus become stroboscopic, which means it is possible to "go" from causality (1) to the absence thereof (3) via stage 2 of the diagram. Acausality (absence) only exists from our macroscopic point of view, i.e., from a certain passage of time. This

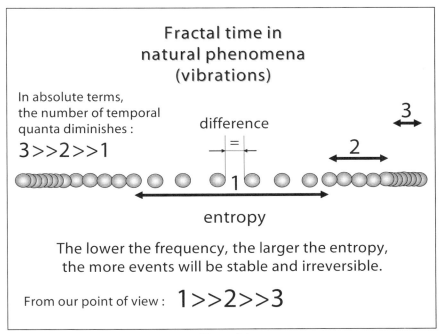

Figure 21

acausality is simply caused by the fact that the absolute amount of information follows the opposite curve. Numerous quanta are unavailable and therefore cannot be inserted into a cause-effect relationship. Causality is relative and variable. Neguentropy (3), negative entropy, would thus be the result of a superposition of time seen of course from a temporal point of view (ours).

We should note that these temporal portals establish contact with space-times of a higher temporal density, which is the seat of the mind's activities. We fall back exactly on the stroboscope of the quantum states. We can also conceive what asymptotic freedom of quarks is all about. Let us go back to the impasses of science after this interlude.

We sense quite well that temporal irreversibility constitutes our physical reality, the researcher affirms. However, proving it is a different matter. It is what Sadi Carnot endeavored in the nineteenth century by opening the path to the second law of thermodynamics. He demonstrated that the conversion of heat into mechanical energy can take place only in a way that is not reversible, i.e., from hot to cold only. The fact that the entropy of an isolated system can only become greater during physical events naturally leads to the notion of temporal dissymmetry. So the concept of invariance has been shattered and that of irreversibility affirmed. I explain this dissymmetry by something I call missing time (next figures).

Does this mean that our senses do not fool us? I am not so sure! Actually, the annoying drawback of fundamental microscopic equations is that they are reversible! Similarly to Newtonian dynamics, the movement towards the future equals the movement towards the past. Neither one is less physical than the other. On the other hand, macroscopic equations that describe the more universal behavior of the matter on a scale close to ours are irreversible! Assuming that microscopic equations describe macroscopic equations more accurately, why would one be reversible and the other irreversible? "Are we still in the same world?" asks the professor.

Ludwig Boltzmann used the laws of statistics to link the dynamics of Newton (reversible law) to the second principle of thermodynamics (irreversible law). This means we no longer have perfectly defined and deterministic trajectories, but position probabilities. The positions and velocity of the molecules can be expressed as mathematical values. Irreversibility would thus be the result of an evolution from a highly unlikely micro-state towards a more probable macro-state. This brings us to the very frontier between determinist and indeterminist causality. Klein concluded that: "The thermodynamic arrow of time only goes from order to chaos." But this chaos does not exist as such. It is a simple interpretation, an intellectual viewpoint. In reality the entropy measures only the misrecognition of all microscopic states rather than the disorder, which is a squandered thought. Nevertheless, it is remarkable to observe that irreversibility is produced by a lack of recognition! In other words, freedom of reversibility would be an attribute of every system (or creature) that has perfect knowledge of a state, but also of a choice! Perhaps that is because the creature is the state, or, rather, consciousness is the state. All knowledge implies we can choose to apply it. The attentive reader will thus realize that every experience is chosen at some point in time ("temporal portals"), at which our habitual causality does not yet exist!

Would not the role of statistics be related to a more or less focused consciousness in one or more states? Are not statistics the mathematic expression of the frontier that exists between determinism and indeterminism? Between strict causality and absolute freedom? Probability amplitude would thus be a simple degree of freedom, of choice. It is tempting to suggest that temporal irreversibility is the nature of complex systems, as Klein did. However, we could state to the contrary that irreversibility is "in fact" and not "in principle"! We see the gap between reality and formalism because the latter fails to prove the irreversibility of time, which for materialist scientists is more than just a pain in the neck. It is an insurmountable obstacle.

In his private correspondence even Einstein seemed to confirm the idea that time is mere confusion: "People like us, who believe in physics, know that the distinction between past, present and future is only a stubbornly persistent illusion." We are beginning to see that time hangs by a fine thread. Why then does it hold on at all? Ilya Prigogine, who challenged the idealistic conception of quantum mechanics that accepts the intervention of human consciousness, viewed it differently. He believed that macroscopic irreversibility is an expression of the fact that the nature of the microscopic level is subject to chance. He wrote: "statistical descriptions introduce irreversible processes and increased entropy, but do not owe anything to our lack of knowledge or to any anthropocentric characteristic. These descriptions are the result of the very nature of dynamic processes." In other words, in his view the microscopic level creates the illusion that there is no arrow of time. The problem is that this has not yet been demonstrated. As a believer in the Big Bang, he felt the world was created thanks to a small group of initial conditions that, in his view, rendered the statistical representation of the universe totally natural, transparent and foreseeable! But what is this multiplicity of initial conditions? How and why would these initial conditions favor the arrow of time? No one is able to answer that question. Therefore, many people feel that the Big Bang never took place, and justifiably so.

"We suffer from countless contradictions, not only in classical mechanics as we have seen, but also in numerous, much more advanced formalisms (special and general relativity, quantum mechanics, quantum field theory, cosmology, etc.)," this French time specialist iterated.

CHAPTER 24

Parmenides or Heraclitus?

FOR EINSTEIN, TIME PARTIALLY TRANSFORMS into space, and vice versa, by switching to another Galilean reference in the ST. Therefore, time loses its absolute status and becomes dependent on dynamics. In other words, the faster a clock moves, the more slowly it will tick. Time dilates. This is called the "elasticity of time." Such a deceleration is observed in unstable elementary particles. Muons — heavy electrons — are a good example. They exist in the high atmosphere thanks to cosmic rays, but also in high-energy collisions. The faster they go, the longer they last. It is interesting to see in this example that, whereas they are born and die in the same location, their lifespan is 2.2 microseconds and increases with motion. The importance of this remark lies in the idea that in the absence of space (the absence of motion), the temporal dilation — when muons disappear — could be much larger, but they must unfold in space for us to see time dilation from our three-dimensional spatial point of view.

This seems to contradict special relativity, but if we consider that the "measured" energy comes from the spatial structure unfolding, stretching out a higher time density than that of the reference frame (it "sucks in" new time quanta), the real energy may be much greater in the case of seeming immobility. A new vision of time then inevitably imposes itself. As space dilates, through motion for instance, we perceive the unfolding of time, because we belong to a space-time fractal where the time quanta are moved apart. As a consequence, history and therefore temporal irreversibility are made of increasingly larger time steps as the considered space grows larger. Causality thus becomes conditional for it depends on the quantity of time in a given volume of space.

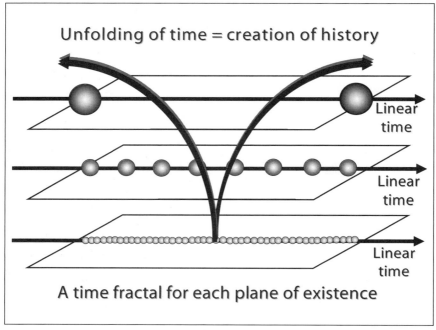

Figure 22

Our physical perception is the source of causality. Read this line again; it is a scientific revolution. The macroscopic viewpoint engenders the cause-effect relation instead of vice versa. The opposite point of view constitutes the theoretical foundations of modern science.

Finally, the sufficiently fast motion of a particle or an object is a temporal fractal "converter" that makes chronons[47] appear where they should not exist. In other words, we measure or do not measure energies that do not exist in the same Galilean reference frame. Part of that energy remains hidden in this brief instant. The entire mechanics of vibratory states, i.e., quantum states, benefits from this new and finally comprehensible explanation. The probabilistic nature of quantum mechanics indeed reflects the difference of temporal quanta between the macroscopic and the microscopic. Reducing the wave packets during measurement provides a temporal coordinate common to these two worlds (micro and macro).

Moreover, a strong indication adds credibility. Since we know that the more there is time, the less there is space in absolute relativity, the possibility of considering minuscule and even null lengths produces enormous problems when we want to study, for instance, the electrostatic field generated by an electric charge, let us say an electron, at

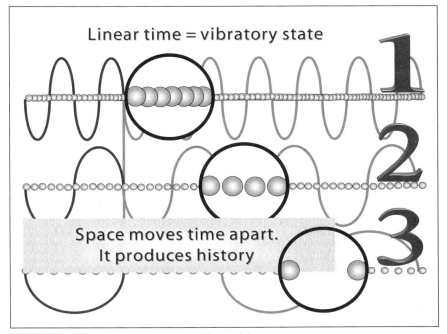

Figure 23

distance r. This field, a variant of $1/r^2$, becomes infinite when distance r reaches the null value. Such divergences or singularities lead to mathematical problems that can be avoided by using various formal procedures (cut-offs) that eliminate these divergences and allow for calculus. Physicists are certainly taking some undue liberties! Dirac showed his discontent with this currently official heresy. I am saying that null distance r corresponds to a very high energy that cannot be measured since it is much too short for the ST of our measuring instruments![48] Null space corresponds to the union (superposition) of time patterns…

If kinetic energy (linked to motion) is naturally connected to time, the intrinsic energy must also originate in a fractal relation of time. This is the exact dilemma of the electron self-interaction, where a cut-off function is introduced to eliminate the divergence of the potential. However, 3D time adapts very well to a discontinuous fractal world. It is true that the inappropriate use of integers does not favor a change in point of view. Non-whole integers represent an interesting path in this respect. In general, every dt notation in science (small time interval) indeed suggests that time belongs to one single proportional arithmetical whole. If time can dilate, there are no infinities but leaps of algebraic unities.

We can study homothetic relations of temporal values to approach an ad hoc formalism, but rather than assuming that ray r of the electrostatic field moves towards zero or that potential and mass (according to general relativity) tend towards infinity, the system changes scales and adopts new laws in the fractal in question. Therefore, the mass of particles does not exist intrinsically, because it partially equals the expression of the temporal fractal values. E no longer equals Mc^2. The fractal energy corresponding to very high temporal densities remains potential for a given lower fractal, without unfolding in it. The Casimir effect, for example, where the spontaneous appearance of electrons (in other words, the materialization of a particle) is associated with two opposing radiation pressure forces, is explained by an exchange between space (spatial compression) and time (the electrostatic potential of the electron, "invisible" up until then). The harmonic frequency state relative to the space between the metal plates in the experiment is a remarkable aspect of this effect.

I should add that the value of the particle spin correlates with its fractal boundary between quantum mechanics and metaphysics. Every non-whole spin (in case of fermions) contributes to a temporal fractal change. This does not apply nucleons, but it does apply to electrons or quarks, for example.

This is a total reversal of our traditional concept. We can indeed measure energy because it has become available on an accessible time scale. This is somewhat similar to acceleration applied to an individual. In a space vehicle, ten g during two minutes will be difficult to endure. However, a one hundred-g force — capable of killing someone several times over — applied during a few thousands of a second will go by totally unnoticed and is harmless. The same applies to the energy hidden in a brief stroboscopic moment. In addition, energy is not only generated by motion, for general relativity teaches us that it is equivalent to mass. In quantum mechanics, this equation is applied to the letter because particle mass is expressed in electron volts! Hence the idea that fractal time, equated with energy, advantageously replaces mass in quantum mechanics (not entirely, and we will find out why). To be more precise, mass is described by the space the particle occupies. It only varies in terms of chronons absorbed by this space.

In this book I am claiming that quantum energy is essentially linked to the duration of phenomena rather than to particle mass, which cannot possibly be measured on this scale, and particle radiation. Please note that mass also means the intensity of gravitational potential.

Gravity is a curvature of the ST that directly influences time flow veloc-ity. Electrostatic potential and gravitational potential both have the same pathology: a field divergence.[49] Even if one of them can be "renor-malized" (addition of infinite counter-terms) and the other cannot, the answer is still the same: time is fractal![50]

The energy of which we speak is constituted of a useful or kinetic part (accessible by instruments and expressed in phenomena) and a potential part (inaccessible because too furtive from our reference frame). This potential energy is the energy of the vacuum or "zero point energy." It could be called present time energy. This energy (in reality present on several fractal levels) is a power source for subtle bodies and for paranormal phenomena to draw the power to take place!

This is how we deduce a causality change linked to the irreversible nature of time. If causality changes, entire science disciplines will have to be revised.

Einstein taught us that time is pliable. We must therefore learn to con-trol its viscosity if we wish to tap into this incredible energy of the vac-uum. For instance, the notion of simultaneity ceases to be absolute. For an observer, an event can unfold in the present moment, whereas for a

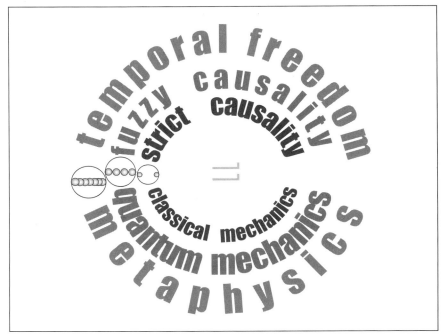

Figure 24

second and third observer, this same event takes place in the past and in the future respectively, providing that at least two out of three individuals move in different directions and/or at different speeds. Each observer thus carries his own inner clock and no one in the universe has the mother clock. So many objects in uniform motion, so many affected clocks. They cannot possibly be synchronized. If time no longer has a standard, special relativity dictates that the principle of causality cannot exist either. This applies to each observer who lives in his own reference frame. The so-called world-line cannot exceed a certain angle, the one that constitutes the speed of light. The question that comes up is: which type of causality can exist between two reference frames, between the physical world and the mental world, for instance?

Physicists use general relativity to describe gravity as a geometric property of the universe. We learned that the density of mass and energy is a condition for the structure of the ST and that it is this structure that determines the dynamics and the trajectory of the objects present in the universe. Such ST metrics, i.e., the trajectory of objects, are vital to understanding the world. "Whether we address velocities (special relativity) or the intensity of the gravitational potential (general relativity) time is subject to phenomena," Klein observed. What I am saying in this book is the exact opposite: phenomena are subject to the passage of time, which allows them to occur or not. However, there exists a natural time flow (fractal reference frame) and an artificial time flow (paranormal). Indeed, we have always seen time and space as passive objects, like the virtual container of the phenomena we study. Nothing prevents us from assuming the opposite point of view and arguing that whoever controls time and space, controls the occurrence of phenomena, such as UFOs, ghosts, extrasensory perceptions, poltergeists and so on. However, how do we control time and space? These phenomena seem paranormal to us, because we do not have such control! We observe as a fact our "limitations" disguised as the norm outside of which everything is refuted. For now, it is important that we study the time factor in phenomena some more in order to find the missing pieces in the universal puzzle.

CHAPTER 25

The time of infinities

FOR COSMOLOGISTS WHO FAVOR the Big Bang theory, which I oppose, the so-called cosmic time is linked to the expansion of the universe. It is the spitting image of absolute Newtonian time. They argue that two observers located anywhere in the universe, who are subject neither to gravity, nor to any acceleration, should be able to synchronize their watches and keep them synchronized for all eternity. It is possible, they say, to determine the age of the universe based on the knowledge that time flows only in one single direction, towards the future.

The problem is the origin of this time! None of the physical laws apply in the first seconds of the universe. They conflict with each other. Hence the abundance of inflation hypotheses consisting, in short, of the image of abrupt and violent phase transition. For water, a phase is a state. It can be solid, liquid or gaseous. Between each state there is a transition when the equilibrium becomes unstable. It is possible to go below zero degrees Celsius while maintaining the liquid state.[51] This is called supercooling. It takes only a micro-phenomenon to turn the water to ice instantly. Therefore, this type of phase transition must have been typical for the beginning of the universe.

In fact, we do not know anything about how the universe came about, except for the fact that it did, and even less about the origin of time. Speculations come and go as to why the universe is made of matter instead of antimatter (in the traditional sense), or why the universe quite simply exists, whereas it also could not have existed. What time was it before the beginning of time? We are told that this question is irrelevant, but that is perhaps because there never was a beginning, just like there will never be an ending. Dates are a human invention!

On the other, particle end of the scale, quantum formalism is based on a very different vision of physics: the wave function of a system. This combines several terms, in this case the position probability and the probability of finding the system in a particular energetic state.[52] The peculiarity is that we can measure only one or the other. The actual measuring of one of these terms cancels out the knowledge of the other, the so-called reduction of the wave packet. While the particle wave function is dramatically changed by the act of being measured, it allows us to calculate only the probability that a certain value is picked prior to measuring. The wave function is assigned by the aforementioned Schrödinger wave equation. However, it remains valid at velocities that are low compared to light speed!

This function has the same characteristics as Newtonian dynamics: it is reversible and deterministic. However, while the equation is neutral, the measuring, i.e., the relation established between the measured system and the macroscopic system of the measuring instrument annuls this temporal reversibility by intervening in the measured system. The measuring therefore creates a temporal irreversibility ignored by the Schrödinger equation. I must admit that this singular time arrow is generated spontaneously, because it did not exist before measuring. Many physicists even think that time becomes irreversible simply because we see things! In other words, if there were not any observers, past, present and future would not exist, and neither would phenomena. Mystics therefore say that consciousness is the eye of God that makes things manifest. This peculiarity has inspired scientists to take an interest in the concept of symmetry.

CHAPTER 26

Is the beauty of the world symmetrical?

THERE ARE THREE TYPES of symmetry: C (Charge), P (Parity) and T (Time) symmetry. The characteristics of a single symmetry do not necessarily correspond to the characteristics of two or three combined symmetries.

The principle of causality, which makes the existence of antimatter inevitable, is the very foundation of physics. This explains why all physical theories predict the invariance of the dynamical laws based on the combined CPT function! This invariance is verified by the mass and lifespan of unstable particles and their anti-particle. The same phenomenological probability is observed on either side of the mirror, even if the phenomenon itself is different. An antimatter world would verify the same laws as a matter world without being exactly the same. In other words, the invariance does not apply to the world, but to the equations that describe the dynamics common to that world. Once again, there is a difference between representation and reality.

However, several catastrophes took place. In 1957, it was observed that the weak nuclear force or weak interaction did not respect the P symmetry. This interaction is one of the four fundamental forces of nature and is responsible for certain radioactive phenomena. Therefore, the mirror-image of this phenomenon...cannot be reproduced! However, that is not all. The weak interaction even violates the symmetry under a charge conjugation without affecting the combined CP symmetry! It was then thought that the CP symmetry could be preserved if the CPT symmetry, and therefore the T symmetry, was preserved. To the dismay of physicists, it was discovered in 1964 that the CP symmetry too was slightly violated during the decay of neutral kaons (singular particles). Because of the CPT symmetry, a violation of the CP symmetry is equivalent to a violation of the T symmetry. This symmetry violation, which remains strange to this day, leads us to conclude that the absolute irreversibility of time (past to future) does not exist for kaons, no more so than the logical causality.

It then becomes obvious that each conceptual system in physics possesses its own temporal system. It is remarkable to observe that by gaining more in-depth knowledge of the infinitely small, time somehow seems to be taking some liberties. In reality, the seemingly logical time arrow reveals only itself in bits and pieces (thermodynamic, cosmic, quantum).

The universal foundation of irreversibility is crumbling and may become just a conditional and relative phenomenon. It is important to understand that a connection can be established between special relativity that dictates the light speed threshold by violating causality and this quantum singularity that does not. The argument of causality therefore cannot be used to defend the unsurpassable nature of light speed and, as a consequence, the dogmas of science.

We could describe the situation as a seeming opposition between history and time on the one hand, and eternity and the absence of time on the other. I am arguing that these two points of view are not contradictory but can exist side by side thanks to 3D time.

CHAPTER 27

Eternity or motion? Causality put to the test

"FOR BERGSON, DISCURSIVE INTELLIGENCE creates a wrong representation of time. It forgets to face up to the true nature of duration, which is the continuous invention, an eternal study and an uninterrupted appearance of everything new," Etienne Klein reminded us. Instead of opposing different points of view, I suggest we incorporate them in a larger vision: beyond physical time, psychological time adapts to the phenomena of the sensory world superimposed by the observer on others that are not of the same fractal level. Is that why an African proverb says that those who have watches do not have time? Plato saw the world as "the mobile image of immobile eternity." Ultimately, there is nothing new under the sun, but it must still be expressed in terms of our scientific progress to give this Platonic definition an objective and constructive consistency. Paranormal phenomena are simply the manifestation of this definition. Like Husserl, I believe that time is produced by our consciousness alone, but it is important to define consciousness if we want to discover what this "product" looks like.

While physicists search for the best way to represent time, they do not unravel, however, its nature. Does it make sense to represent something that is indescribable? The problem is that by adjusting time to a flux consisting of infinitely close moments elapsing one after the other, we create more distance between us and the reality of metamorphosis, where the information flow varies depending on the object studied. I think that time is part of phenomena instead of something separate. Time and phenomena are so closely related that it is safe to assume that time creates phenomena.

The evolution of scientific thinking thus increasingly affirms the influence of what constitutes the abstraction of the universe, i.e., space and time. This new vision allows us to look at phenomena, including the unusual ones, from a different angle without changing the generally accepted laws. In fact, we are interested in what is outside the norm, such as paranormal phenomena and UFOs. We all know that the "marginal" constitutes our future, because otherwise we would just remain stuck in contemporary notions. To change our point of view, we must accept that causality is variable, going from strict causality to zero causality (in the physical sense of the term). We therefore need to apply fuzzy logic, the laws of chaos, synchronicity and fractals. I will show you several indications proving the tangible existence of a third possibility, of a phenomenological gradation and of variability in the cause-effect relation. This causality change — from absolute reproducibility to absolute willpower — will be expressed in various ways depending on the number of causes and effects involved, and the proximity of the cause or the effect, depending on the indetermination (inability to identify one or the other), and more simply through the absence of relations.

In fact, causality is a matter of complexity. The greater the complexity of a system, the less causality is expressed "individually." Causality becomes the system, as observed in thermodynamics. Therefore, a systematic analysis provides the best formulation of causality. The system is defined by an inherent causal mode. The human body is a good example. Depending on the purity and form of the system connections, cause and effect will appear clearly or not and may disappear completely in a hyper-complex inter-connective network such as the brain. The network needs such complexity to generate the connections it needs — as we have seen in neurogenesis (production of neurons), i.e., the connections indirectly requested by the "network owner." Every connection is a causal link in itself. This is the fundamental quest of artificial intelligence: controlling causality by creating it and making it disappear. Creativity is a divine power. It supplants causality by its own nature. Therefore, God is not a cause, but the Principle Creator, i.e., the Willpower He shares with us. Physics picked linear time by pure convention to observe the a priori nature of causality. However, if it is relative or variable, we can accept that cyclical time with a circular geometry is useful.

Causality may disappear for one system, but not for others. Time travel can thus become possible without changing the cause-effect relations of other systems, where causality is necessary and/or rendered compulsory due to the imperfection or simplicity of the system. I am defending the idea that the simultaneous unfolding of the three dimensions of space is the source of causality and creation, and does not allow any retroaction in the past, because the degrees of freedom in space (and the space between chronons) are simply too large. On the other hand, in a simpler system with two spatial dimensions, these retroactions are possible under certain conditions.

Klein reminded us that in classical physics, the principle of causality is expressed simply by the fact that time is presumed linear with a well-defined course. In special relativity, it is guaranteed by the impossibility to transmit energy or information at a higher velocity than light speed. In the quantum field theory, the constraints of causality are expressed by the "commutation rules" of field operators. These commutation rules, he said, prevent particles from moving faster than light speed in the vacuum on the one hand and ensure that the creation of particles precedes their annihilation, on the other. However, what defines propagation in a non-local universe, as generated, for instance, by the superposition of states? That is a painful question!

These constraints (commutation rules) require the existence of particles mathematically described as particles "catching up" with the course of time (see the Feynman diagrams). In other words, antimatter would be the "material" trace of the fact that time is presumed to move in a single direction. The drawback is that antimatter has an extremely short lifespan and exists in very low quantities only. The assumption of a single temporal direction and the constant "materiality" of antimatter leaves us with many questions, because no one has ever proven experimentally that antimatter can exist for a long time. Antimatter seems to be only the signature of a fractal spatio-temporal boundary. Antimatter does not exist as such, but it is still produced every day. Is this not a contradiction?

It is only one side of the space-time story that takes shape when we observe the oneness of microscopic structures. The quasi-encounter between matter and antimatter shows the enormous energy of higher temporal fractals. Antimatter engines cannot be compared to classical propulsion systems. In general, the assumption that UFOs use propulsion means adhering to an obsolete, inertial vision. However, throwing fission bombs, and more even antimatter bombs, is like declaring a war to ETs. We will find out why.

Let me fast-forward a bit. If the world-line of an object (notion of special relativity) is exceeded, we will go faster than the speed of light. On the other hand, if an electron crosses this world-line, it becomes a positron, i.e., an anti-electron. All antimatter therefore seems to be a sign of a causality that goes against ours. As a consequence, we need antimatter to explain the causality of the physical world. Please understand that the prefix "anti" justifies the use of causality — as we have seen in the discussion about CPT symmetry — which justifies the use of our equations. Antimatter eliminates "the activity of the vacuum" that this book attributes to the mind. Are we sure that such radical causality exists? We could see antimatter as simply being the absence of causality of the physical world instead of causal symmetry manifesting itself in inverted causality. In the standard model, they need each other to exist. Therefore, antimatter would not be worthy of its name.

It is strange but Feynman retracted his own statements on the matter. He initially thought that antimatter had a temporal flow that was the opposite of ours. Remember that antimatter cannot exist in our physical world for long. Our best attempt produced only fifty thousand atoms of antimatter during a few microseconds in an extremely strong magnetic field (keeping matter and antimatter apart). As a reminder, and to give you an idea of the minute quantities of antimatter stored, one cubic millimeter of matter possesses several hundreds of billions of atoms.

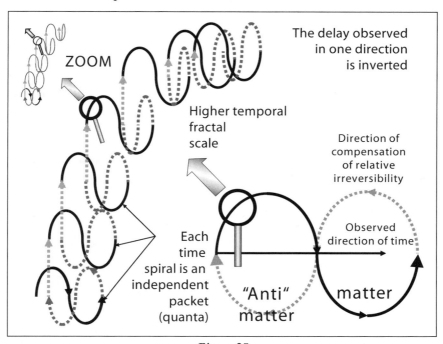

Figure 25

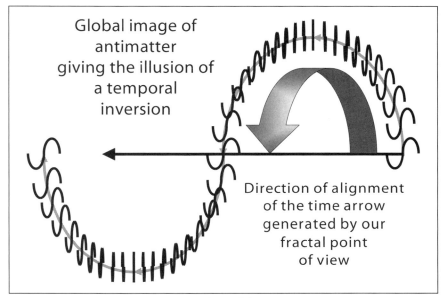

Global image of antimatter giving the illusion of a temporal inversion

Direction of alignment of the time arrow generated by our fractal point of view

Figure 26

I am arguing that antimatter is not the opposite of matter but of non-matter. This comment is illustrated in the following fractal figure.

This gives you a general idea. Antimatter may appear to be the opposite of our temporal flow, but it compensates for the cyclical and circular nature of events.

In this figure, the wavelength changes in the center of the "antimaterial" sinusoid of the whole suggest that each frequency must correspond to some kind of temporal alignment of quasi-identical frequencies (instead of strictly identical), but with inverted charge.

This temporal alignment is a simple compensation of linear time for the cyclical time we are developing.

Cyclical time wants a phenomenon to come back exactly to its point of departure after covering a period. Since the effect cannot precede the cause in linear time, this contradicts the irreversible flow of time. To confirm this thesis, it so happens that every particle, each having its own and very specific vibratory level, has an antiparticle. This symmetry is absolutely remarkable. Actually, the existence of a causality violation due to a small violation of the T symmetry for neutral kaons has been proven. I believe that this violation is an indication of the existence of this slight delay between the unfolding of the sinusoid and temporal alignment.

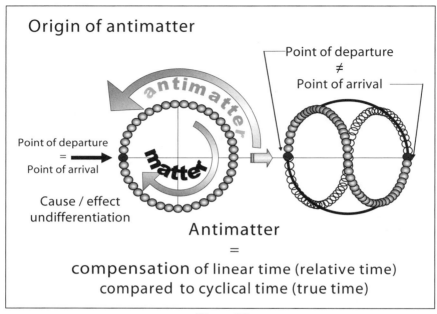

Figure 27

If antimatter makes up for the difference between cyclical time and linear time, it will thus disappear after the energy level reaches a certain point or, to be more specific, it will adapt to the signature of a higher temporal density, with the proviso that this compensation takes place at a more subtle level than the frequency of the particle in question. It turns out that photons do not have an antiparticle!

The "encounter" between matter and antimatter generates such an enormous amount of energy, because matter originates from antimatter by the difference in time density, i.e., non-matter. This non-matter is a time sequence generated by a time flow that exceeds the matter flow, generating energy as a result of the fractal change. The higher temporal density emerges in the lower density. It must then manifest itself by a huge discharge of energy effects. We have seen that there is accessible energy and potential energy. Antimatter therefore causes the latter to appear.

When it comes to 3D time, I avoid contact between "antimatter" and matter to avoid the conversion of temporal density of non-matter (antimatter) into that of microscopic matter producing effects in our macroscopic world due to its acquired spatio-temporal instability. Is not the experience of the creation of antimatter so short exactly because the temporal "antimatter" flow is so fast?

The world-line threshold associated with light speed then becomes a fractal boundary, i.e., a link between time and space in the sense of their granularity. Quantum physicists integrate antiparticles in diffusion matrices, because the stability of matter (specific fractal time flow) forces these "antiparticles" to return, not in a time direction opposite to ours, but in a higher time flow than the one of the atomic scale, i.e., in a physically acausal world, where no temporal flow can emerge (superposition of quantum time). Non-matter is therefore located on a different fractal time scale (higher time density) than matter. There is no symmetry, but a temporal fractal change from one subtle level to another less subtle level. More concretely, antimatter is realignment, compensation of the entropy caused by a temporal flow.

On the other hand, this observation makes us believe that the causality is inverted because the "particles" disappear, probably in an opposite spinorial direction considering the temporal freedom acquired in the higher temporal flow (antimatter). In reality, the prefix "anti" comes from the electric charge opposite to that of matter particles. The question is: what is the nature of this electric charge. In my opinion, it is simply some resistance of space or time related to the fractal scale of the atom, which will be discussed later.

Finally, do not forget that intermediate bosons are virtual particles[53] going from particle A (creation) to particle B (annihilation), which explains the interactions on the microscopic scale. A virtual particle is but a simple mathematical formalism. In other words, we create the causality we need in order to explain causality. This is a dogma that will be reduced to a strict minimum by the twenty-first century. The validity of many theories will soon be scrutinized.

We seem to have wandered off topic in the last few pages, but you must understand that it is impossible to clarify the UFO mystery without searching the maze of fundamental scientific thoughts. It may be a bit of a trial, but I see too many superficial books on ufology that elegantly avoid the fundamental problems and merely address beliefs. I feel that time is key. That is why I have been elaborating so long on this issue. At the end of this part, you will see where this is going. It is the individual path towards enlightenment that matters in the healing of Earth and humanity. So let us look up at the sky to receive this light.

CHAPTER 28

What do the stars tell us about time?

IF ETs EXIST, THEY MUST COME from the stars. However, do we have an accurate perception of the cosmos? In fact, the most important question is if the standard model of the Big Bang reflects reality, for it creates or destroys a large number of deductions. Big Bang equals initial conditions.

In an article published[54] in 2001, David Albert pointed out that "the initial conditions in question are presented in a remarkably simple and elegant form called statistical mechanics. We do not speak of a unique physical situation, but rather of probabilities, of the odds that a certain, specific configuration will appear. These probabilities play a key role in the scientific deduction eventually established of the temporal asymmetries on macroscopic scales." This is a breakthrough in scientific explanations: asymmetry exists because we have been lucky! The universe as we know it exists, the past comes before the future because God played dice…before they even existed! Almost apologetically, he continued: "Every strategy applied to explain temporal asymmetries in terms of initial conditions…is therefore 'slightly' embarrassing: on the one hand, these temporal asymmetries are the very models and paradigms of physical laws. On the other, we are accustomed to thinking that the initial conditions in physics depend on the coincidental, the serendipitous." Indeterminism creates determinism!

In two sentences showing his excellent sense of irony, wit and humorous understatement, this lecturer justified my position with impressive clarity. We must seriously rethink the current models and paradigms. It is easier to replace the Big Bang model with a more solid model. Furthermore, I am defending the idea that consciousness is the heart of the symmetry phenomenon. That is why we need to experiment and learn that we mentally build the course of time from what we learn in life (evolution by learning). This is the true meaning of individual and collective learning, the fundamental form of the evolutionary archetype that sends the idea of dynamics and therefore of time flowing in the direction of progress, back to the universe. This need comes from our sense of separation. The Big Bang would be impossible from this point of view alone. At the end of the article, Albert said that there exists "a certain number of suggestions aimed at changing quantum mechanics in such a way that this kind of interpretations [note: intervention of consciousness due to the psychological experience of a physical phenomenon] becomes valid. Some of these proposals demand that fundamental equations take a statistical form and do not behave like invariants during a temporal inversion." As I said before: everything boils down to statistics, because everything depends on the degree of freedom accessed by the consciousness that observes the world! That is why causality is variable! Indeed, the absence of invariance of the T symmetry decimates a great many certainties. Synchronicity, and thus its underlying psychic mechanisms, will inevitably affect the hard sciences and the soft sciences (e.g., human sciences). The connection with the perception of reality will significantly change the dogmas of cognitive sciences.

One single page may have been enough for us to start doubting the ET clichés widely spread by the movie industry.

How can causality be variable when we still see the stars in the sky above us? I would like to discuss a recent article presented in *La Recherche,* also in the edition about time. Does cosmic time exist?, Marc Lachièze-Rey asked. He presented the problem as follows. "What defines the properties of time?" The answer to this and many other questions means replacing current physics by another larger framework and using new concepts. Relativistic cosmology strictly applies the concept of space-time proposed by Einstein. However, what is the time of the relativistic ST? It is impossible to determine the duration of a phenomenon in absolute terms, or to speak of simultaneity. This does not promote the idea of cosmic time, which would consist of using one and the same reference: the origin of the universe. This situation also contributes to the erosion of the Big Bang theory.

Everyone can define their own time that will be different from all the other observers depending on its motion (position, velocity and acceleration). The time specific to an individual or object is therefore the only "physical" one. Of course, those who are close to one another, and whose differences in velocity or acceleration are small, will make only a slight or no relative distinction between their clocks, which is what normally happens on Earth. In case of particles, the differences are much more noticeable. If we follow a moving particle, its lifespan may seem very long. However, if we look at this particle from the outside, its lifespan seems shorter. Observing a particle from the outside inevitably signifies that we see it from a different temporal flow, i.e., a different velocity.

Therefore, there is no simultaneity between our physical body and... what constitutes its essence! How then can biochemists, neurologists, psychologists and psychiatrists see a causal continuity between certain phenomena, both internal and external from a physical point of view, and our perception of it? We should always start our research by studying the nature of time to establish the academic truths that feed off the tautology "temporal irreversibility/causality." We therefore possess several "passing times" depending on the space scale on which we observe them, as special relativity keeps insisting. The division into sectors of science often prevents it from glimpsing a coherent and comprehensive vision of fractal spatio-temporal reality.

Our own time, however, cannot be used in star-dating methods, since only what is in our immediate surroundings, at our rate, can be compared or synchronized with our clock. This explains why we can date only the moment at which we perceive the light caused by this explosion. However, astronomers use a synchronization technique to define cosmic time and subsequently deduce the age of the universe: they look at their watches!

They suggest that gravity, the source of local spatio-temporal distortion, is uniformly spread throughout the universe (homogeneity and isotropy), allowing the global convention of our Earth time to date the history of the universe. Having an individual (or a planet) with a much higher velocity and whose time moves more slowly is not a problem if a conversion protocol has been established. For instance, if his second takes half our time, it is safe to say that his universe is not thirteen, but twenty-six billion years old. However, what about someone whose "second" is billions of times shorter than ours (from our point of view), knowing that the speed of light is not a threshold, not even for Einstein?[55] In that case, the universe is eternal, so eternal that there is no beginning and no end. Thanks to this cosmic time, we can express the rate and acceleration of cosmic expansion (or not), as well as the dilution and cooling of inherent matter. Needless to say, this cosmic time is the foundation of cosmology.

However, it is quite possible that it will soon crumble at the edges. A fact is a fact. Everything we see of the universe happens today and on Earth! The history of the universe is based merely on speculation. The cosmological principle that is supposed to reflect the universe about three hundred thousand years after the Big Bang is nothing other than the extrapolation of the radiation existing today! Inflation, which allegedly explains the first moments of the world, does not at all fit in the theoretical framework of particle physics and will also, quite understandably, never be justifiable in laboratories.

First of all, physicists do not know every existing particle typology in the universe (particularly when we discover some that are not supposed to exist). Secondly, they do not know the number and distribution of black holes, essential factors presumably playing a role in gravity. The calculation of homogeneity and isotropy takes place in the observable universe instead of the entire universe. Actually, there is not enough observable matter to take into account the dilation of the universe, probably because the universe simply does not dilate at all!

In cosmology, the principle of Occam's razor seems to be used with…reluctance. At this time, there is no objective reason to assume that the seventy percent of missing mass are uniformly spread since their location is unknown. The discovery of dark matter should have refuted the Big Bang model. To save it, however, cosmologists hold onto the concept of unseen, hypothetical, exotic matter to avoid explaining that, in the opposite situation, an enormous quantity of deuterium (hydrogen isotope) should have been produced by the primordial universe, which is inconsistent with the model itself.

Observations of distant supernovae suggest that the universe is in accelerated expansion, as they proved less bright than the standard model anticipated. For the universe to be in accelerated expansion, a new form of energy called dark energy is required, which has never been seen other than in speculations made by those who support the Big Bang model. This decrease in brightness could quite simply be explained by galactic dust produced by condensation of iron needles in supernovae remnants, as the Indian astrophysicist Jayant V. Narlikar proposed; a phenomenon confirmed by laboratory experiments. He also argued that the Big Bang does not explain why a redshift deviation exists between two galaxies materially connected by a filament. The probability of this being part of some smart backup plan is extremely low. Redshifts are one of the principles of the prevailing model.

This astrophysicist regretted the arrogance of those in favor of the standard Big Bang model, which he compared to religious fanaticism.

He thrashed the discriminating practices contrary to other proposed models, both in publications and in the allocation of research budgets. Students who think outside the box of the Big Bang model have little chance of obtaining a research position, he therefore commented: "It may not be religious fundamentalism anymore, but I have coined the name 'scientific fundamentalism' for such a closed attitude."

The religious dimension may not be a stranger to that approach. The idea of a beginning of time and of the world was suggested by Georges Lemaître, a Belgian Roman Catholic priest and part-time lecturer at the University of Leuven. However, Buddhist thinking, for example, is apparently more capable of accepting a universe without beginning or end.

The expansion of the universe was presented after Alexander Friedmann and Lemaître proved the existence of redshifts, the "official" translation of the recession velocity of a star or galaxy. The velocity sweeps them along in the expansion of the universe caused by the Big Bang; a so-called electromagnetic Doppler effect that consists in a frequency shift of the white light of stars towards the red spectrum caused solely by the relative movement of this star moving away from Earth. The measured apparent frequency is therefore lower than the real frequency. The Indian astrophysicist recognized the expansion of the universe without actually determining a beginning. These two statuses are not incompatible. Narlikar explained: "You should know that the expansion of the universe is only directly observed until redshifts of 4 or 5…which corresponds to a past era, where the density of the universe was only about two hundred times higher than the actual density, while a redshift of 10^{29} corresponds to a density multiplied by a factor of 10^{87}! How do we verify the validity of our physical laws on such a high-density scale? This however, requires a gross extrapolation beyond known physics…."

Please note that Fred Hoyle's quasi-steady state model anticipated the appearance of new matter as recognized by high-energy physics. In fact, the Casimir effect clearly showed the spontaneous generation of particles in the vacuum. Narlikar, who sides with Hoyle, expected to see blueshifts of fainter galaxies to accredit the thesis of his model; the spectrum shift that the standard model could not explain. Moreover, he anticipated the existence of forty to fifty billion-year-old stars that would be at the origin of cosmic rays.

Therefore, if the Big Bang never took place, the notion of cosmic time could be seriously challenged, because the history of the universe would not pivot on a beginning from which the temporal asymmetry originated. Another difficulty is Planck time (10^{-34} seconds), called the Planck era, prior to which the relativity theory and the quantum theory were clearly incompatible. So the alleged birth of the universe must have taken place before this Planck era. This is where a new and metaphysical physics will emerge.

General relativity deals with cosmological problems in a relatively simple manner by smoothing out, homogenizing the singularities that represent stars, galaxies or black holes. The homogeneity of matter and the isotropy of space are the very principles of cosmology even if they are only approximate. Galactic clusters (pile-ups) and super clusters, consisting of millions and millions of stars, hardly seem to lessen the effects of scientific fundamentalism. It is true that the visible millions of light years in the universe are but a lump in the primordial soup. People therefore hope that quantum gravity can simply be applied to quantum cosmology and that objects in the universe fit in a specific framework (black holes, galaxies, stars, etc.). They just forget a few minor contradictions. How can we assume that the level of homogeneity, suggested by the cosmic rays principle, was greater in the beginning of the universe and at the same time indicate the expansion rate, which is an essential factor of dilution and therefore of homogeneity over a long period of time? It would be easier to imagine that space is neither homogeneous, nor isotropous by taking into account its fractal nature. This would have a remarkable consequence. According to this fractal topology (volume orientation, reduction rate, number of iterations), space travel might be facilitated by following specific space corridors, like the air corridors that exist in commercial aviation. What applies to the entire universe is also applicable to Earth, where certain telluric energy sites constitute narrow passageways between several fractal levels, also called inter-dimensional portals. We could even envision that certain ET races are more inclined to visit us than others because we would be on their way, like a roadmap where the junctions are a matter of geography.

Another deteriorating factor is that those in favor of the standard cosmological model consider the gravitational instability a fundamental temporal asymmetry of the cosmic evolution: the origin of the universe is highly homogeneous, the present state is not. They claim that this instability is caused by imperceptible fluctuations of the matter that produced the stars we see in the sky at night. Therefore, everything is homogeneous, in which case there is no cause that creates effects, but there are also fluctuations that cannot come from a cause! This causality, the foundation of all sciences, therefore does not have a cause!

What happened to the antimatter produced in the alleged first seconds of the universe? It should be just as spread out and "material" as the matter we know, because as space expanded, it fell apart without touching matter for as long as thirteen seconds after the Big Bang, while waiting for the temperature to drop to three billion degrees. However, there was no antimatter! What about the apocalyptic vision of one hundred billion degrees, one hundredth of a second after the birth of the universe? That temperature is a matter of specific collisions. Astrophysicists speak of photon collisions at light speed producing particles and antiparticles. Let me ask a bold question. Where do these photons come from? Why do they change if they are supposed to be part of the expansion? Why were they born with two constants, the Boltzmann constant and Planck's constant?

I think we should not look for the explanation in this overly mediatized Big Bang model!

The precursory signs of the collapse of the Big Bang model are becoming noticeable. God died with Nietzsche, so why not the Big Bang? To illustrate this argument, I would like to refer to a debate between H. Reeves, C. Césarsky and J. P. Luminet that took place in Essonne in January 2004 focusing on "refuting the Big Bang." I should also mention the Coherent Raman Effect of Incoherent Light (CREIL)[56] proven by Jacques Moret-Bailly, a professor of optics. He argued that the birth of the universe never took place because in virtue of the quantum effect:

   a. Light waves of distant (allegedly very old) quasars travel through a much diluted cloud of hydrogen atoms. The distance between the atoms induces a redshift of background emissions.
   b. The thickness (cumulative effect) of the hyper-diluted gas cloud is sufficient for the redshift.
   c. Instead of explaining Hubble's law (the redshift of frequencies) by the Doppler effect (stars moving away), he explains it by using the CREIL (stimulated non-thermal emission).

Therefore, if the universe is not expanding, it never started to expand in the first place and there never was a Big Bang. The universe is stationary!

Maybe these debates among experts will not change the world (but maybe the world of astronomers and astrophysicists). Will the absence of the Big Bang give us an edge? Consider this! If time never began, the time arrow is no longer relevant! We have to eliminate all of our causality concepts and tell ourselves that this world is one big illusion! Nothing more, nothing less…

Both contemporary science and our everyday certainties are therefore on the verge of a breakdown (variable causality). Imagine that, based on new theoretical principles, we succeeded in controlling free, non-polluting and unlimited energy. The current notions of work, salary, social struggle, politics, health, economic imbalance, scarcity and abundance, unemployment, stress, human drama and pollution would be radically eliminated. Now that would constitute a real Big Bang! That of a better world…

CHAPTER 29

The metaphysics of space-times

LET US RETURN TO THE SUBJECT of temporal irreversibility and to Lachièze-Rey,[57] who said: "The phenomena, or rather their descriptions, are reversible or not [note from the author: more so than time], and we have understood today that the seeming irreversibility is caused by the conjunction of two situations:

1. we are incapable of rendering a complete description of a macroscopic phenomenon: we can only do it statistically.

2. Our description of the evolution of a phenomenon is inevitably dissymmetrical because we know the initial state, but not the ultimate state: we are the ones who add a temporal asymmetry to the description."

His point of view is very interesting, because he stresses the idea that the consciousness that establishes the description is the cause of the problem. In other words, since we (but who are we?) are unable to describe something other than the one-directional flow of time, the time arrow is as we describe it. It is a surprising form of fundamental tautology affecting the inferences of every scientific discipline, which invites us to leave the matrix and see the universe differently. However, how do we get out? If science states the source of its powerlessness so clearly, then why does it keep denying the existence of precognition? Knowing all the information of a system in a high temporal density allows for reversibility and thus the ability to foresee the future before it happens, simply because the universe is also a system and not just a story!

This explains why "present" quantum cosmology that endeavors to describe a global wave function cannot reject the Big Bang, allegedly the origin of the expansion of the universe, because it actually generates the master time arrow. This brings us to another question: how could the world have classical features, based on gravity and cosmology, and quantum features based on the other interactions? We can definitely not afford to skimp on a new approach towards space, time and matter any longer.

For general relativity, gravity is space-time geometry. The ST is therefore dynamic. For quantum physics, all that is dynamic is indeterminate and fluctuating. According to Lachièze-Rey, the immediate consequence is that "in a quantum gravity theory, the ST cannot be determined. There is no geometry and no time flow. The notion of geometry must be replaced with a quantum notion, just as the notion of particles in quantum mechanics must be replaced with the notion of the wave function." This is what I mean by saying that we must think outside the box of geometry and its spatial nature in order to understand time. The problem with the wave function is that we do not say what it represents. We speak of probability amplitude. What is its status? Just a gamble (what is the cause of the emergence of temporal asymmetry?) or intervention by a presence (human or otherwise), or even of true willpower? What about a universal wave function with infinite parameters? Does that make sense? Let us go back to my previous argument.

One of the important cornerstones of quantum mechanics is the Heisenberg uncertainty principle, which dictates that the position and the momentum of a single particle cannot be determined at the same time. This uncertainty is a fact and not a principle. In fact, the underlying ascendancy is the wave-corpuscular duality, but no one explains this duality. Quantum mechanics always speaks of probability amplitude and the existence of chance is presented as a new principle. Probabilistic functions are an adequate formalism in their application, but do not explain anything. They list possibilities in accordance with a variable probability of them actually happening. In other words, science explains the nature of things based on a law that does not exist! Chance! What is science without laws? Pseudo-science! How do we explain chance? We do not. We say "it is a coincidence and that is all there is to it." That is science: the absence of explanations about the origin of things. Therefore, the key to solving the problem lies in explaining the nature of chance and its "density," i.e., the place it takes in the occurrence of phenomena.

Chance is essentially a spatio-temporal scale problem in the framework of absolute relativity, i.e., "the more there is space, the less there is time," and vice versa. Chance is the translation of the relevance of time in phenomenology. To be more exact, it follows from the comparison of a fast time flow in another, slower time flow. In the microscopic world, time is preponderant. In the macroscopic world, space is preponderant.

Therefore, the real problem is finding out what the probabilistic nature of units of measure (position, energy, etc.) intrinsically represents. It is not enough to say: "the probability of this happening is…" We must be able to explain why the probabilistic mechanism itself has to take place. Let me illustrate this comment. All the grains of sand in an hourglass cannot fall through the aperture at the same time because it is too narrow. It is this narrowness that prevents us from being aware of every "action" at the same time. The great difficulty in precognition experiences is to ascertain whether the information obtained from the future (in the upper part of the hourglass) regards the person consulting or someone else, or, in case of sufficient empathy between the seer and the person consulting, whether the predicted events follow a precise chronology. In other words, does the sand come from the right, the left or the middle?

3D time is not opposed to the experiments conducted in physics, but to their interpretation. In other words, some scientists have the question right in front of them without bothering to find an answer. It is therefore enough to simply study quantum mechanics to find out what it wants to tell us.

Even the most experienced physicists never explained the relevance of this probability. The explanation is very simple for those who apply 3D time. There exists a time flow in the microscopic world that is so radically different from ours (because it possesses such a large quantity of information), that the measurement performed in the macroscopic world (hybrid wave function between the measured particle and the measuring instrument) has to take into account the probability that the measured physical magnitude is more or less close to the common temporal coordinate between the microscopic and the macroscopic. In other words, will the grain of sand follow a vertical trajectory to reach the aperture of the hourglass or not? You can try all you like to get all the rain to fall (time on the microscopic scale) in a glass (time on the macroscopic scale), but the latter will not be able to contain it all at the same time. Everything outside the glass is potential energy for the glass, i.e., the whole of probabilities of position, energy, etc. These probabilities really exist on the scale of microscopic time. They are not exactly probabilities anymore, but events out of reach of our perception, including the perception of our measuring instruments. What is most difficult to understand is that there is a counterpart for every one of our seconds. As a consequence, the law of conservation of energy is in reality a law of energy decrease (or choice).

What is valid between our scale and the atomic scale is also valid between atoms and quarks (see asymptotic freedom), and so on between quarks and the vacuum. The more we go into the infinitely small (so the higher we go in the temporal hourglass), the more the isolated grain of sand stands a chance of being far from the vertical axis. However, this axis exists only when information (a grain of sand) has to come down. It comes down only when it is measured by instruments and, more in general, when it is perceived, including in an extrasensory manner. This is why it is virtually impossible to say when a premonition takes place in our macroscopic world in the natural course of events.

It is only logical to assume that chance is unused creative potential, ignored potential energy, applied when we choose and create. This "chance" relatively increases at the fractal level in question when there is less space. The infinitely small cannot be a law unto itself. That is not in line with the beauty of the universe. While the macroscopic world is bound by the laws of the spirit, the microscopic world is subject to the spirit of the laws. The chaos of life is a source, a pretext for self-realization, like a gift God has given to His creatures to exercise His powers. Gradually, chance is replaced by synchronicity and intuition, by visualization and cooperation, by the control of space and time, in short, by willpower, the power to create. The principle of least action (see the Feynman path integrals) is gradually replaced by the principle of creative choice, by gaining access to knowledge. The principle of least action is therefore foreseen by God so that a minimum of cohesion exists before free will. This is the primordial stage, our pure and untouched playground. However, God would not be Love if he did not share! "Chance" is indeterminism left to our discretion, i.e., the power (and the will) to initiate. Chance is God's love of incarnation! It is the new no man's land to conquer. That explains why too much formalism impairs the evolution of our consciousness by stripping it of the very essence of its awakening.

Let us talk about formalism. The approach to the various paths that were explored (Regge calculus, loop quantum gravity, spin networks) does not present anything workable right now. In these interpretations the ST does not exist, but should appear along with the results of new geometries such as algebraic topology, fibred space or noncommutative geometry. We will see that one of the greatest enigmas of physics —

finding out why gravity is so weak[58] compared to other interactions —
remains impenetrable, because we have to discover that time is three-
dimensional, fractal and discrete. In other words, gravity no longer
exists in the infinitely small. It is useless and even inefficient to ask what
quantum gravity looks like. Superstrings, which help us to explain this
anomaly (weak gravity) and other microscopic parallel universes, will
always remain in the realm of science fiction. Reality is much more surprising and much less materialist! It is rather painful to become aware
of the fact that conceptual instruments, such as the group theory, can be
and are used to say everything and anything. Too many physicists have
been seduced by the siren call of the mathematical realm of imagination. The more it is complicated, the more it seems true, for the mathematical stratospheres are an ideal means to curtail debate. The truth is
more pragmatic. It is accessible to everyone, because God did not create
it just for the happy few. Nevertheless, the idea that the super wave
function could be considered the quantum superposition of several STs,
with very specific geometry, looks very much like the concept I am
defending.

I indeed think that the universe has a fractal structure. Some examples of ST systems, or fractals, include galaxy clusters, galaxies, con-
stellations, planetary systems, planets, minerals, plants, animals,

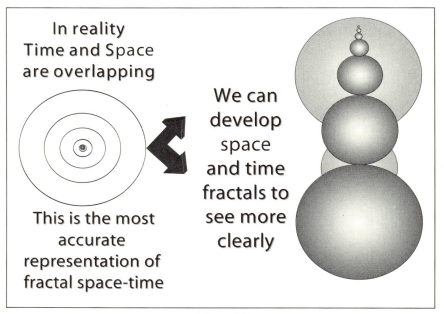

Figure 28

bodies, organs, cells, molecules, atoms, quarks, photons, astral planes, mental systems, spiritual systems, etc.

These fractal systems of nature are not mathematically perfect thanks or due to exchanges of grains of time and space that exist between iterations. These exchanges allow us to have the phenomeno-logical experience and to actually be able to create it. In other words, everything is interaction.

Every scale level is a ST in itself, in which both time and space can be represented by a specific number of grains (quanta) of time and space. Each level is therefore capable of managing a specific amount of infor-mation (position, energy) depending on the structure of the system, whether it is considered isolated or not. This granularity has one simple property: the larger the number of grains of space, the lower the number of grains of time, and conversely. In other words, on the microscopic scale, the time quanta appear in great numbers, even more so because the spatial scale is small. The larger the number of grains of time, the less causality there is, because more events occur at the same time! The infi-nitely small could be renamed "the infinite at the same time." This is the problem of the non-locality of particles, so-called synchronicity. The rel-evance of events can be diverse. The universe does not create different paths of cause and effect (no parallel universes offered by a very gener-ous Creator, which is the antithesis of the amply proven principle of least action); the universe is made of sequential prisms of one and the same reality (we speak of spatio-temporal prisms).

CHAPTER 30

Time quakes in space

WE KNOW THAT THE PARTICLE does not exist in quantum mechanics. The particle is what is called a misuse of language! The particle is a probability amplitude of presence. Moreover, if quantum gravity exists, or quantum cosmological gravity, space and time should not exist. A quantum state is therefore not a particle, but a superposition of possible situations.

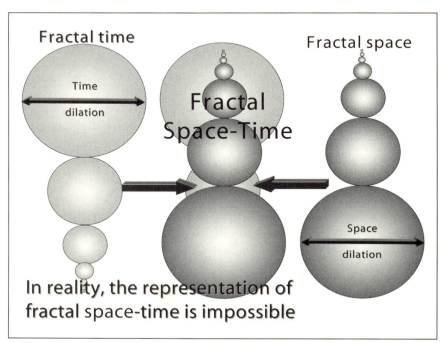

Figure 29

157

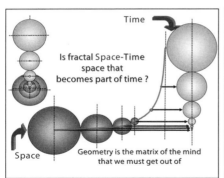

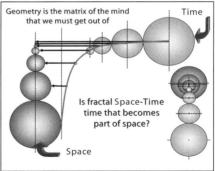

Figure 30   *Figure 31*

I just said that the universe does not correspond to an exact geometric configuration of the ST, but to a superposition of STs. There would not be a time flow. Causality does not exist without a time flow.

One of the greatest difficulties of fractal ST is to make a clear representation. In fact, this may be impossible with a simple geometric approach.

In a quantum experiment, the measuring evolves the system towards situations that suggest the presence of particles. In a way, the measurement creates particles. If we follow the same line of reasoning, the observation of the cosmos creates ST, just as quantum observation creates particles. The problem between the two is that the observer is both part of the system (the universe is by definition what encompasses all) and outside the system (that is the definition of an observer). However, if the effect is the same, does not that mean that consciousness only changes the scale and that in both cases it is part of the system? One could ask if the universe is not the observer of its own behavior and reduces the wave packet to a classic description of the ST. These ideas have been explored in the framework of quantum decoherence, which has led to new interpretations of quantum physics. I am arguing that consciousness travels through STs and that we do not need the Big Bang to explain temporal asymmetry. This asymmetry is simply caused by the fact that we (the individual is manifold in nature) occupy several STs at the same time while traveling through these STs, a voyage we call evolution. According to the old traditions, we are made of several different bodies. These different bodies correspond to just as many spatio-temporal (or fractal) prisms. The asymmetry of passing time is caused by the fact that we are viewing an ST (material world) from another ST (spiritual world)![59]

The best evidence is Einstein's "train" thought experiment or Gedankenexperiment. He wanted to know the behavior of photons traveling at the same speed. Nothing happened. Phenomena take place only because different STs meet. These phenomena allow us to access higher STs and therefore gain more freedom.

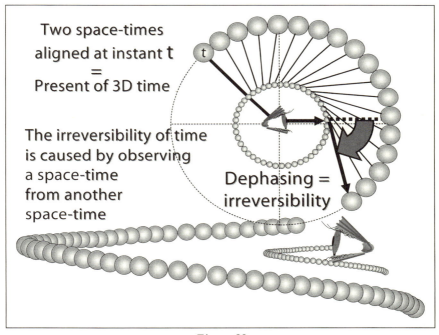

Figure 32

CHAPTER 31

Alice in fractal land

A FRACTAL IS THE REPRODUCTION of shapes on ever smaller (or larger) scales. Nature comes in numerous geometric (spatial) fractals. We can find them in snowflakes, sponges, cauliflower, sea shells, coastlines, the human body, mountains, clouds, ferns, leaves and trees. In general, we can see them in every realm and manifestation of nature.

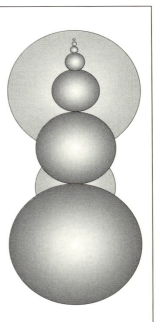

Fractal

=

Self-similarity
by changing scales

=

The same « shape » is multiplied
as it clones itself while
growing larger or smaller

=

space-times
of <u>absolute relativity</u>

Figure 33

Please note that the constructal theory[60] also elaborates on the discontinuities on the macroscopic scale. This engineering theory shows that exact shapes must be used to lose the least amount of energy.

Let us first look at geometric fractals. They possess properties such as a non-whole dimension that is strictly higher than the topological dimension, non-differentiability (impossibility to define the tangent) and the presence of infinities. A topological dimension is a classic dimension: point (0), line (1), surface (2), volume (3), hyper-volume (4). A homothety (magnification factor) is the repetition of a topological dimension. A fractal dimension is expressed by the ratio of two logarithms: the number of fractals (p iterations) and the magnification factor (q):

$$\text{Log } p / \log q$$

I am not going into detail here, because it would become even more complex. However, this equation gives us a good idea. Let me simply say that the fractal dimension is, of course, non-Euclidean. The fractal values lie between 1 and 2 when we follow a curve or between 2 and 3 when we speak of volume. It is remarkable to observe that the microscopic world contains fractal objects, such as the protein molecule (a value of 1.7). In 3D time, the fractal nature of time only regards the "time density" dimension as the homothety of a single topological dimension. For comparison purposes, fractal time is to conventional physical time what the fractal dimension is to the Euclidean dimension. Moreover, I think that the fractal nature of space inexorably implies the fractal nature of time, because the two are closely related in special relativity. By accepting the universality of the latter as that of geometric fractals naturally spread across the universe, we also accept the existence of fractal time as the only logical conclusion. Most calculations using Minkowski space-time are validated, give or take a few approximations, because fractal space is usually juxtaposed to fractal time giving the illusion of linear equations; hence the use of integral functions. If space indeed diminishes in the same fractal ratio as the increase of time and, of course, at the same time, then a linear function is perfectly appropriate. The changes will be clear. However, if the transition from one scale to another does not take place simultaneously for space and time, significant differences will be observed, for instance in case of 1) gravity on a very large and very small scale, 2) residual gluonic interaction (different color charge for quarks) permitting strong interaction, 3) residual electromagnetic interaction connecting two atoms, which is the origin of all manifestations of life and, in general, but on a grand and spectacular scale, 4) all UFO and paranormal phenomena. Finally, special relativity is a particular case of absolute relativity. It is an increase and a correlative exact decrease of space and of granular time.

The particularity of the fractal dimension in geometry is that it rapidly increases the absolute length or surface that become in fact theoretically infinite. The surface of our lungs, of which the alveoli unfold in fractals to help absorb the air in our blood, is actually the size of a soccer field. Still, on the outside, on our scale, our lungs would fit on a small table. In the same way, the time we perceive is not the real time, but time as we perceive it on our temporal scale. Similar to the image of our lungs, we absorb subtle information (air) and integrate it into our body (blood). Just like most of the air from our lungs returns into the atmosphere when we exhale, the information of our psychic experiences (e.g., dreams, remote viewing, etc.) returns to the collective Akashic memory when we become aware of it. Fractal time may be infinite in its iterations. We will see that this does not apply to entanglement, which is a factor of universal oneness.

I prefer to use the term ST instead of fractal. They have the same meaning. A fractal vision of the universe, both for space and time, is not only enormous, but also has great demonstrative power.

According to Einstein, problems arise when we have to connect remote events: what would the fact that two distant events occur simultaneously mean? The terms of 3D time actually dictate that when STs are separated by a very large scale, it is very difficult or even impossible to synchronize the duration of that flow going by in each of these STs.

The spatial proximity only has meaning on a specific scale, i.e., a specific ST! The motion dynamics of each of these STs is indeed irrelevant. A one-meter difference between two objects is small compared to a length of one thousand meters, but extremely large on a scale of one millionth of a millimeter. In other words, the phenomena are quite different depending on the scale we use. The same applies to time.

Since we all possess our own clock in a specific ST — different observers have different velocities and acceleration — each of us also and a fortiori possesses his own clock in two different STs, where the differences in velocity and acceleration are much greater.

This piece of information is vital to understanding the notion of spatio-temporal distortions, such as psychic paranormal phenomena.

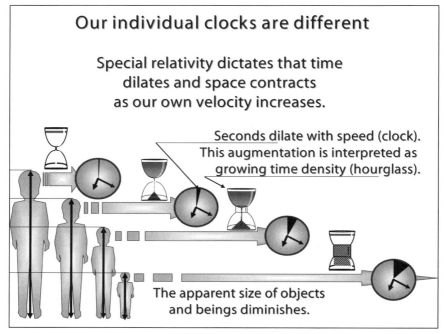

Figure 34

We can therefore deduce that the macroscopic and microscopic effect of a physical or psychic event cannot be simultaneous in two specific STs. The following figures explain the essential concept of missing time.

If the ratio log p/log q is constant, the absolute value of the amount of information (physical units or number of sections) is quite different between two scales. Just like there is a difference in length between a coastline on our scale and on the microbial scale (missing length for man), there is a difference between two temporal fractal iterations. This difference is missing time. However, we need to understand that higher time (mind) is not included in lower time (matter) because we look at it from this physical time. The time flow of respective temporal sections at each repetition is therefore quite different. The time differences will become evident when we compare them; hence the missing time. Since nature essentially manifests itself cyclically, the temporal behavior is represented by concentric circles in the following figures (see figure 36).

It is funny to compare the closed circles of the frequency sinusoids stretched out as helicoidal springs by the temporal protocol (second) of the time flow, defined before as the product of consciousness.

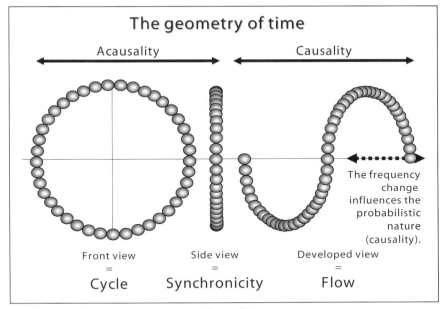

Figure 35

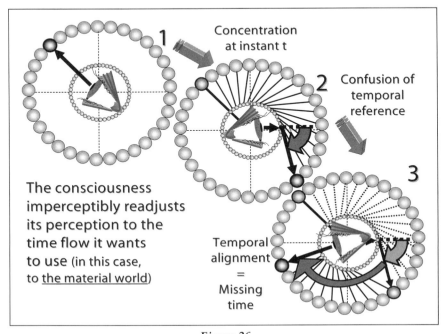

Figure 36

Missing time is quite common, but usually remains imperceptible, because we would constantly and simultaneously have to compare two specific time flows. It is virtually impossible to be in two STs, i.e., to focus on two things, at the same time. In daily life, these time flow differences are small (apparent simultaneity), but not in paranormal phenomena, when radical changes take place. The cycles are then very far apart.

The cause-effect relation is completely disrupted even when temporal irreversibility is absent! We can wish for something that we feel takes too much time to materialize, but we can also experience something that we will not wish for until after it happens from our terrestrial point of view! It is therefore wise not to become attached to the result of our wish, because it usually manifests itself in an "illogical" way.

However, in high time densities, where willpower originates, the wish and the result are both instantaneous. We can understand that traditional science is eager to fight the monster (parapsychology) that is bound to destroy the current form of science. Psychologists know that

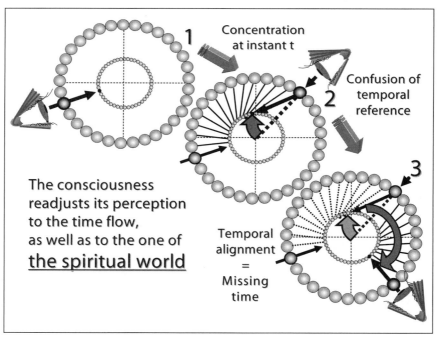

Figure 37

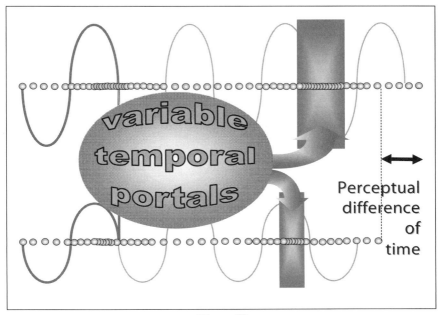

Figure 38

laughter (sarcasm) is a form of protection and often hides an unadmitted fear. Fear does not eliminate danger, it attracts it.

When we take measurements in quantum experiments, there is necessarily a delay due to this distortion. This brings me to the following two statements. First of all, temporal irreversibility is caused by the fact that the act of measuring concerns at least two STs (actually a much larger number). Secondly, assuming that the distortion is homogeneous, what is measured either took place in the past or will take place in the future, but becomes the present for the observer. This is hardly relevant in the understanding of a local system, but may be a source of great error when it comes to some more general interpretations.

Subjectivity is personal and non-imaginary because every person's consciousness is at instant t in a specific ST, which causes perceptual distortions compared to another person in a different or slightly shifted ST.

In "normal time" these distortions are negligible. You will thus understand what signifies the "norm" to which many people refer since they disregard these disparities.

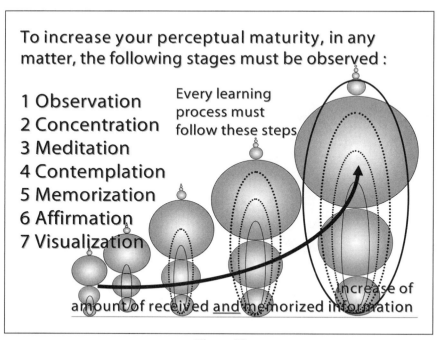

Figure 39

However, in high temporal densities, in dreams, hypnosis, remote viewing or deep meditation, the differences can be considerable, because the probability amplitudes of magnitude "action" S are stretched out prior to Planck's constant h. "Only different in your mind," as Yoda[61] would say!

Hence the growing importance of perceptual maturity in evolution.

CHAPTER 32

The axioms of 3D time

TIME HAS BEEN SUBJECT to various three-dimensional theories that all apply different definitions of temporal dimensions. Several names are mentioned in this respect, including Bartini, Tifft, Lehto, Kozyrev and Shikhobalov. Scientists from the East, particularly Kozyrev, conducted very advanced research on time as early as the 1960s. As substantiated by countless scientific examples, it has been recognized that different scientists sometimes discover the same things at the same time, or in different eras, but independently from one another. Be that as it may, superior space-times constitute the center of ideas accessible to all. Nicolaï Alexandrovich Kozyrev was an astronomer. Almost fifty years ago, he took an interest in the nature of time. Assuming that the rotation of stars was connected to their energy output, he embarked on a crusade to decrypt physical time. He and some other Soviet colleagues grew fascinated by the secondary effects of gyroscopes. A spinning motion (like the rotors of an alien vessel) seemed to lead to different time flows. Similarly, Yuri V. Nachalov explained that "H. Hayasaka and S. Takeuchi have attempted to explain the effect of antigravitation as the manifestation of torsion fields generated by the spinning gyroscope."

Kozyrev discovered astonishing physical properties of time. In an article published in 1967 entitled "Possibility of the experimental study of the properties of time[62]" he presented the results of a series of experiments he had run on scales and gyroscopes based on the effects of vibration, and even on temperature or latitude change. He focused attention on the fact that a spinning gyroscope causes deviations similar to the power of a lever in comparison with the laboratory frame of reference, which of course had nothing to do with the motions of precession or nutation already well known at the time. He also showed, probably most importantly of all, that the weight varies. He explained how these variations are the result of a significant differential in the passage (density) of time, of which he said that it is rarer near any cause and denser near any effect. In other words, the experimental facts indeed suggest the existence of what Kozyrev called density of time, a kind of intrinsic temporal viscosity rate.

However, the Russian did not go so far as to talk about time dimension. He mentioned only the singular property of time. It should be noted that Kozyrev briefly iterated telepathy to illustrate this property. What is bothersome in his writings, though, is that his three principle axioms are based on the strict causality he emphasized in his conclusion. He seemed to set aside the quantum-mechanical uncertainty relations while giving priority to the constant C_2 to link up the smallest possible quantity of space (x) and the smallest possible quantity of time (t):

$$C_2 = \partial x / \partial t$$

We now know that quantum behavior transgresses the causality principles of classical mechanics. Kozyrev had based his interpretative structure on a minimum causality (C_2). However, even he admitted: "In atomic mechanics $C_2 = 0$. The equations (6), obtained by refining principles of Newtonian mechanics, are approximate and do not provide for the critical transition to $C_2 = 0$. They simply indicate that additional effects unforeseen by Newtonian mechanics will take up a very important part. Causality becomes completely intertwined (fuzzy) and the events of nature remain to be explained statistically...Newtonian mechanics equals a world with infinitely stable causality relations, whereas atomic mechanics represents another critical case of a world with infinitely weak causality relations...For instance, we can expect the manifestation of quantum effects in macroscopic mechanics..."

This last stage is the very foundation of paranormal phenomena and UFOs: the manifestation of quantum effects in macroscopic mechanics! If he confirmed that the causal relations are weak in quantum mechanics, then what is causality?

The principle of the exclusion of a third possibility once again suffers a heavy blow. According to this principle, the causal relation either is or is not. This means that the relation is determined by the consciousness that observes it, in other words on our point of view. Let us return to the credo: is the coincidence of statistical mechanics causal?

I think the superposition of quanta is due only to the observation of a fractal seen from another fractal, which results in the absence of physical causality at certain levels. The void is simply the center of superior fractals that are inaccessible from our macroscopic space-time, where mental energy (a new form of causality) is rooted. In response to Einstein, who said that "God does not play dice," this book shows that "God has given the dice to His creatures to be in His image."

Interestingly, Kozyrev's experimental work demonstrated a relation between harmonics and the weight changes and deviations, which determined the validity of the fractal nature of time. It is a fact that the harmonics, being natural and complete frequency multipliers, do not correspond to the incomplete fractal dimension but to the "magnification factor" in logarithm q (homothety). Therefore, the resonance of any vibrating objects affects the time flow of these objects. This does not apply only to quantum mechanics, it also applies to our macroscopic world.

Finally, we should credit Kozyrev for deriving the relation between time and parapsychological aptitude: "It is possible that our psychological perception of temporal void or of substantial time is not only of a subjective nature, such as the perception of time flux, but also an objective physical foundation."

This seemingly anodyne phrase inflicted in reality a "scientific blow" to human sciences that Kozyrev did not exploit in his article. In matters of ufology, the psycho-sociological hypothesis is about to collapse like a house of cards. It is becoming but a simple antediluvian belief in comparison with the fantastic powers of the nature of space-time, being the heart of all information in the visible and invisible universe.

Like Kozyrev, L. S. Shikhobalov wanted to know what can be obtained from a substantial conception of time.[63] The Russian scientist referred to an old opposition between a relational and a substantial conception of time. He wrote: "According to the first one, there exists no time 'per se' in nature and time is no more than a relation (or a set of relations) between physical events. In other words, time is a specific manifestation of the properties of physical bodies and changes occurring in them. The second conception, the substantial one, assumes, vice versa, that time is an independent phenomenon of nature, a specific kind of substance, coexisting with space, matter and physical fields. The relational conception of time is conventionally associated with the names of Aristotle, G. W. Leibnitz and A. Einstein. The most ardent adherents of the substantial conception of time are Democritus, I. Newton and N. A. Kozyrev."

As strange as it may seem, I think both approaches are valid. Time is "transported" by natural systems while being the framework in which they are generated. Actually, Shikhobalov reached the same conclusion. He compared thesis and antithesis and proposed a more general conceptual framework acceptable to all. Referring to the metric form of Minkowsky, he asked a pertinent question as yet unsolved by modern physics: "what is the cause of the time stream tempo concordance (metric form value concordance) in different points of space-time?" He saw specific structures of space-time substance in physical matter and fields. Substance structures! This means that space-time, and more specifically time, is the very essence of nature. Controlling that essence is therefore a condition for these phenomena to occur. In that case the comparison of two Galilean frames of reference (special relativity) does not suffice. The influence of space-time precedes the phenomena instead of vice versa. In his conclusion of a mathematical, forty-five-page article presenting his new model, he wrote: "this conception can give an understanding of the essence of space and time, the basic concepts of natural science, which would be deeper and more adequate to reality than the existing one."

Neither Kozyrev nor Shikhobalov addressed three-dimensional time. However, by suggesting that the passage of time is not continuous, they have opened the path to a very different vision of time. I should also mention Robert Ludvigovich Bartini (Soviet-Italian, 1897–1974), who apparently proposed a conception of 3D time. Bartini was a rather mysterious and strange individual if we are to believe the stories about his professional career. This aeronautic engineer collaborated with the Soviet secret services. However, he was imprisoned for ten years and subsequently rehabilitated. An article found on the Internet provides the following curious commentary: "many who knew Bartini quite seriously suspected he had come from outer space." He saw the dimensions of time as:

1. date of a time: change of history or time erosion.
2. Rate of a time (T/Te, with T being the local time in an experimental system and Te being the physical time on Earth).
3. The arrow of a time.

Let me add a word of warning with regard to the definition of these dimensions. It would indeed be easy to show that two out of these three dimensions constitute but a single one (the date and the arrow of time). This is one of the reasons why my conception of time is different.

Many Russians have researched and still research the nature of time. Vadim Chernobrov, who currently works at the Faraday Lab in

Saint Petersburg and who referred to Bartini, has conducted temporal experiments with what he calls a time machine. These experiments and his results are disputed. Nevertheless, it is important to keep track of what is concocted behind the scenes. Is it not true that this former employee of the spacecraft department of Moscow's Aviation Institute (propulsion department) has distilled false theories (Bartini's thesis) to obscure a genuinely advanced theory on extraterrestrial technology in Russia? Vadim Chernobrov seems to have gravitated to Soviet Black Programs. He said[64]: "…Since 1967, some research work has been conducted at Moscow's Aviation Institute under the direction of professor Felix Yu. Zigel (until his death in 1988) on UFOs with a specific technical form. Following this 'preliminary research on anomalous phenomena in the atmosphere,' performed with state budget funds, a great deal of valuable information has been assembled in a file on these phenomena…, established based on authenticated cases of traces and fragments, of videos and photos, and telemetric images of UFOs taken between 1987 and now. There is data on the subject of the influence of certain parts of these objects and their bodies (the exterior) on the rate and direction of time…"

I should add that Chernobrov's remarks, made based on his experiments, open astonishing perspectives. The principle of his time machine can be compared to Russian nesting dolls. He injected electromagnetic waves to flow from the periphery towards the center of a device of concentric spheres equipped with electromagnets. He measured temporal changes in the center of this device, which may have been weak,[65] but sufficiently explicit to deduce the existence of temporal density. It is peculiar to observe that this logic concurs with that of absolute relativity: "the less there is space, the more there is time." He also said that "experiments have shown that man and time mutually influence each other profoundly. The effect of the operator on the experiment has been established but has not yet been studied in its entirety…" The passage of time has a tangible influence on us and conversely.

He also observed some toxic effects on biological systems. He wrote that these are not related to the process of time displacement, but rather to the value of the time flow rate according to the different body parts concerned. This shows that the natural temporal passage is not identical in every part of the physical body. We will see why this is important when I address the cognitive abilities of our brain. This explains why the temporal bubble of a UFO, the time flow of which can vary, has a more or less considerable impact on our ability to respond or not (motions and perceptions) around a vessel, and even around ETs who, being biological systems, "carry around" specific time flows. We also transport various time rates, but the differences between them are not of the same magnitude. He added that "...space sectors, of different time flow rates, have unclear boundaries. When the time rate change is sufficiently large, the human eye can see the sector of the other time rate as a white mist, and as a radiant mist when it is even larger, which can be considered a sign of danger to biological systems..."

A radiant mist visible around the boundary means that what is inside this temporal egg cannot be seen clearly. In the next chapter I have reached the same conclusion on the mere consideration of a fractal temporal deviation. The immediate consequence of this phenomenon is that, both in theory and in practice, it is impossible to see and photograph the distinct outlines of UFOs in the sky, whether in motion or not, and of entities (ghosts for example) present in a denser temporal field. Therefore, UFO photos that are too clear are forgeries!

Another scholar from the East, a Belarussian academic called Albert Veinik, embarked on an adventure of establishing temporal technologies. He developed his own theory based on the existence of chronons, generally known to the scientific community as Planck time (5.4×10^{-44} seconds). Veinik wrote that time is not continuous, but discrete. Remember that special relativity adheres to a continuous vision of time. Veinik considered time to be a sequence of quanta. However, he did not specify the relation between them, and that is a big problem. My vision actually suggests superimposing quantum time to mend this missing relation by positioning these quanta onto the very sinusoids.

Following in Chernobrov's footsteps (temporal influence on biological systems), Veinik suggested medical applications by changing the time flow. His discoveries may very well remind you of the miraculous healing power of ETs often mentioned by abductees, i.e., people who have had a close encounter with ETs inside their vessel. Moreover, Veinik seems to have perfected a propulsion principle based on asymmetrical centrifugal force. He ran experiments that showed the possibility of reactionless antigravitation motion by means of creation of different velocity of time flow in different parts of mechanical systems.

Veinik suggested that every substance possesses a chronal charge that is nothing more than the intrinsic number of chronons present in this substance. This approach appears valid because it suggests that refraction and reflection observed on substances through which light travels are directly related to this chronal charge.

The Snell-Descartes law stipulates that light does not move in a straight line when traveling from one environment to another. This law is based on the principle of least action. Pierre de Fermat (1601–1665) proposed a principle on which all laws of geometrical optics had to hinge. Light waves traverse the path between two points that takes the least time. One century later, Pierre-Louis de Maupertuis argued that light does not take the shortest distance, that of a straight line, nor does it take the shortest time. Light does not follow either of these paths, but that of the least amount of action, i.e., the most efficient route. Maupertuis standardized this principle for all bodies going from one point to another. He called it the principle of least action. Feynman actually reapplied this principle to quantum mechanics. The action of a mechanical system is the following quantity S:

$$S = \int_{t_i}^{t_f} (T - V)\, dt$$

where T and V are kinetic and potential energy respectively, and ti and tf are the moments of departure (initial) and arrival (final). S is minimal for the trajectories described by Newtonian mechanics. T-V is the so-called Lagrangian of a system. It contains the dynamic information.

Two useful aspects immediately jump out to support my case. The moments of departure and arrival have meaning only if expressed in accordance with the same time scale. We know that special relativity modifies the notion of temporal reference (particularly that of simultaneity). Moreover, the dt factor also depends on the considered time scale.

In the hypothesis of a body that undergoes a change of spatial scale, and therefore of time like UFOs do, it is clear that their trajectories have absolutely nothing to do with our traditional inertial physics. Such bodies will seem utterly magical. Showing up sometimes here, sometimes there, without any apparent displacement. We should not forget that the integral of a function disregards the fractal nature of space and time by straightening out the curves.

Let us return to the discussion of more general aspects. I would like to briefly mention the Institute of Time Nature Explorations located in Moscow.[66] Here a group of acclaimed scientists aim to unravel the nature of time and produce future technologies in the fields of aerospace, medicine and energy via a considerable number of contributions. This institute seems to have taken a keen interest in the developments of 3D time as laid down in this book.

In the West we find, among others, the American astronomer William Tifft and the Finnish scientist Ari Lehto. Tifft[67] was fascinated by the redshifts of stars and galaxies (light shift toward the red end of the spectrum). He considered the possibility that these are not caused by the recession speed of celestial objects, but by a strictly temporal effect. He wrote many articles, including one dedicated to three-dimensional quantized time in cosmology.[68] He developed a model based upon three-dimensional time consistent with properties of particles, fundamental forces and other cosmological effects. The basic equations describing period-doubling sequences, resembling forms of Kepler's third law, may have broad implications with regard to the structure of matter, space and time. The American believed that quantized time can explain quantized redshifts of galaxies, the missing mass of the universe, discordant redshifts, and the dichotomy between quantum mechanics and conventional dynamics.

Ari Lehto also published an extremely interesting article[69] in this respect. The Finnish physicist clearly stated his approach: an agreement between the calculated values and the measured ones is obtained by assuming space and time to be symmetric, that is three-dimensional. He argued that electrons and protons are not subject to transformation and are the only two stable particles. Unlike objects in the macroscopic world, and unlike other particles, they inexorably keep their properties of spin, electric charge and mass. It is remarkable that the extraordinary continuity of these particles is what contradicts the temporal flow concept on which causality is based (time variation). It is this materiality that kills the materialist vision of the world, which is based on the relations between physical values, i.e., on rational time.

The expression: "nothing is created, nothing is lost, all is transformed" is nothing more than a popular belief. These particles appear, disappear and, in the meantime, are not transformed. The conservation of energy is a relative conception. In addition, and that is something to be reflected upon, the life span of a proton considerably exceeds the presumed age of the universe. Lehto suggested that the cyclical conception of time, the oldest in the history of mankind but also the one most in disagreement with the linear and causal conception of time, is perfectly compatible with quantum mechanics, but also with the stars and in general with every body in stabilized rotation. Particles are influenced by two events only: their birth and their death. Therefore, Lehto proposed a (3, 3) signature rather than (3, 1) to characterize space(3)-time(1). According to him, some suggested the existence of continuous three-dimensional time. However, Dorling has proven that, in this case, matter would lose its stability. He concurs with Roland Lehouc of the Atomic Energy Authority CEA.

However, this stability does not resemble any of the properties of rigid bodies. There is a permanent fuzziness: cloud build-up (electrons) + gluonic elasticity (quarks). The effects of the interactions (containment of the atomic nucleus, electronic connections between atoms and subsequently molecules, the manifestation of life) actually constitute the residue of these interactions and of a slight imbalance of the forces. This slight disparity allows the universe to be as we see it. This explains why physical theories have been interested in this entropy, in this permanent chaotic motion, in this irreversibility of time and its cause-effect relations.

Ari Lehto followed a quite different approach and went back to basics as described by the ancients a very long time ago: cyclical time. This is indeed the foundation, because matter (electrons and protons) determines that cyclical or periodic time rules. Periodic time contravenes the irreversibility of time, i.e., causality, both in the past and the future. However, how can temporal periodicity and irreversibility exist side by side? The author showed in his article that periodic time can be used to describe phenomena that are not dependent upon time flow. According to him, it is important to start by symmetrizing the degrees of freedom of space and time. In other words, the topology (3, 1) is not in conformity with the totality of observational reality. Symmetry (3, 3) allows for the asymmetry of phenomena subject to temporal flow while allowing those that are not to exist also, which is the case for the elements in atoms.

E. Cole has shown that ad hoc transformations between two Galilean reference frames can be obtained by using either complex coordinates (as in Minkowski space-time) or six real space-time coordinates. The major difficulty is the physical understanding of the extra time dimensions. Therefore, he suggested the use of a formal framework to classify extra dimensions of 3D time.

The Italian school has also made progress in the study of three-dimensional time. Lehto observed that Demers, Mignani, Recami, Dattoli and Vysin have studied coordinate transformations, electromagnetism and tachyon monopoles in a six-dimensional space-time based on observable time:

$$T = sqr\ (t^2_x + t^2_y + t^2_z)$$

Pappas has taken an axiomatic approach (3, 3) where each space coordinate corresponds to a temporal coordinate, each pair being independent of the other two-dimensional coordinates, with the produced space being the direct sum of the three two-dimensional coordinates.

Lehto argued that in classical, continuous space-time we should be able to obtain infinite energy with an infinite frequency when dx, the small spatial part, nears zero. This was contested by Pauli and Weisskopf. As a consequence, Planck energy (1.2×10^{19} GeV) should be the largest local energy around. In parallel, the very foundation of quantum mechanics (the ultraviolet catastrophe) dictates that space variation should be proportional to time variations, based on light speed. So cyclical time, Lehto felt, had to follow Planck's law. He replaced the frequency by t (cyclical time):

$$E = h.t$$

Lehto said that non-linear forced oscillators generate factor 2 subharmonics. This phenomenon is called period-doubling. M. I. Feigenbaum extended his research to incorporate all universal behavior. The maximum local energy corresponds to a minimum period. Lehto argued that all the minimum local energy must be obtained by period-doubling. According to him, the existence of the process of period-doubling was underlying stable-particle systems. He thus took ratios in base 2 of the energies and lengths characteristic of different physical phenomena. The periods of a simple period-doubling system then obey the equation:

$$x/y = 2^{\pm M}$$

where M is an integer and x and y can be any system period. This equation can also be used to find out whether a system is a period-doubling system by solving for the exponent M:

$$M = \ln(A/B) \, / \, \ln 2$$

where A and B are measured values, lengths or energies, for instance. Attentive readers will not be surprised to see the expression of a fractal in this equation. M is in fact a logarithmic "binder" (neperian in this case) that increases with powers of 2. Lengths and energies, Lehto said, have their corresponding periods obtained from the relations r=ct and E=h/t.

In his article he presented a series of very important tables. Based on the previous equations, he proved the existence of ratios of permanent natural phenomena (stationary), such as planetary orbits to the electron Compton wavelength, and electron rest energy to the energy of the cosmological essence of radiation (3K-background radiation). One might note that these phenomena both originate from the microscopic and the macroscopic universe. An underlying temporal law therefore crosses the spatial scales, showing that M must be of the form:

$$M = N/3$$

where N is an integer. This means that the A and B ratio is as follows:

$$A/B = 2^{N/3}$$

Lehto showed that this relation is true for a three-dimensional, period-doubling system in the case of permanent phenomena. These calculations prove extremely close to observational data obtained via the classical method of one-dimensional time. Nevertheless, Lehto deduced the three-dimensionality of time from the only asymmetry that exists between space and time. He did not provide specific definitions for these dimensions, as length, width and height are given with regard to space. Therefore, his consideration of values 0, 1/3 and 2/3, derived from the calculations in line with the observations, seems the theoretical foundation of this three-dimensionality, which he presented as degrees (3) of freedom of time. Lehto limited this freedom to the permanent physical entities (stationary in time) he related to period-doubling phenomena (harmonic oscillatory of "binder" 2).

Lehto stressed that both Einstein ($E=Mc^2$) and Planck ($E=hf$) considered energy a scalar quantity that has a magnitude, but not a direction. According to them and to Lehto, energy is therefore not vectorial, as in space vectors. Lehto discovered that time is needed to define particle kinematics (such as macroscopic objects) and that dynamics is a one-dimensional flow from the viewpoint of the observer. As a consequence, he felt 3D time cannot be considered a generalization of one-dimensional time. His mathematical model is therefore based only on a cubical lattice, the constant of which increases with integral powers of 2. The unitary scale used is that of time and the Planck length.

Furthermore, Lehto emphasized that quantum numbers can theoretically take any non-imaginary value. In practice, these are often powers of 2. They are called values of the second kind. Lehto described it as follows: "the (n+1) t period may be obtained from the simplest Mandelbrot set (with constant = 0) : t(n+1) = t(n)* (t(0) = 2 in this case)." However, when discussing his own contribution, he added: "this article does not deal with period-doubling processes leading to the quantum numbers of the second kind"! Of course Lehto also brought up fractal progressions. In my opinion, he used the fractal nature of time to cut himself off from the most important aspect of true three-dimensionality.

Nevertheless, Lehto clearly showed that the "grains" of space should be separated from the "grains" of "time" in a lattice made up of quantum steps using the Planck scale. As a consequence, velocity becomes a relation between the quantum number of space and the quantum number of time. However, he subjected this approach to the need for conversion of space into time via light speed value c. He thus returned to using the traditional vocabulary for interchangeable quantum objects of type space or type time, as in special relativity.

Note that speed value c is expressed in kilometers/second. We have already seen that the second is considered a convention. We also know that whereas this speed cannot be exceeded (we will see what this restriction means in the framework of absolute relativity), it can be slowed down. These two aspects are essential to the outcome.

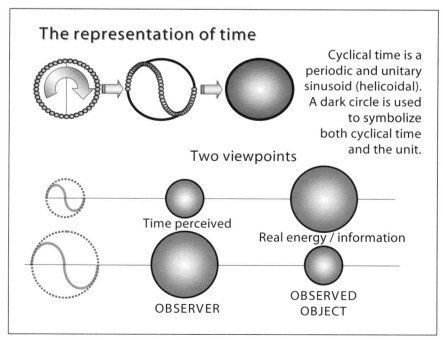

Figure 40

Lehto used E=ht to define the energy generated by cyclical time, knowing that this is the largest possible frequency (c marking the boundary). He thus opened the door to a very inspirational way of reasoning. The "t" period is the inverse expression of the frequency. A frequency is a number of periods per arbitrary time unit. This means that the only natural temporal reality in the universe is the period itself. This period is in itself a time quantum presented as a packet for each of the frequencies of our arbitrary temporal convention.

In most figures (but not all), time is represented from the viewpoint of the observer, i.e., a smaller circle while the frequency is higher. In other words, quantized time, quantum time, is the period itself, any period.

This is exactly how physicists visualize quantized energy, a discrete multiple of Planck energy. Therefore, I am saying that time is energy and vice versa. On the other hand, whether we use our senses or our measuring instruments, the perception of energy is necessarily related to a difference between quantum values of time, i.e., between two periods, one holding the other.

Our normal reasoning forces the appearance of time flow by sketching the orthonormal reference that includes the cyclical sinusoid. In a

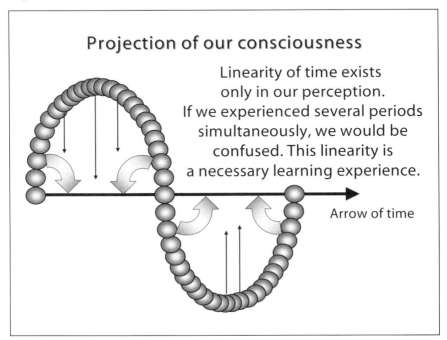

Projection of our consciousness

Linearity of time exists
only in our perception.
If we experienced several periods
simultaneously, we would be
confused. This linearity is
a necessary learning experience.

Arrow of time

Figure 41

way, the abscissa is the projection of our consciousness in the perception of events.

In other words, the right question is not how many periods exist per arbitrary unit (hertz), but for any given superior period (numerical relation). The only temporal reality is: number of periods x per period y! This is actually shown by the tables of the Finnish physicist. The result can be an integer, odd or even, or a fraction. Even better! The sequence relations between periods positioned inside one another like Russian dolls, characterizing a given phenomena or object, can follow an arithmetical or geometrical progression. These progressions can either be seen as the harmonics signature related to neguentropy or as the opposite, the signature of an evident entropic chaos, i.e., chaotic system behavior.

In the following figure I have displayed the connection between missing time and entropy. As this is the visualization of a principle, it is clear that the effects have been exaggerated considerably.

It is essential to understand the overall reasoning, which argues that our subjective perception of time (personal rather than imaginary) is directly linked to our feeling with regard to time flow. By force of

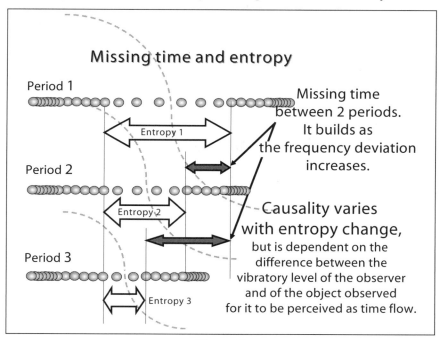

Figure 42

habit we associate reality with the fact that it needs to be experienced for a sufficient period of time. Our mind thus takes an unconscious shortcut between reality and its continuity in our perceptions. An event unnoticeable in time simply does not exist. Remember that there is a persistent tautology between causality and temporal irreversibility.

We should distinguish between what our mind can learn from advanced physics and our personal daily experiences. The description of general relativity and the standard model of quantum mechanics just will not suffice to acknowledge the phenomena we experience. When we speak about quantum mechanics, the vast majority of respondents think of consequences that do not affect them, such as lab experiments or nuclear weapons. Only a few will remember that they are made up of billions and billions of leptons and quarks, or conceptual virtualities. We transport time and space as described above. Therefore, our consciousness navigates from one quantum level to another and between fractals of reality.

The deviations described in figure 43 illustrate accurately the different perceptions between an average psychic life and an evolved psychic life that has access to very high frequencies. The perception of the time flow of high vibratory states (therefore possessing energy) is synonymous to fundamental reality for those who perceive this flow. In other words, it is necessary to be sufficiently close to a specific level, in vibratory terms (psychic life), to experience this flow and thus its content. This explains the disbelief when confronted with testimonies about extraordinary experiences.

For those who are at too great a distance (the majority of the population in the waking state), these experiences do not exist, because they occur extremely briefly and much too fast for our traditional conception of the world. The "superior" entropy (perception of the temporal flow of very short periods, a synonym for extrasensory perception) will be close to zero.

The other way of presenting fractal time is by adding up the intrinsic entropies between two very different vibratory states. The direction of the entropy then becomes our subjective perception of the passage of time. Curiously, this subjective impression of time flow is caused by the existence of intervals of temporal emptiness. Is that not incredible? What we believe to be time is in fact the absence of time! This sounds like the old mystic belief that only the present exists. In fact, past and future are the result of temporal flow. If the latter is nothing but a sequence of non-existences then what does not elapse, remains. In other

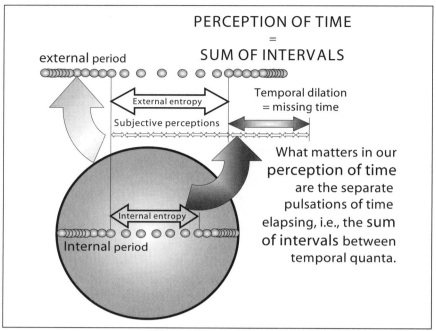

Figure 43

words, this permanence is the present. This present can be translated by the common link (point of departure = point of arrival) that connects consecutive periods, the slower to the faster ones. This direction of the third temporal dimension is extremely difficult to understand.

This present connects sequential concentric periods and thus frequencies to one another, meaning that the present is the line of harmonics. We are living an extremely persistent illusion. Nevertheless, this widespread subjectivity is caused by our need to see causal relations. Subjectivity is thus the source of objectivity as mentioned before: our mind needs the temporal emptiness (= causality) to understand the world in which we live and move forward.

These developments show us that the consciousness of time is highly relative. This is what absolute relativity is all about. This characteristic of consciousness has considerable implications. Clearly, on this side of the spatial atomic scale, space and time still exist. Since there is no more "matter" below that threshold, the 10^{17} remaining grains of space and the 10^{26} eternal grains of time are inevitably the center of an activity. However, which one? What is both non-material and present on a huge playground? We have known the answer to that question for a long time: the mind!

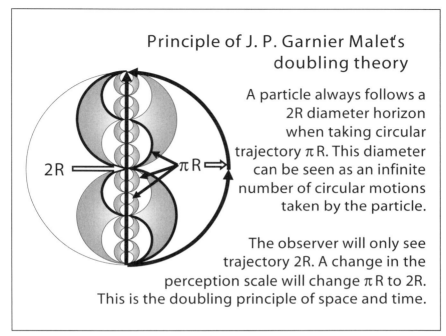

Principle of J. P. Garnier Malet's doubling theory

A particle always follows a 2R diameter horizon when taking circular trajectory π R. This diameter can be seen as an infinite number of circular motions taken by the particle.

The observer will only see trajectory 2R. A change in the perception scale will change π R to 2R. This is the doubling principle of space and time.

2R   π R

Figure 44

Whereas it is vital to base the understanding of time on rational and strict principles, it would be incomplete without a more worked out vision. The quoted scientists have given valuable clues. However, they did not develop a comprehensive view combining the material and the spiritual, which would allow us to understand more easily the direct link between the experiential and the invisible world.

Nevertheless, a Frenchman has laid out an interesting theory and associated it with our evolutionary capacity, i.e., our ability to concretely and spiritually change our future. He also travels France to give personal development training courses. Jean-Pierre Garnier Malet, who holds a doctorate in fluid mechanics, has written articles[70] and a book[71] on the so-called doubling theory.

This theory emphasizes several important points. It transforms πR and 2R by changing the scale of perception. Dividing π by 2 gives us approximately 1.57, which is very close to a fractal dimension.

The Frenchman summarized his theory as follows: "The doubling theory…completes the basic principles of modern physics without throwing away existing laws…A doubling gives us the possibility of anticipating the motions of any particle. As it takes place in an imperceptible time, this anticipation gives a potential to the particles that use

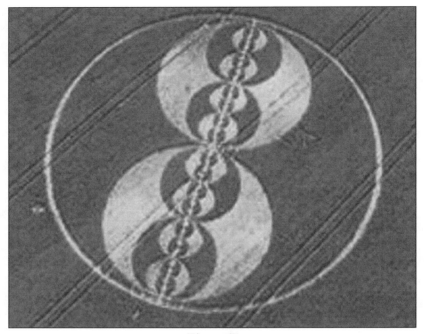

Figure 45

a temporal differentiation in horizons embedded into the same doubling transformation. This strictly observed, instantaneous potential of doubling particles is the result of a fundamental property of time stressed by this theory that may solve numerous paradoxes and more in particular the EPR paradox."

On the website that presents his theory and book,[72] Garnier Malet compares the doubling principle with the knowledge of ancient traditions.

The Hermes symbol of prophecy (caduceus) and the scarab, symbol of metamorphosis of ancient Egypt, bear a striking resemblance to this principle of modern physics. Similarly, crop circles convey an unambiguous scientific message.

Of course, we could also see this as yin and yang or the alpha and the omega, as Garnier Malet did.

To an average person, time is a series of moments of observations intersected by times of non-observations. He called it stroboscopic time. This means that time is discontinuous and that the stroboscopic frequency is an essential characteristic of the nature of time. The author introduced the concept of horizons as follows: "In this theory, a particle in its horizon is always a horizon of particles: as Russian dolls, a particle can be the horizon of internal constituents and its horizon can be also a constituent of an external horizon." So particle = horizon and horizon = two particles twice as small. The term particle is used here in a broad sense. It can be a planet or a proton. In other words, the container is always the content of a larger container, and the content is always the container of other smaller contents. This physicist linked up time and space, defining time as a periodic motion of a space in the horizon of the observer. The figures he used in his theory describe the particle motions according to the scale in which they are observed in relation to sequential particles-containers.

Time dilation occurs at the exact point where a particle crosses a curved line and another crosses a straight line. In this sense, a horizon is an observation boundary and the interactions demarcate time flow deviations. Similarly, the result of an interaction can be anticipated as doubling time elapses more quickly than time on the scale in question. As a consequence: "this anticipation, for which the first rigorous definition was established by Robert Rosen, can therefore be considered the result of a doubling of space and time."

Garnier Malet's reference to temporal relativity hinges on the embedding of horizons or particles, which explains why discrete time is dependent on the viewpoint of the observer. This adds considerable weight to the idea that, from time to time, time flows as described above, in the same way as intuition leads us there: "with discontinuous energies and masses in a discontinuous universe, a discontinuous time seems logical. Thus, Heisenberg's uncertainty relations ($\Delta E \Delta t \geq h/4\pi$) and Einstein's equation ($E=Mc^2$) would use only discontinuous and quantifiable sizes. Einstein talked about time as a succession of moments, but he never used a time discontinuity that is the cause of relativity."

Therefore, the exchanges of interactions would correspond to time accelerations and decelerations. This concurs with Kozyrev's observations. He showed that time was rarer near a cause and denser near an effect. This remarkable fact is the result of the doubling generating possible exchanges of trajectories (and therefore information) between internal particles (accelerated time) and external particles (decelerated time). Slowly but surely, our ability to change our macroscopic world by intentional and mental anticipation is being revealed. Of course, this exchange will remain unobservable since it takes place in the accelerated time of a horizon characterized as virtual by Garnier Malet, in the sense of unreal from the viewpoint of the observer (and his measuring instrument).

Therefore, as accelerated time (that which reaches a point more quickly) exists side by side with the observer's real time, it would be legitimate to argue that the future is visible (premonition/precognition) in the present; as is the past for that matter. One might posit the idea that, due to the propagation of the waves of the past and thus the dilation of their wavelength, the perception of the past takes place in a spatially very large horizon. We also see that intuition finds its roots in the future, where time is accelerated, and usually guides us in our decision-making. In scientific terms: "periodic reconstitutions on a radial axis transform a non-observable circular motion into an observable rectilinear motion. The fundamental doubling motion of embedded consecutive horizons produces apparent translations that are the result of different simultaneous rotations." If the embedding of horizons leads to an acceleration of time, and therefore of motion, the question is: how can we generate it artificially? The answer lies in nature itself: a rotational motion. Subsequently add the change in the vibratory state of a body. This is what resonance frequencies are used for in technology every day. Such combined solutions are applied in UFOs. The Frenchman suggested three different time flows, or horizons: internal, intermediate and external. Past, present and future. He challenged the notion of straight-line propagation,

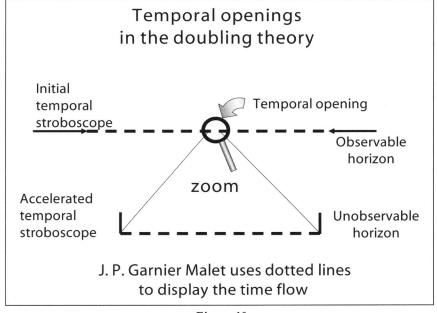

Figure 46

which should not be confused with the physical observation of a recti-linear trajectory that applies only to a given scale. In fact, this tangential propagation takes place on a horizon smaller than the observation scale. The internal horizons, which he called "temporal openings," are defined by stroboscopic observations.

Due to our perceptive inability, each non-observation interval is in itself a stroboscopic series of observations/non-observations. My next figure is inspired by J. P. Garnier Malet's theory. The particles are defined by their speed of motion in a given horizon. They seem to be at rest while they go through a "temporal opening," whereas the particles are really part of a horizon where time flows more quickly. Nevertheless, the arguments proposed by this physicist fit in with a strictly dynamic vision of bodies. He did not mention the states of resonance or intricateness. However, he did point out that the fundamental doubling motion applies to both quantum mechanics and relativist mechanics in cosmology. I think the following sibylline sentence is essential: the propagation of a particle is just an appearance in a given horizon. It is important to understand that all mechanics is due for an overhaul. Just like Lehto, one of the very first who brought up the doubling principle, Garnier Malet specified that the durations of the temporal openings are connected to the periodicity of a particle. He even went one step further by presenting the notion of a spinback, which consists in a triple rotation of the particle or of horizon Ω_0. A spinback can be radial or tangential, the first being an anticipation of the other.

I advise experts to visit this physicist's website[73] for a detailed study of the formalism used and to learn more about his description of the seven juxtaposed horizons.

In his theorem of the three horizons of doubling, he argued that a doubling transformation requires three particles (internal, intermediate, external) embedded into seven stroboscopic times.

I am sure the following crucial element will pique your interest. Garnier Malet defined the maximum radial velocity of the horizon/internal particle Ω_6 during doubling as follows: "During time τ of 4x54 = 216 spinbacks ($\pi\rho$) of particle Ω_6, the motion of this particle accelerates from 1 to 10^6, whereas horizon Ω_0 accelerates from 1 to 10^2.... The application of the doubling theory to the solar system has thus enabled the theoretical 'calculation' of the following velocity in kilometers/second:

$$C^2 = (216\pi\rho/\tau)\ 10^4 = 54\pi^{5/2}\ (\pi R_T/4\tau)\ 10^6 = 299\ 796\ \text{km./sec.}$$

where: $2\tau = 365.25 \times 24 \times 3600$ sec $=$ one year (2 spinbacks)." It is not that difficult to see that the speed of light is related to a deviation of temporal fractals. The big question is if the seven stroboscopic times described by this physicist equal the maximum deviation of a doubling transformation. Considering the incredibly small size of the Planck length (10^{-35} meters), it would be quite acceptable to argue that this velocity c is a boundary between two reference frames (Ω_0 and Ω_6), without being absolute.

This boundary is caused by a number of horizons (7) in a fractal dimension that I call time density. You will have noticed that the Frenchman applied his calculations at the scale of the solar system. This means that the number of fractal horizons that separate us from quarks, for instance, must be much larger.

In other words, ET technology is subject to a time dilation larger than the seven steps described by Garnier Malet. This is how UFOs are able to travel the galaxy with a measurable factor of c without going against the generally accepted laws of physics.

Stating that ETs are not interested in exceeding the speed of light simply means they do not reason from an inertial frame of reference, as we are used to doing. Their vessels do not generate a continuous

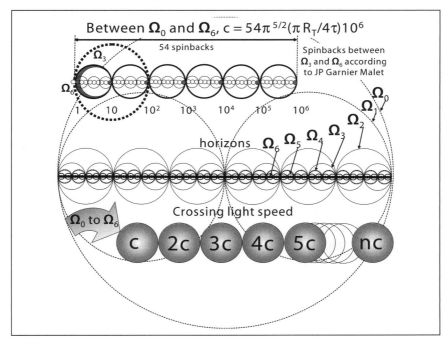

Figure 47

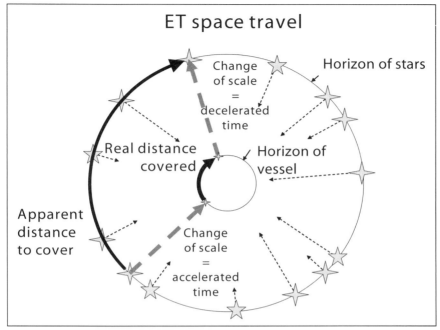

Figure 48

acceleration like a material space probe (i.e., remaining in our horizon), but on the contrary, they reach a non-existent speed in our scale. This non-speed is related to the non-observation times where particles seem at rest. While at rest they do not show any Brownian motion. This is the phase known as the Bose-Einstein condensate, even if the temperature does not equal absolute zero. This allows ET vessels to change scales and make use of transfers of the group of seven maximum horizons. Such transfers are designed to generate, from our point of view, a rapidly multiplied value c.

We have seen that a period or cycle — a motion that returns to its point of departure — is the actual time quantum. However, this quantum, like a packet, may take numerous values varying from extremely large to incredibly small. Nature generates many different cycles. One of the most widely spread forms is produced by the rotation of bodies, which constitutes the link between inertial reference frames (motions) and sinusoidal changes, i.e., time fractals (vibratory states).

In other words, UFOs use variable-velocity tori and rotors enveloped by a spinning electromagnetic field. This means it is now time for explanations.

PART

2

TIME FOR EXPLANATIONS

CHAPTER 33

Personal growth through understanding

UFO AND PARANORMAL PHENOMENA are perfectly controlled by beings that are part of non-material densities of existence. Using the term "paranormal" is in fact misleading. These phenomena are absolutely normal in the whole of possibilities offered by the nature of space and time.

Our modern physics must be rendered one-dimensional again to be understood. Countless physicists, such as Maddox, have endeavored

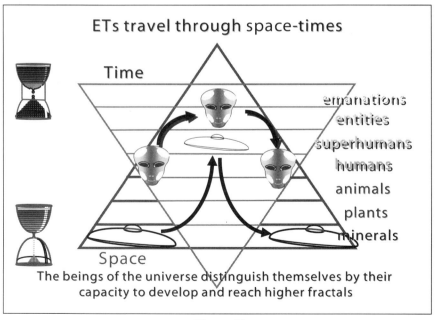

Figure 49

to do so without necessarily having an exact vision of what needs to be reconsidered.

The following two antagonist principles add paradox to contemporary science:

1. The principle of intrinsic reproducibility justifies the use of equations.
2. The principle of irreversibility of time explains causality: equations would not exist.

Equations do not describe reality. They describe what is acceptable. However, if a phenomenon is irreversible, it cannot be reproducible! The conditions have changed. Either an event does not have a cause and can be produced at will, or an event has a cause and cannot be repeated because it is irreversible. It is not strictly reproducible, as long as there is a will to reproduce it or it is cyclical. In other words, everything is produced (and reproduced) at will and outside the flow of time. We need only to study the essence of this will or the conditions of reproducibility (gradual and willful rejection of "disruptive elements"). As a consequence, either nothing is natural or we change the definition and everything is natural when it is done willfully. This is why so-called supernatural effects exist. These are actually the best evidence of the existence of God as Higher or Divine Will with power over every phenomenon, including the most deterministic ones. The difference between determinism and indeterminism must be explained by a distance between the source of will (or intention) and the phenomena (the acts of intention) we bear witness to.

Remember Kant, who said: "each act is always both the effect of a cause according to a certain degree of determinism and the cause of an effect according to causality through freedom. Paradoxically, every act is therefore both free and determined." The dilemma of causality exists because we are utterly convinced that the entire universe is governed by strictly impersonal laws of cause and effect. We are discounting the fact that beings have the power to produce these facts. In this case, not only is the cause not physical, but it cannot be isolated either, unless physicists conduct a long study of occult sciences and occultists and psychologists take up fundamental physics. In absolute relativity, causality is quite simply variable. It is more or less existent.

There are a few indispensable steps towards understanding. The following arguments are based on the evolution we have observed:

1. Newton described time and space as absolute, in which the dynamics of reality took place separate from phenomena.

2. Einstein described time and space as relative in the whole called "the ST" transformed by objects.
3. However, I am arguing that the objects are transformed, that phenomena take place as a result of the space and time of which they are part or that they move through.

Newton thus preceded Einstein, who did not dismiss his ideas but placed them in a relative context. That is what this book is proposing. As we have already seen, the density of time relativizes all equations! However, what happens in case of growing degrees of freedom? Should we adhere to the reproducibility of scientific facts decreed by the philosophy of the Enlightenment? Did you not understand that growing degrees of freedom and deterministic reproducibility are incompatible?

While respecting Penrose's so-called superb theories,[74] I am proposing a new vision of the universe. The problem of understanding the current boundaries of science is that we need to make a distinction between reality (facts), concept (understanding of reality), representation (equation) and verification (measuring instruments). Scientific faith was based on equations that became like the icons of religious faith. The excessive formalism alienates scientists from the primordial conceptions of reality, causing the latter to be forced into equations at the cost of an impressive complexity. This complexity can be replaced by the new paradigm of decreasing causality. The gradual disappearance of this causality means that something else will take its place: intention! The gradual disappearance of deterministic causality deprives equations of their relevance in the explanation of reality, for equations are meaningless without a cause-effect relation. That is the way of quantum mechanics.

There are three basic thought forms that constitute the foundation of physics: logicism, formalism and intuitionism. Neither completely satisfies all the criteria used in establishing the evidence, particularly since Gödel showed the incompleteness of formalism, which is the basis of scientific research. Hervé Barreau summarized the situation as follows[75]: "the price of intuitionism is the inaptitude to cover the entire field of classical mathematics. The price of logicism is the obvious impossibility to connect even the most recognized arithmetical foundations and the price of formalism is that it does not satisfy anyone, leaving mathematicians to live this adventure at their own risk and peril." Physical magnitudes thus lose much of their significance. Therefore, it is an utter waste of time to focus on mathematical formulas alone without adopting the method used by great minds such as Einstein — he also borrowed a great deal from others — i.e., the thought experiment, which is basically what this book is all about. There are several approaches that describe the relevance of mathematics, stating that it is either the absolute expression of the universe or the rudimentary product of human thinking. Nevertheless, one of the fundamental contributions of mathematics is the notion of invariance, i.e., generalized symmetry, a sign of coherence and therefore of profound reality.

This "great symmetry" exists between space and time: what one loses the other gains. The allure of Einstein is the extraordinary elegance of his formula $E=Mc^2$ that generously allows for the symmetry between energy and mass, and even the expression of light speed. I am proposing a symmetry that only includes space and time, considering that — simply put — energy is the expression of time (or more exactly of a time differential) and that mass is the expression of space (a space differential), knowing that constant c also expresses both. Energy and mass must be quantified in order to be used as representations of time and space. This new approach profoundly changes our possible interpretation of observations.

The great novelty of absolute relativity is that time, in motion for instance, does not grow less with space, but actually increases. Paradoxically, a lot of time passes at the same time during apparent immobility, but the time flow is subject to the relative space occupied by the object we study. It is the difference that exists between potential and kinetic[76] energy. Energy is the actual expression of time. As a consequence, motion becomes related to a decrease of space occupied by the object, i.e., the logic of relativistic effects.

The most unsettling aspect of absolute relativity is the inversion we need to apply to our perception of time. The characteristics of time are in fact contrary to entropy (more information) and neguentropy (structuring of information). We therefore need to take the opposite approach to time: the less time passes, the more there is of it.

This new vision leads to several important conclusions. The ST in question is in itself a structure written as "quantity of space over quantity of time," which are therefore absolute instead of conventional quantities.

This object takes the properties of velocity. In our standard language, velocity induces the idea of motion, showing us that motion is actually a singular interpretation of a fractal differential where the notion of information becomes of primary importance. This ratio will be more or less close to 1. Each structure is in itself an information

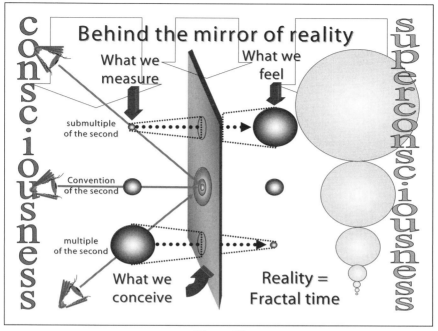

Figure 50

exchange system. Hence the existence of virtual particles in quantum mechanics. These virtual particles can then be considered real quantum entities belonging to a higher spatio-temporal fractal where time is highly dilated, whereas in quantum physics these virtual particles appear and disappear immediately. All information systems overlap in a fractal way like Russian dolls. Therefore, each system is partially autonomous just like classical mechanics. The different degrees of information exchange constitute degrees of causality. Causality thus becomes changeable rather than absolute. This variability in the cause-effect relation implies that we must reconsider the current equations describing a strict causality by nature, except when they are probabilistic, for instance in their representation as a diffusion matrix. In fact, causality, the very foundation of scientific thinking, decreases as the amount of time increases, both in relative terms — compared to space — and in absolute terms. Hence absolute relativity!

CHAPTER 34

Infinite piano symphony

BEFORE PRESENTING THE SOLUTIONS offered by 3D time and absolute relativity, I would like you to imagine the universe as a huge piano keyboard with an infinite number of keys. Every key corresponds to a sound, or frequency. A beautiful melody is made of harmonious chords. We consist of a large number of chords, both on the inside and the outside. We emit and receive these notes. Gaining awareness means recognizing the notes that we emit and receive. The greater the number of these notes, the more expansive our consciousness is. To be more precise, consciousness is the ability to resonate with the largest possible number of notes.

In physics, this grand piano is called the electromagnetic spectrum and we speak of electromagnetic waves. Every wave is called light rather than sound, because electromagnetic waves are known for their ability to travel at light speed in the vacuum. After discussing temporal portals, it should be clear that this velocity is nothing other than a barrier between two fractal scales. Therefore, the argument of this barrier c preventing ETs from visiting us becomes void.

The place we attribute to the brain in interactions with our surroundings remains to be defined correctly. Experience shows that our consciousness is delocalized (nonlocality in QM) and is not located in the brain pan, even if there is a connection (we will see which one later). It forms a whole that could be called a field.

Matter itself is composed only of electromagnetic waves. It is also made of fields. A wave is characterized mainly by a frequency and a wavelength. These two magnitudes are directly proportional because one is defined by the opposite of the other. In the infinitely small,

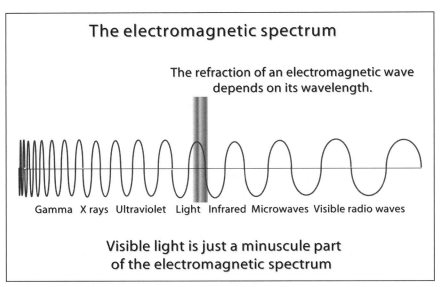

Figure 51

wavelengths are very weak by definition. The shape, the propagation and the properties of waves are diverse. Therefore, the universe is made of countless wave networks interacting in accordance with these criteria. From a scientific point of view, materiality does not have any significance as such. The boundary between materiality and immateriality is a problem of scale and interaction. Ultimately, a wave is simply a space-time ratio.

The most astute readers will find that their knowledge is put to the test. You may even be in denial. The biggest problem of understanding reality is grasping the true meaning of time. We can approach reality if we consciously make the effort to retreat from the world. Nevertheless, do not worry if you are not quite familiar with the following explanation. It refers to scientific and spiritual prerequisites. Read this part at your leisure. Some words or sentences will appeal to you more clearly than others. We are used to saying that "what is conceivable is stated clearly." However, as we have already seen, reality is not in conformity with its description, because the latter cannot encompass it by nature. Feynman, one of the greatest physicists of the twentieth century, said: "I can say without the risk of being mistaken that nobody understands quantum mechanics...Do not keep saying to yourself, if you can possibly avoid it, 'But how can it be like that?' because you will get 'down the drain,' into a blind alley from which nobody has yet

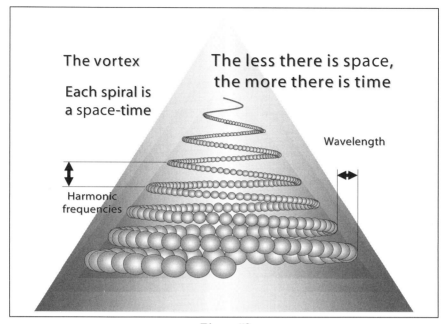

The vortex

Each spiral is a space-time

The less there is space, the more there is time

Wavelength

Harmonic frequencies

Figure 52

escaped. Nobody knows how it can be like that"[77]. As we reach the end of this chapter, I hope that some of you are beginning to grasp the nature of reality. Welcome to our future…

CHAPTER 35

Space and time: beneath the cobblestones lies freedom

CONTRARY TO WHAT WE BELIEVE, particles do not exist. They manage a punctual ST that can behave like a wave. We speak of "quantum entities" instead of particles.

It is impossible to discuss time without discussing space. A new notion of the granularity of space and time emerges. Just as there are grains of energy (quanta), there are invisible grains of sand in the spatio-temporal hourglass. In a way, temporal grains are energetic grains. In the case of discrete (discontinuous) space, the theoretician Alain Connes pictured non-commutative geometries allowing for the presence of spatial structures showing a discontinuous nature (hyperfine mesh network structure) without violating fundamental symmetries. The spatial coordinates have been replaced by noncommutative "algebraic operators." Therefore, the order of their use is not random. It seems as if these geometries restore the usual properties of space on the largest scales, particularly the spatial isotropy, i.e., invariant under rotation. Please note that meshed networks were invented to react to the axiomatic constraint of the absence of divergence! In other words, we created the means to prove us right! At the same time, the wings of the paranormal are arbitrarily clipped by preventing immaterial phenomena to occur. The problem with these noncommutative geometries is actually that they suggest a configuration without time and space; the very negation of universal dynamics. Nonetheless, they suggest that spatio-temporal fractals have a pseudo-hermetic boundary (see below for the anti-return valve of strong interaction), while leaving an open door to exchange. Discrete time seems to pose problems. While observing time quanta, a kind of temporal particles, it is indeed difficult for us to imagine the nature of the intervals between every particle, called chronons. Is this non-temporal time? Did time stop? I think the problem cannot be formulated in these words, but in terms of information and, as we will see, in terms of the unavailability of energy. If there is no information, there is no time. On the other hand, if there is a great deal or even an infinite amount of information, there is an infinity of temporal quanta.

That is the very principle of fractal time. In other words, the infinity of time is the opposite of the infinity of space. Temporal quanta appear as space quanta disappear, which would explain the existence of energy — related to information — and why it is unavailable in certain parts of space. Those are the premises of the solution offered by absolute relativity.

Klein argued: "Thanks to the standard model of particle physics we can now describe the behavior of elementary particles and their interactions on scales close to 10^{-18} meters.... However, at much smaller distances a new physics is required. Its elaboration will definitely change our representation of space and time." That is exactly what I am trying to do.

CHAPTER 36

Absolute relativity, or the end of the quest

IN THE THEORY OF ABSOLUTE RELATIVITY:

1. Information structures the ST, and vice versa.
2. Consciousness creates the world.
3. All is one and one is all.

In absolute relativity, the occurrence of phenomena is subject to the flow of time. This reasoning is opposed to what we accept today: by

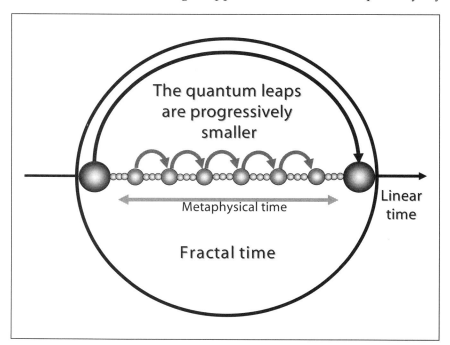

Figure 53

controlling time and space, we control the phenomena. I am arguing that time has three dimensions connecting general relativity and quantum mechanics, as well as the material and the spiritual. I have called it 3D time. The triple definition is as follows:

THE DIRECTION OF TIME: direction of the time flow. This is a sequence of time that establishes the cause-effect relation. More concretely, it is the time arrow. It describes the visible transformation of matter and events. The direction of time is not linear, but discontinuous.

The direction of time has two directions that can be represented by a graphic axis of a function. The most acceptable is therefore the natural arrow of time going from past to future. The second direction goes from the future towards the past, which is more difficult to interpret because it occurs beyond a specific flow rate (see density below). The inversion does not apply to every fractal scale.

The keyword is transformation. It is the direction of the fluctuation of time units during an exchange of information or in motion. Time unit: temporal quantum (Qt).

THE DENSITY OF TIME: Fluidity of time flow. The relative quantity of time affects the behavior of matter and events. It describes their

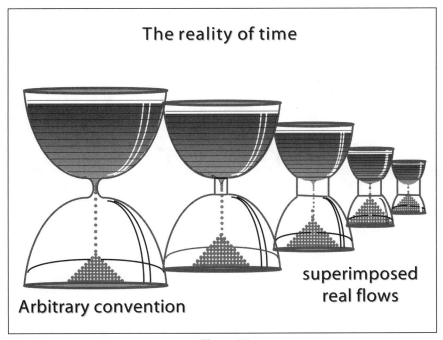

Figure 54

transformation rate. The density of time is not linear but discontinuous, thus fractal, and implies that events are more or less present in quantities of time defined by convention.

In other words, in a density of time D, there is less information than in a density D+1. Density can be represented by a graphic axis describing the transition from one density to another.

The keyword is velocity or rate (of transformation). It is a quantity of time units during an exchange of information or in motion and can also be interpreted as the possible (or potential) amount of information or the number of movements per conventional time unit (second).

Time unit: temporal quantum (Qt).

We need to understand that in one second there is a variable quantity of time units. The higher the time density, the greater the number of time quanta. All time densities pass at the same time (the example of the hourglass), both in the past and the future, but on different spatial scales. The more temporal density there is, the farther we go into the past and future.

THE PRESENT OF TIME: alignment of temporal quanta in the harmonic frequencies. The fluctuation of the present is connected to the

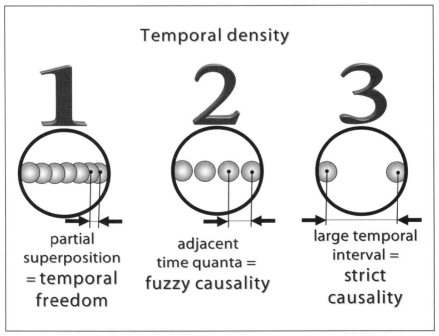

Figure 55

cyclical nature of events when they return to their initial point. The present is not subject to the direction or density of time, but constitutes the link between them. It is a common number of time units between different time densities during a transformation in a balanced state. The present allows us to go from one density to another.

The keyword is permanence (the non-transformable). Time unit: temporal quantum (Qt).

The cycles of nature were so important in ancient cultures because cycle conjunctions can establish a link with the highest time densities and therefore with more or less spiritual entities, depending on a person's ascension skills.

Ultimately, 3D time is nothing other than the introduction of variable causality. This variability imposes two fundamental principles:

1. The continuity of interactions only manifests itself in a well-delineated and thus fractal spatio-temporal reference frame.
2. The number of parameters and therefore the amount of information introduced to a system produces a complexity that defines the degree of causality.

Therefore, as a system grows more complex, causality gradually disappears. It appears that the spatio-temporal parameters of quantum

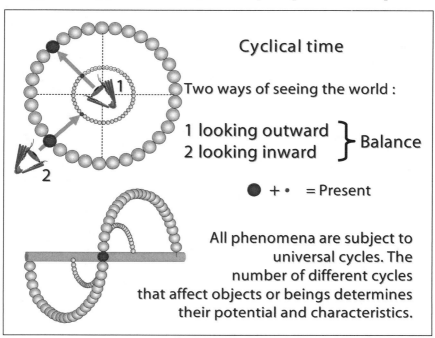

Figure 56

mechanics are much more complex than the access to large scales, which justifies their aleatory or probabilistic nature. In other words, 3D time takes into account the variability of causality by measuring the interval between subsequent time quanta. This means that traditional time does not exist during this interval in this ST. The primordial time unit (time quanta) is taking leaps, called discrete time in scientific literature. On the one hand, this interval is occupied by different STs (of a higher temporal density) and on the other, only phenomena have an intrinsic reality, since 3D time — just like 3D space — is also a conceptual tool guiding us towards a better understanding.

These intervals pose a logical problem. How is it possible that differential equations, fully satisfactory in terms of reason, can contravene the alleged non-linearity of the motion of celestial bodies, for example? This issue is at the very core of Zeno's paradoxes,[78] which, according to Bergson, must be seen "as the symptoms of the ways of the human intellect in its absurd proposition that movement is made of immobilities."

We are often inclined to think that the continuum is not subject to space and time, and that every phenomenon occurs in space and time to be perceived and therefore measured. The measurement is actually what prompts us to validate or invalidate theories. If I may say so, we measure a form of aporia induced by science. The decrease of space and time attributed to the intervals suggested by Achilles' race[79] argues that the fluctuation in question is arithmetical and linear. Bergson said: "that it is enough to go with the movement, in other words to scrutinize what Achilles did, to put yourself in his shoes in order to retrace each of his steps as an indivisible act that contributes to giving the race its natural order." In this case, the indivisible act comes down to considering the ST (also called horizon) defined by the phenomenon (the race) that does not take place in the microscopic universe, but on a (macroscopic) battlefield. In other words, velocity itself defines the passing time intervals for the Greek runner. Putting yourself "in the shoes of UFOs" means no longer being part of our plane of macroscopic observations. The UFO is part of the stroboscopic time of non-observations. It is there, but we cannot see it!

CHAPTER 37

Time is energy

THIS BABYLONIC CONFUSION is the principle cause of misunderstandings. Providing a clear definition of what represents each idea and each word that constitutes this idea is an integrated part of knowledge (but not of transcendental knowledge). Not only does time not escape this need to define what we are talking about, but according to Ludwig Wittgenstein, "a word has not got a meaning given to it, as it were, by a power independent of us, so that there could be a kind of scientific investigation into what the word really means. A word has the meaning someone has given to it." Therefore, in absolute relativity, the physical magnitude of time is… energy! From this point of view, it makes sense to say that time does not exist. However, it also makes sense to say that energy does not exist and that our consciousness of time "represents" other temporal densities as energy. Could we actually receive energy if we were on its frequency? The effects only exist because of the vibratory differences. Our sense of separation from others is merely caused by the belief that we are defined by our vibration alone. That separation is just a belief, even if it is persistent. The science practiced today is a belief, because it claims to be outside the studied object, whereas scientists are part of a specific horizon.

The mere fact of observing the energy of a process is indicative of a time density that is different from ours in the system in question! All is energy, particularly matter. This means that everyone, including the laboratory assistant, expresses but a very small portion of this energy while remaining part of the whole. The consciousness expressed by our ego observes the separation and not our intrinsic energy or time. This consciousness can vary as we please, according to our desires and our ability to switch between STs (e.g., via deep meditation). Desire is the foundation of all needs, as we have seen, which is what our different bodies (physical, etheric, astral, etc.), superimposed like Russian dolls, are used for. They express a specific need in the sense of Maslow's hierarchy of needs.[80] Those who would like to use free energy technology must understand that such devices simply access different time densities at will. In other words, free energy technology controls frequencies by composing a melody with the harmonics of a particular environment, taking into account that the energy of the vacuum corresponds to temporal densities that are inaccessible from the macroscopic universe. Rotating fields are the key to free energy and define the present, being the only link between fractals, i.e., between different temporal densities.

CHAPTER 38

Towards a new formalism

THE AXIOMS OF 3D TIME open the door to a new formalist approach called absolute relativity. What follows is simply a research path that probably needs to be developed further. What matters is the reasoning behind it. First, I would like to provide a few fundamental equations, starting with the Planck equation:

$$E = h.f$$

Planck's constant h is expressed in joule-seconds. This physical magnitude is therefore subject to the definition of time. One joule is a unit of work or energy, defined to be the work done by a force of one Newton acting to move an object through a distance of one meter along its own line of action. This indicates that we are subject to the definition of space. In a fractal universe that strips space of its isotropic nature, the scale in question will cause significant deviations. In addition, force is mass multiplied by acceleration, the latter also being subject to space and time. What remains is mass, the nature of which needs to be defined. Experiments confirm that h is constant, which is justified by the quantum behavior of particles. The study of time has shown us that time accelerates, which we interpret as an increase of the time quantum number.

We believe that every condensation phenomenon (Bose-Einstein condensates) eliminates space in favor of time. This elimination of space is confirmed by the absence of particle motion. Moreover, according to the logic of the doubling theory, the motion of a "container horizon" (container particle) does not exist for the "contained horizon" (contained particle). This motion does not exist because space does not exist above the given horizon. If you can picture this motion, it exists only intrinsically by changing scales. However, the actual scale change is the inverted fluctuation of time and space. In other words, absolute space disappears due to the fractal fluctuation of time.

This logic would dictate that the ultimate phase of space is an absence of itself, whereas time would be a form of motionless permanence, a continuous light purified of all movement (motion requires space). This is evidently not easily accepted by the mind, but quantum experiments are particularly counterintuitive.

Therefore, Planck's constant should be expressed only through time. Please remember that although we may object to this innovative approach, there is a great conceptual void on the nature of space and time below the quark scale. However, this conceptual void represents almost half of the universe in terms of the number of scales. If h is a constant, it must be written as a ratio, in this case the ratio between the times of two, directly adjacent or overlapping horizons (fractals):

$$h = t_0/t_1$$

where t_0 is the smallest quantum time and t_1 is the smallest quantum time that contains t_0, h being an energy constant, whereas the energy must be expressed by a temporal fractal ratio. Ari Lehto expressed frequency f by unitary cycle t. This cycle can only be t_0 in our expression. The energy is thus expressed by:

$$E = \frac{t_0^2}{t_1}$$

where t_0 is the smallest quantum time and t_1 is the smallest quantum time that contains t_0. We can extend this formula by considering two fractal scales t_s and t_{s+n}, where s is the index of the source fractal and s+n is the index of the number of fractal iterations between the source horizon (not necessarily the smallest possible) and the target horizon of the larger spatial scale (the observer). As a result:

$$E = \frac{t_s^2}{t_{s+n}}$$

It is important to pay attention to our definitions of certain terms. The logic of the horizons distinguishes between the point of view of the observer and of the object in question. In this case, $t_s > t_{s+n}$ because the absolute value of the number of temporal quanta is used. However, t_s

<< t_{s+n} in apparent duration for the observer located in t_{s+n}. Nevertheless, by strictly adhering to the traditional scalar logic of energy, E — included in this expression — corresponds to the energy measured in the fractal space of the observer/measuring instrument. When we change space and time, as UFOs do, E becomes a vector.

Let us move on to the Compton wavelength:

$$\gamma_c = h \ / \ mc$$

where h is Planck's constant, m is mass and c is the speed of light. After having defined h, we can now express m by using c in accordance with a new approach solely centered upon space and time.

We have seen that the doubling theory suggested rewriting light speed c. This formulation considers seven iterations between t_s and t_{s+n}, where n=7. The speed of light is constant for a given horizon as it represents a maximum deviation between two fractals separated by seven iterations. One of these two fractals can be the observer's target fractal.

Therefore, the point of view (i.e., the horizon) of the observer determines the standard velocity of light. We have seen that the space quantum number decreased while the time quantum number increased. This has a peculiar, but not unexpected consequence.

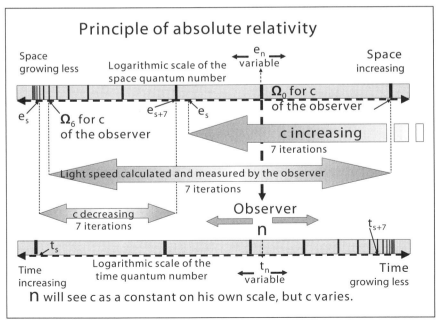

Figure 57

As we probe deeper and deeper into the infinitely small, the more this velocity decreases, while keeping the seven iteration interval, because the distance to cover is so much smaller that there are fewer space quanta per fractal level (space disappears). Experiments confirm that this velocity is decreasing when light moves through matter.

However, in astrophysics c could be considered much greater on distant spatial scales, because the horizon of galaxies would increase c in accordance with the fractal principle. As a consequence, galaxies may be much farther away than we think and some stars may be closer than expected.

Translating the group of seven iterations changes the space-time ratio of c.

Please note that the difference between t_s and $t_{7+n'}$, where n' is the number of iterations separating the observer from the target horizon of c (Ω_0 in the doubling theory), produces a multiple of c, not necessarily in integers, but a whole of positive natural numbers, if this translation takes place towards the infinitely small and the speed of light decreases correlatively. In other words, the temporal dilation of the horizon corresponding to t_s compared to our physical time is clearly higher than the

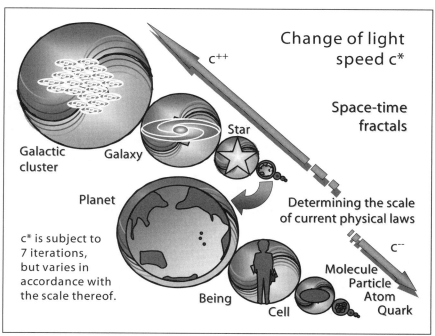

Figure 58

one predicted by special relativity at the threshold of c. It is vital to understand that our common temporal units, such as the second, cannot be used as such anymore. Cycle ratios are no longer sufficient. We can use frequencies to improve our representations, but they would still be a weak and distorted expression of the primary concept.

This results in the following conditions:

1. There is no observation/measurement possible outside the seven iterations of c.
2. We measure the 'fractal distance' between object and observer/ instrument.
3. There is no distinction between observer and measuring instrument if the observer keeps a physical point of view (same scale, same motion as the instrument).

C is both the resultant of a maximum temporal fractal deviation and the resultant of a maximum spatial fractal deviation. Value c can therefore be expressed as:

$$C = \frac{E_{F7}}{T_{F7}} = \frac{\dfrac{e_{s+7}}{e_s}}{\dfrac{t_s}{t_{s+7}}} = cst$$

where e_s and e_{s+7} are the space quantum numbers with $e_{s+7} \gg e_s$ being an absolute value (which feels intuitively right) and $t_s \gg t_{s+7}$ (which does not feel intuitively right). When e_s tends towards zero (towards the infinitely small), c tends towards zero because e_{s+7} is following the same motion. That tendency is even stronger in this numerator because the space quanta disappear faster due to the scale change, as already observed. It clearly remains a paradox. How can space quanta disappear when a fractal progression zooming in on smaller scales should cause them to multiply?

This is the most difficult aspect to understand. The essential difference between space and time is indeed that one is finite in the horizon of an object-system, whereas the other is only finite in terms of the information it can provide. As a consequence, the number of iterations of a spatial fractal is limited by the system itself. Beyond this boundary, the system disappears from an ontological point of view. We are beginning to understand that objects usually qualified as matter, i.e., having a reality in space, are gradually becoming less efficient in transmitting the information they are supposed to transmit.

As the information trajectory grows longer (remember the principle of least action), prompted by a permanent increase of spatial iterations, the chance that the system-object can resist the laws of evolution leading to more information diminishes. If space is fractal, it expresses itself by using the systems of creation. Every system is not a perfect representation of its fractality or every object would look fractal, such as ferns.

Systems do only what they were designed to do. The already acknowledged principle of least action therefore consists in multiplying the occurrences that inform a system without passing through space and producing a great deal of S actions, but through time. It is therefore easier to create the system while keeping its function intact. This so-called redundancy can be found in every information system. It is present in the security systems of airplanes, where alarms are doubled, tripled and even quadrupled, and basically in every complex and intelligent system. The complexity and intelligence are translated by a network that decreasingly uses physical links, and therefore space quanta, in favor of accelerated time. In other words, the more time there is, the less space there is. Nonetheless, everything is subject to scales, the absolute values of which remain to be determined.

It is clear that exotic matter used by ETs, for example, is a material system with potentially more than seven spatial iterations exceeding the threshold of c. This property allows them to dematerialize. Let us return to rewriting the value of c.

In the same way and in accordance with the aforementioned equation, c tends towards zero when t_s moves towards infinity (and towards the infinitely small). We have seen that c is constant for a given horizon, that of the observer. The problem is to determine the value of a space quantum number and a time quantum number. The choice of Planck scales seems a first possibility, but may not necessarily be sufficient.

Many ask if it makes sense to think that in the absence of space, time could still exist and even increase. As long as we think solely in terms of motion, the answer is no. In terms of information, the answer is yes. Do not forget that motion is changing information, but only from our perspective. Motion is nothing other than a specific type of information. The question is what the information looks like when it is not subject to motion. It constitutes the quantum memory of all that ever was, is and will be. This memory is reality, whereas motion is subjectivity stretched out by fractal unfolding. Consciousness thus becomes a receptacle of one or every piece of information for the purpose of choice, contemplation or being.

After this indispensable digression, let us study the nature of so-called weighty mass by returning to the Compton wavelength:

$$m = \frac{T_{F1}}{\gamma_c \dfrac{E_{F7}}{T_{F7}}}$$

where T_{F1} is the fundamental fractal ratio h (Planck's constant), γ_c is the Compton wavelength and E_{F7}/T_{F7} is the revised expression of c (see above). As the name suggests, the Compton wavelength is the expression of space. In a formalized form it is written as e_n, where n is the index of a given horizon allegedly situated between e_s and e_7. This produces the following equation:

$$m = \frac{T_{F1}}{e_n} \times \frac{T_{F7}}{E_{F7}}$$

which clearly shows the following astonishing expression:

$$\text{mass} = \frac{\text{time}}{\text{space}}$$

The most unusual property of mass is its ratio to space as the traditional equation indicates, since h and c are constants. What is new is that it is reduced to a product of temporal ratios compared to a product of space ratios, similar to the opposite of velocity and thus creating the illusion that weighty mass equals inert mass, the opposite of acceleration. In reality, it is a time-space ratio that is independent of the physical magnitudes in question and therefore without size. If we do not want the nature of mass to be influenced by the scale on which it is observed, gravity and all interactions in general should be expressed solely in terms of time and space. If mass is subject to space, the only reality is that of volumic mass, written as:

$$\text{volumic mass} = \frac{\text{time}}{\text{space}^2}$$

This expression is similar to the inverted picture of acceleration. Of course, volume is cubic force. However, space is not isotropic because it is fractal! Therefore, the moving body is fractal in one single non-whole fractal dimension. The factor is a variable horizon, but it is not the only one changing in the expression above if we consider that c (E_{F7}/T_{F7}) decreases when the spatial scale grows smaller, and vice versa. It is clear that mass is relative to the horizon on which it is observed. This approach distinguishes between weighty mass and inert mass and as a result, challenges the traditional interpretation of Einstein's equation

$E=Mc^2$. It is indeed possible to prove that value m in Einstein's equation is the inertia. In the new formalism it is written as follows:

$$m = t_{s+n} \times \frac{e_{s+7}^2}{e_s^2}$$

Inert mass m is growing because quantum space e_{s+7} is much larger than e_s. Since e_{s+7} is in square, its influence is preeminent on t_{s+n}, which diminishes along with space. This expression clearly shows that inert mass is essentially subject to space. The expression mentioned above does not take into account $\sqrt{1-\beta^2}$ (where ß is v/c), which completes Einstein's equation in the denominator. When we replace v and c by their formulation in absolute relativity ($v=e_n/t_n$ as expressed above), two things become clear: v tends towards c or c tends towards v. Indeed, v/c is no longer a ratio lower than or equal to 1, but a quantum value ratio higher or lower than 1. The first situation describes the point of view of the observer, which is the observational measurement. This is written as follows:

$$\sqrt{1 - (x > 1)}$$

which is an imaginary number. In the second case it is written as:

$$\sqrt{1 - (x < 1)}$$

which is a natural number. This clearly shows that the point of view of the observer does not correspond to reality.

Usually, weighty mass and inert mass are mixed up on our macroscopic scale because c is large. However, as we probe deeper into the infinitely small, and the so-called weighty mass grows, inert mass disappears completely, either because c diminishes, or because the observer is located in an intermediate horizon between e_s and e_{s+7}. In both cases e_{s+7} is written as e_{s+n}, where n < 7. On the other hand, on the large scales, inert mass increases, but weighty mass diminishes. The expression of a force (f = m.a) is therefore written with the following magnitudes:

$$\text{force} = \frac{\text{ratio of time}}{\text{ratio of space}} \times \frac{\text{space}}{\text{time}}$$

This shows that a force, i.e., an interaction, is affected by time-space ratios. Depending on the value of these ratios, the intensity of a force (on a specific scale) compared to other forces is therefore different. That is definitely true, particularly between gravity and strong interaction.

We can compare this vision to Heisenberg's quantitative uncertainty relations that limit time Δt, during which a boson is able to exist. The Heisenberg inequality is written as:

$$\Delta t < h/mc^2$$

which leads to the following new formulation:

$$\Delta t < \frac{T_{F1}}{\dfrac{T_{F1}}{e_n} \times \dfrac{T_{F7}}{E_{F7}} \times \dfrac{E_{F7}^2}{T_{F7}^2}} = \frac{T_{F1}}{\dfrac{T_{F1}}{e_n} \times \dfrac{E_{F7}}{T_{F7}}} = \frac{T_{F1} \times e_n \times T_{F7}}{T_{F1} \times E_{F7}} = e_n \times \frac{T_{F7}}{E_{F7}} = \frac{\gamma_c}{c}$$

In other words, the Compton wavelength is divided by the velocity of light, of which the resultant value is definitely related to time. The lifespan of a boson is subject to a distance (γ_c) that lowers the velocity of light (c) as it grows smaller. Therefore, there is a boundary below which it is impossible for us to measure the existence of a boson, since it is considered from the perspective of the observer (i.e., of traditional formalism). This is where strange phenomena suddenly occur without a visible cause and without being influenced by mass. That is the most important observation from our point of view. In the new formalism however, time quanta are more prevalent than space quanta, which is in line with absolute relativity.

The following diagram explains my arguments:

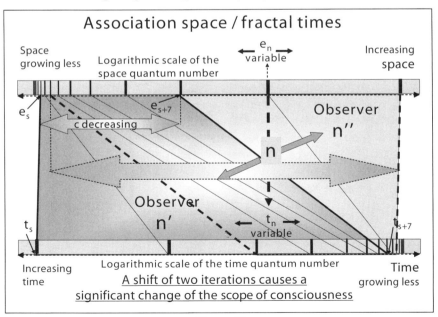

Figure 59

Moving fractal space and time closer together requires us to associate a given temporal flow with a given part of space (horizon or spatial scale). This is the general framework of the universe. An observer can thus easily change his point of view and move from one ST to another. This changed point of view, e.g., by means of psychism, influences his perceptions to a certain degree depending on the number of shifts (iterations) realized in either direction (towards the right or the left in figure 59). It is not astounding that Einstein's thought experiment led him to believe that an observer traveling at light speed (the large arrow in the figure) sees the photon as immobile. The velocity expressed by the space-time ratio has become (quasi) zero compared to its old frame of reference (n). Nevertheless, things are slightly more complex in absolute relativity.

Either three observers n, n', n" are as positioned in the figures mentioned above (n is between n' [microscopic] and n" [macroscopic]), or the light speed of the observer is also c_{obs}. It follows that:

1. if n' or n' $\in c_{obs} \Rightarrow$ n' or n" can be observed by n.

2. if n' or n" $\notin c_{obs} \Rightarrow$ n' or n" cannot be observed by n.

It is clear that 'observed' means measurable in this case. Observer n sees n' at velocity S'/T according to his degrees of freedom of space, with S' being the quantum value of space n' and T being the quantum value of time n. The spin of a particle greatly resembles the boundary of two intrinsic degrees of liberty by a rotation around itself. This explains the aforementioned instants of non-observation (in fact T') and its orbit around the nucleus in the classical configuration of atoms. The movements at constant or accelerated velocity are therefore perceived by the observer if and only if they take place outside the plane of rotation. The velocity is interpreted as an observable ST differential (as it is located outside the plane of rotation), and the acceleration as a change of this differential. Once again, energy

$$E = t_s^2 / t_{s+n}$$

applies to a given horizon (that of the observer); hence its apparently scalar nature.

In absolute relativity, we need to distinguish between time and space, just as Lehto did with his cubic lattices. The fractal values of space and time are translated into a scale of quantum values, specific for each one, or $f_s = \log p_s / \log q_s$ and $f_T = \log p_T / \log q_T$. We now know that these logarithmic scales are inverted. For the observer, the velocity of "object" n' or n" is therefore expressed in two ways:

$$v' = \frac{f_E}{\frac{1}{f_T}} \times \frac{E}{T} \qquad \text{or} \qquad v'' = \frac{f_E}{F_T} \times \frac{E}{T}$$

with v' if the observer measures a horizon lower than his own (microscopic) and with v'' if the observer measures a horizon higher than his own (macroscopic). S and T are the quantum numbers of space and time of the observer's horizon. This means that v' and v'' are not only velocities, but deviations between the measured ST and the observer ST. The problem is to correctly calculate S and T, as well as the number of iterations and the magnification factor of S and T. Please note that this reasoning concurs with the reduction of the wave packet, for the act of observing (or measuring) from our horizon actually deletes T' from our perception.

This development, even if it is new to this budding formalism, allows us to understand a vital property of the acceleration of UFOs. They produce a logarithmic time scale slip by using the spinning movement of two inverted disks, before a spatial scale change appears in a delayed reaction.

It may be necessary to consult Garnier-Malet to find the relation between Ω_0 (10^2) and Ω_6 (10^6) or Lehto to find the x-y relation (x/y=2±M where M=1n(A/B)/1n2, where M is of the type M=N/3) and assess the ad hoc factors that must be taken into account. At this time, we do not know exactly the number of iterations and the magnification factor for S and T used by the ETs. Nonetheless, it is not difficult to see that an

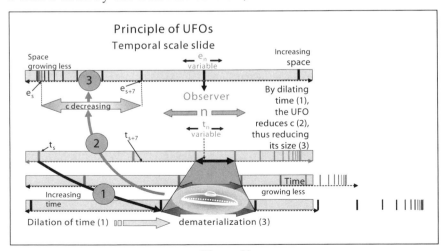

Figure 60

exponential acceleration is perfectly possible (inverted function of the logarithm). It is also clear that the velocity attained by UFOs does not even come close to c before the latter is changed by the horizon change. It is exactly this horizon change that allows for the reduction of inert mass. The most important arguments opposed to the impossibility of such accelerations, and in general to the UFO phenomenon, therefore lose their relevance in the light of fractal space-time.

Please note that the rotation of the internal UFO disks, which we may see as cold plasma of coherent light, limits the movements of the space-craft on their rotation plane as the rotation reduces the spatial degree of freedom, just like particle spin. Therefore, UFOs move very slowly as long as the horizontal plane coincides with the plane of rotation.

As a consequence, the acceleration of the craft must take place on a different plane, either in a direction close to the perpendicular of this plane, or by tilting the vessel (by slightly changing the rotation veloc-ity of the two inverted-rotation disks). In such a configuration, instan-taneous ninety degree turns correspond to an incline change realized in high temporal densities. ETs change the position of the saucer to align it with the initial vectorial component and subsequently generate

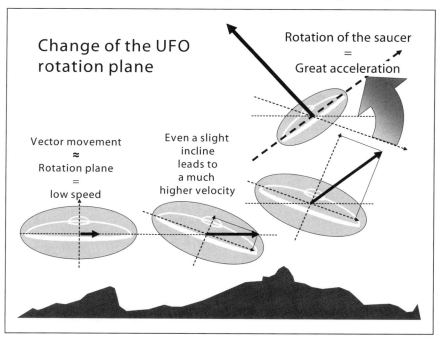

Figure 61

a vector perpendicular to the vessel. This is a well-known gyroscopic effect. This allows them to accelerate much faster, as observed by numerous eyewitnesses. I should also mention that the position of this rotation plane compared to the Earth horizon is absolutely irrelevant, because gravity is always quasi-zero for the craft. Therefore, ETs are not tilted to one side due to an absence of gravity. Of course, this only applies as long as the vessel does not land on terra firma, where it must align to the Earth plane.

CHAPTER 39

Constraint and freedom: from separation to oneness

A REMARKABLE THING ABOUT THIS three-dimensional vision of time is that an increased time density gives us more freedom, whereas universal information converges in complex systems. However, the presence of space between time quanta means that the law of cause-effect prevails because temporal leaps are larger. Inversion becomes impossible. Objects become tangible. As you can see, we are faced with a surprising, progressive duality that was however, well-known in ancient mysticism: constraint/separation versus freedom/oneness.

Contemporary science is founded on causality and therefore on the reproducibility of phenomena. This is true for the physical world of classical mechanics, but the degrees of freedom in quantum mechanics are much larger. The "evidence" is thus based on physical laws allowing for the reproducibility that we have already characterized as one of the terms of the scientific paradox. In addition, establishing proof requires the validation of measuring instruments manufactured in accordance with confirmed laws instead of potentially new physical laws. It so happens that these measuring instruments are part of the macroscopic world of man and of its causal consequences. It is a vicious circle. To establish the reality of a phenomenon, we use instruments that can only refute it when it is governed by unknown laws, or rather when it is acausal from our physical point of view. However, scientists acknowledge the vulnerability of proof as it is historically untrue to argue that it can be absolute. The person refuting the facts is actually responsible for delivering the proof. The law of large numbers, e.g., when it comes to paranormal phenomena, provides very strong evidence. This is not a matter of belief, but of fact and therefore of logic.

Precognition (or premonition) is an example of a paranormal phenomenon ordinarily refuted because it violates our sacrosanct causality. It is therefore categorized as coincidence. Our future destiny is partially visible for those with the (sometimes temporary) ability to see. We use the same arguments by saying that an event must take place before we know that it was a premonition. Please note that scientists merely describe what will take place with the help of equations! They can be certain only when it actually occurs (which is not always the case), but they a priori know in advance (that is why theories exist) what will happen up to a certain degree! Just like psychic mediums! It is this "minuscule" difference between premonition and fact that leaves room for…quantum free will. The problem is that this degree of uncertainty increases along with the degree of freedom of the object we study. The odds that a fact comes to pass following a prophecy are therefore considerably lower than in classical mechanics; hence a large margin of error (despite the skills of the seer). As a consequence, the potentiality of an event depends on the intention associated with it. This depends on the subject in question, whether or not his consciousness is evolved, i.e., his ability to access high temporal densities, and whether or not he accepts the suggestions (hypnosis, self-hypnosis or deliberate choice).

More concretely, a premonition looks just like a past memory, but regards the future in accordance with the laws of karma. Intention can erase only this "later memory" and not the memories from the past, because that intention was already designated. It cannot contradict itself. That would be self-denial. We can change the course of events only if the intention is unspoiled. When it comes to future events, it must also be well directed. That is why many cannot dissociate themselves from an apparently undesirable or inescapable destiny.

As our consciousness expands, karma loses its grip. Past-life memories are therefore useful only to discover previously made choices that still mysteriously affect us. How can we explain that we are more or less "fortunate" in life? When we gain a better understanding of ourselves, our point of view can change. Respecting our own self means learning which choices we should make, which then become a source of incredible power. That is why we learn more from our mistakes than from our successes. They inspire us to move forward. Why should we give them a moral meaning when they are a driving force? Because of the guilt and constraint it generates, morality prevents us from taking an objective look at the consequences of our choices. It slows down our evolution. However, ethics — the principle of evolution — constitute a sincere and personal scrutiny of consciousness, which inevitably leads to constructive decisions, both for the self and for the community of which the individual is a natural and inseparable part. A decision is always related to the information level of the individual with regard to himself and his environment. Ethics are as such related to the attained density of time where the information is stored. The highest degree could be called the Inner Master, who observes and guides the ego. In other words, the best method to practice ethics is to call forth the most enlightened state of consciousness in ourselves without worrying about other people's advice that can never perfectly fit the unique individual reflecting upon and making the decision. Many call this ultimate state of consciousness God...

What essentially causes an event to take place or not? Freedom! As a being is able to access more degrees of freedom, a fortiori the freedom of time, he becomes less constrained (including by the laws of karma). When we evolve, we develop a great fondness for life and its great variety of expressions. You probably noticed that mineral phenomena are more easily predicted than plant phenomena, which are much more predictable than human phenomena. I am leaving it up to you to reflect upon my enthusiasm and my arguments. You need to understand that karma exists only because we are incarnated and influenced by the time flow on Earth. Occultists argue that we choose our incarnation before we are born. Prior to birth, our state of consciousness corresponds to a high temporal density and therefore to causality through freedom. The problem is that this state of consciousness is not identical for everyone, as there are many levels in the astral and spiritual world. The same applies to this freedom.

CHAPTER 40

3D time: unreal

THE THEORY OF 3D TIME has probably won over many readers in favor of the time density dimension, rather than the other two. Understandably, considering the doors it opens explaining, among others, the acceleration of UFOs. When a vessel flies off it seems to accelerate to amazingly high speeds. However, this is just an optical illusion! The occupants of these machines would not be able to survive these amazing accelerations, no matter what their physical constitutions are like. As a consequence, we should not focus our

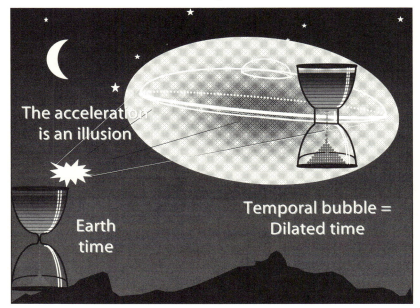

The acceleration is an illusion

Earth time

Temporal bubble = Dilated time

Figure 62

research on variable space but on variable time. If an object seems to accelerate at 100 m/s^2 to us, it really moves at 10 m/s^2 to its occupants (for instance), because their seconds change densities. In other words, the first of their seconds will be the same as ours, but the next will expand and become one of our minutes and so on, thus reducing the acceleration to an absolute minimum.

To us they seem to accelerate extremely rapidly and eventually disappear into another time density, rendering them just as invisible to our stroboscopic eyes as we are to plants when we walk fast. Not only is the acceleration of UFOs seen from our perspective an illusion created by a differential of temporal density, but it also causes an illusory reduction of their size, which adds to our impression that they are at a great distance. Do they shrink to the size of a World War II foo fighter[81] or crop circle luminosities[82] witnessed in recent years? I do believe so. In reality they go much farther than that.

A legitimate question would be whether ball lightning, of which the mechanisms of manifestation are undetermined to say the least, are not partially of ET or paranormal origins, just like orbs (luminescent balls of light).

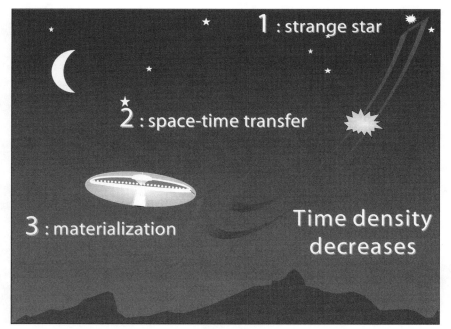

Figure 63

The direction of 3D time seems most evident because it corresponds to our usual way of thinking. There are two time arrows: from the past to the future and vice versa, as described in the section on antimatter.

On the other hand, with regard to the present — which basically means connecting different densities by means of vibratory harmonics[83] — I think entanglement or quantum correlation may be a neverending source of wonder. Entanglement has been the object of many scientific articles, particularly after the experiment of Geneva conducted in 2002 when some journalists wrote that time stopped. The objective of this experiment was to take the next step in the study of entanglement, which I will discuss later on. This experiment showed the interference of two photons leaving in different directions, even opposite ones.

I am arguing that the properties of two particles are complementary, whether or not the spin of one of them is altered, for a simple reason that I have never seen iterated explicitly by any scientist before: it is the same particle! In addition, this can be true only if the experiment is interpreted based on, among others, the concept of 3D time. There is absolutely no need to apply any hidden variables, local or otherwise, that have divided physicists so much. Unless the non-local hidden variable is 3D time. When we see two photons, there is actually only one! The separation occurs because we see things from the viewpoint of another ST, the laboratory. We should keep in mind that time multiplies while space progressively disappears. In fact, these photons respond to the wave function (probabilistic function) that enables particles to be potentially in several different places (hence quantum decoherence). In the case of the entanglement experiment, the pair of photons was obtained by going through a present coordinate very distant from ours, i.e., in a quasi-absolute instantaneity for a single localized harmonic.

This ability to isolate (interference suppression) one of many parameters of quantum mechanics experiments (motions in particular) allows us to control such very high frequency harmonics. The supernatural is the mere occurrence of conditions that favor higher quantities of harmonics. The more there are, the rarer the phenomenon will be. A harmonic is indeed an integral multiple of a frequency. The greater their number, the greater the sensitivity required. The ETs have actually achieved such control in UFOs. The difficulty lies in the alignment with infinitely small and extremely specific frequencies, equaling high temporal densities and thus the fractal distancing of our ST. Understanding the above is so important that we need to take it one step further.

CHAPTER 41

We are God!

YOU ARE NOW BEGINNING TO SEE the implications of this situation. We see two particles, where there is really only one. Bilocation phenomena are based on the same principle. The "simple" problem is caused by the perspective from a certain space-time. In other words, the more there is space, the less there is time and the more the separation is visible, generating new properties in beings, systems, wholes and scientific objects. Cellular division works with the same

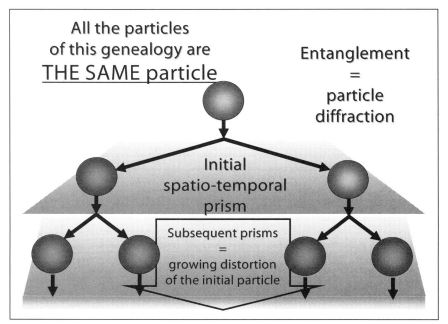

Figure 64

space-time shift principle: the more a cell reproduces itself, the more space it occupies, while gradually switching to another ST up to the point that a new system (organ) appears in a new time density by breaking away from the previous one.

The complexity is not caused by the number of system elements, but by their ability to generate information, i.e. to converge into a single structured and homogeneous whole. This is the definition of neguentropy. It is also the meaning of life. Nature forms unique individuals by structuring their being on ever more subtle planes as they participate in this structuring process themselves. That is the definition of evolution!

Therefore, what matters is the structure that generates its own causality, which explains the growing importance of self-control and will (the ability to acquire intention). Logically speaking, bodies, such as crystals or the human body, have more or less potential to communicate or interact with different STs. Now you understand why brain connectivity is so complex.

It is common knowledge that the brain consists of neurons linked by synapses. A more uncommon aspect of the brain is that neurons screen the countless superimposed signals they receive and only transmit a small part. The fact that this information circulates at a

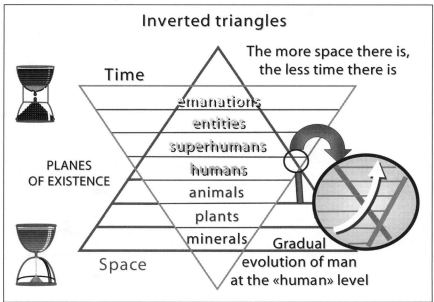

Figure 65

mere 100 m/s — which represents an extremely short time on the scale of neurons — does not mean our knowledge potential cannot exceed this transmission capacity. It simply means that the choice of information is made before it is screened. In other words, our focus on a specific object clearly influences the nature of the information and the horizon of which it is part.

The brain has the ability to connect with very high temporal densities. It is a structuring, interconnecting instrument, but it is not consciousness itself. Our consciousness taps into the information it finds in the greater unifying structures of the infinitely small (from our point of view). Incarnation means we need the brain! In this physical organ time passes much more slowly than in the high temporal densities where we existed before birth. This physical temporal flow is naturally compensated by an astronomical number of possible connections enabling the information to circulate faster.[84] Therefore, the brain is a spatio-temporal elevator allowing the individual to retrace his origins and establish a mind-matter connection. The experience of incarnation is indispensable to the movement of conscious unification of souls that were previously united "in principle" rather than "by their deepest

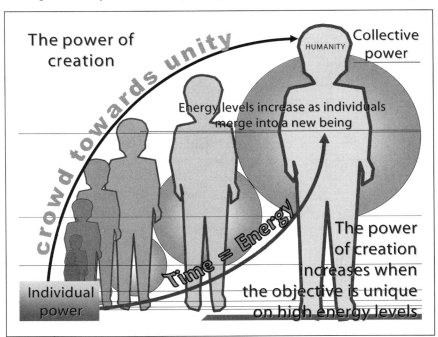

Figure 66

desire." The fact that we direct our own intention, in the sense of unification, gives such reality and relief to the soul that it can exercise the autonomy and powers stored in the spatio-temporal expanse (high time densities), where the necessary energy can be accessed. We must indeed direct our intention to co-create our experiences and control causality. Such control is exerted in parapsychological phenomena.

Humanity is in fact one single being. We are God, but we see and believe that we are separated from Him as long as we stay in our ST. This is the cause of our identity problems[85]: "show me your ST, and I will tell you who you are."

We are beginning to see beyond the matrix. We must genuinely break free from the observer state to understand that what seems to exist on the same plane, an apple and a pebble, for instance, may not be there at all. We see the objects as such because we are part of a higher ST. Other, higher time densities exist next to ours, compared to which we are "physically" similar to the apple, or even the worm living inside. What happens when we observe something through a microscope with tunnel effect? We observe higher STs, just as astronomers see lower STs through their telescope. The difference we attribute to either is the "visible" proportion of objects.

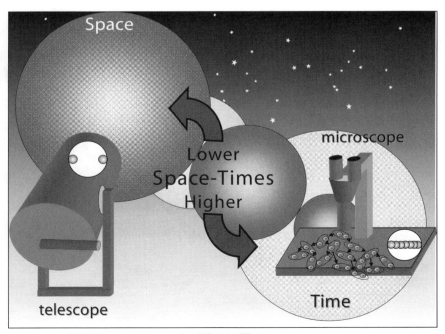

Figure 67

These proportions are completely subjective! We take the idea that one thing is bigger or smaller than another and declare it the truth. Even if it is true in our reality, it is also an utter illusion! We compare incomparable objects, each belonging to a different ST, where different time flows exist and the associated space is subject to the perception of the motion related to a specific flow. How does an elephant see its own size? Or an ant?

Do you remember what things looked like when you were a child? Did not everything seem huge? Every human observation is subjective, because it is inspired by anthropocentrism. It has nothing to do with stereoscopic imaging problems. Comparative analysis is a shortcut used by our intellect, for space and time alike. Moreover, our culture and behavior constantly require us to judge and be judged. Rather than questioning the measuring instruments, I am questioning the interpretation of the results, which is inherent to an artifact existing in a specific ST, subjecting us to and locking us into the matrix. We irresistibly, but unsuccessfully attempt to separate ourselves from an environment of which we are an intrinsic part! I am arguing that the only way to make progress is by looking inward, by allowing us to access higher time densities. This temporal view frees us from the matrix!

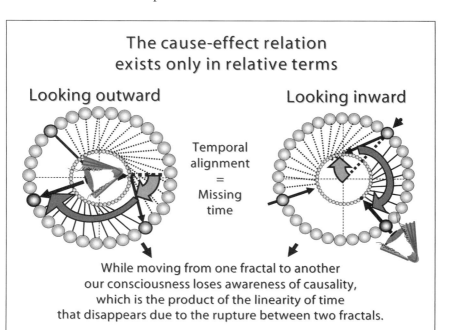

Figure 68

This innovative road to understanding sheds a bright light on quantum mechanics, the purpose of which can be summarized as keeping records of the spatio-temporal reproduction of all that is unique. In other words, everything already was, is and will be, and we simply cannot see this uniqueness because we are in the matrix of a specific ST.

We are not human brothers and sisters. We are the same human being in another ST! That human being is called humanity. Those who have mastered this concept will consider this a philosophical and scientific earthquake. Only a changed perspective renders us capable of understanding the other universes that surround us in the fractal ocean of reality. These parallel universes are not separate. We separate them with the illusion of the macroscopic dream. In general, we are under the spell of a permanent sensory illusion, simply because our physical senses have adapted to this spatio-temporal level (physical body), just as our mental senses have adapted to other spatio-temporal levels. Hence the debate over the nature of things (human/non-human; mortal/non-mortal). A great philosopher once said: "we are not human beings having a spiritual experience; we are spiritual beings having a human experience." That is the most important difference between causal relations and interdependence.

CHAPTER 42

God is very discrete, and so are ETs

LEE SMOLIN'S ARTICLE[86] "Atoms of Space and Time" clearly shows that the theory of loop quantum gravity[87] characterizes space and time as discrete (discontinuous). This seems to be a prerequisite for the unification of interactions. This theory is incomplete at the moment, particularly because of the three-dimensional nature of time. It is opposed to my vision of gravity, which increases as space expands.

One of the most important elements of this article with regard to ufology is the fact that the "discrete" (discontinuous) nature of space causes higher-energy gamma rays to travel slightly faster than lower-energy ones, which is similar to the doubling theory. If the difference seems a priori relatively tiny on the Planck scale, its effect steadily accumulates during a billion-year voyage, leading instruments to measure particles and waves of the same stellar burst at different instants. It confirms that the state of matter defines the temporal field in which the matter is located.

If the dematerialized state of vessels causes them to be partially located in such a gamma spectrum, space travel may be much faster than we think, despite the parallel implications of a varying light speed and the effects of special relativity in which space contracts. For more information about this subject, please read *Faster than the Speed of Light*,[88] written by the controversial physicist and Cambridge professor João Magueijo.[89]

Of course, this also has implications for our observation of UFOs that emit numerous wavelengths, including gamma, depending on their materialized or dematerialized state (simply luminous or even invisible). You should take into account that countless gamma-ray flashes have been registered in the cosmos since the Cold War traveling in all directions around the Earth, at least one per day on average. Do these intense flashes have a distant or nearby source? The truth is that this remains a mystery. It is argued, probably justly so, that almost seventy-five percent of these bursts are of extragalactic origins. They are associated with supernovae transformed into neutron stars. However, only some thirty out of tens of thousands of flashes have been studied. In the year 2000, NASA registered approximately three thousand flashes showing huge energy levels. Do not forget that the thesis of objects moving away from the source is related to the standard Big Bang model. It is only logical that one of the models used specifically to explain flashes refers to the collapse of a star to a black hole. Quantum physicists think they can identify these famous black holes by reducing them to a much smaller version — in other words, by penetrating still further into the structure of matter — in the Large Hadron Collider (LHC) project scheduled at CERN in 2007.

However, the proposed and generally accepted model is impaired[90]: "an as yet unappreciated mechanism causes part of the accretion energy to transform into ejection energy." Yes, you are reading correctly. How can a powerful mechanism that pulls in matter also eject it? In other words, matter located beyond the Schwarzchild radius circling around the black hole, using a sufficient amount of energy extracted from the plane of rotation and therefore from the centripetal force and directed to one of the black hole poles, allegedly causes spectacular collisions similar to the birth of the universe. If we follow this imaginary experiment and accepting this model for a moment, the question is why these collisions produce gamma rays? How do we explain low-energy bursts, such as GRB031203, that are inevitably closer by? What about the shortest flashes that are incompatible with this model; bursts of which we have only been able to locate a single one so far? Why are the curves of visible light and gamma rays of these bursts non-correlated? I would like to invite astronomers who say they have never seen a flying saucer to solve this enigma. We might just as well acknowledge that the temporal density changes realized by ET vessels, which may seem brief from our point of view, produce these gamma-ray bursts, including remanence effects and temporal delay. The huge amount of energy observed would then be caused by the extreme proximity in the sky of the source of these flashes. In other words, it is quite possible that invisible vessels fly around the Earth leaving traces of their existence for astronomers to find every day. Of course, they are not aware of that.

Therefore, human observations are subject to:

1. parameters intrinsic to the vessels depending on the granularity of their ST;
2. distances that separate the observers from the UFO. For the same UFO, we could therefore have several different descriptions depending on the influence of its temporal field. The greater the distance of the vessel, the weaker its influence.
3. The mental state of the observer, because this state "translates" a temporal density.

A sentence in Lee Smolin's article sparked my interest: "Any concentration of energy distorts the geometry of space time." Based on eyewitness accounts, we can extrapolate that UFOs possess extraordinary amounts of energy. This explains their perfectly logical ability to distort the ST surrounding the vessel and to change how we may see it. I should point out that the temporal bubble — with a higher temporal density than ours — paralyzes nearby observers when they approach a vessel, as they are simply not part of the same time density as the bubble. In accordance with 3D time, countless eyewitnesses report paralysis caused by the inability of the physical body to adjust to the faster time flow in the temporal bubble of this vessel.

To make us well aware of the relativity of our point of view, Smolin adds that the theory predicts that there are 10^{105} atoms of volume in every cubic meter of space, much more than there are cubic meters in the entire observable universe (10^{91}). In other words, one hundred thousand billion times more! The average size of a "being" in the universe, i.e., the average between the alleged size of the universe (10^{18} m) and the Planck length (10^{-35} m), is that of…an atom (10^{-10} m). In other words, one single person is an entire universe.

A quantum computer with a storage capacity of one kilobit of physical memory would thus behave like a virtual machine endowed with 10^{1024} memory bits, exceeding by far the number of atoms in the visible universe! This means that information can circulate much faster than we can ever imagine. After all, one cubic meter (our body, for example) is more easily traveled than the cosmos! In fact, they need each other to exist, because they are both overlapped by the present. The potential number of connections realized by the synapses of our brain thus exceeds the number of atoms in the universe!

The variability of causality seems of the utmost importance. If time has three dimensions, then energy is a vector traveling from the future into the past, rather than a quantity. Cause-effect relations are subject to the entropy of a specific ST. As we probe deeper and deeper into the infinitely small (or move up in the time densities; hence the term "ascension"), the entropy will seem higher from our perspective. What we observe is the amount of entropy, which, as you remember, is the unawareness of the instantaneous states of particles (i.e., variable space-time). We know that the cause is indiscernible from the effect on the quantum scale. This means that physical causality disappears in STs where the density of time is significantly superior to ours. In this respect, freedom of mind plays an important role. It creates and un-creates as it pleases. The article "Relation of uncertainty for time," written by Alexander K. Guts, shows the existence of a temporal zone where neither cause nor effect can exist.

The philosophical implications are powerful: causality is deter-mined by the space-time that we occupy. So as the density of time increases, particularly that of the mind, the existence of this physical cause-effect relation becomes more and more unlikely. To close the loop: entangled photons do not need a cause and God is not a cause either. He simply is! Please remember that our equations cannot be used to find out how ET vessels work and are therefore incomplete or fail to describe reality. In principle, only the scientific theories are refuted, not the sci-entific observations. There is no reason to make an exception to that rule of common sense. Since the current theories are incomplete, the follow-ing scientific tour may be somewhat incoherent, showing us that when we use the new absolute relativity to explain UFO phenomena we may soon have a "Theory of Everything".

CHAPTER 43

Shedding new light on science

SPECIAL RELATIVITY TELLS US that space and time are relative, but that a given space-time is absolute. From the viewpoint of an immobile observer, the more an object approaches the speed of light, the more it grows smaller and time dilates. Consider the following orders of magnitude to get an idea of proportions. If we travel for one year at fifty percent of c, one year and two months will have passed on Earth. At ninety percent of c, two years will have passed. However, at 99.999% of c, Earth will have aged 224 years! Space is even more amazing. A missile of ten meters at rest measures only 8.7 meters at fifty percent of c. At ninety percent of c, it measures only 4.4 meters. However, at 99.999% of c, it is barely 4 cm long. If we continue, it will disappear from sight altogether. It simply becomes too small for us to see.

A rapid change of relative velocity therefore gives the impression that an object shrinks or grows, and that it slows down or accelerates correlatively. This is exactly how UFOs seem to behave, except that there is not always displacement in the same way light travels. It is the local environment of the vessel that allows for such behavior. Therefore, we might ask if motion itself, as it applies to bodies in general, is not an illusion. We just need to find the mathematical "trick" that allows this process to take place. The trick is to establish a relation that does not require the use of motion compared to a Galilean reference frame, but describes a state compared to a physical reference frame, i.e., on a specific fractal scale, each fractal scale being a specific ratio between a quantity x of space and a quantity y of time. The motion of an object, in terms of displacement, is simply a specific and remarkable state relative to the perspective of the observer, who literally has enough time (a sufficient amount of time) to detect a displacement

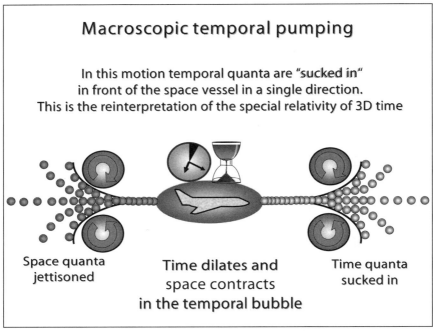

Macroscopic temporal pumping

In this motion temporal quanta are "sucked in"
in front of the space vessel in a single direction.
This is the reinterpretation of the special relativity of 3D time

Space quanta
jettisoned

**Time dilates and
space contracts
in the temporal bubble**

Time quanta
sucked in

Figure 69

phenomenon. In other words, nothing moves; everything contracts or expands. We just need to know the proportions. Harmonics provide a controlled response with the proviso that the whole of a body is subject to this homothetic translation (magnification or reduction factor). In paranormal phenomena we do not detect displacement, because we, as observers, do not have enough time. Einstein's entire theory is based on the postulate of scale indifference. That explains his mistake.

Please note that in absolute relativity the speed of light is the boundary of space-time exchange established by motion. The latter is simply a transfer mode of space quanta to time quanta. Nevertheless, and this is the very principle of absolute relativity, space-time transfer (or vice versa) is essentially caused by "local" exchanges realized between spatio-temporal fractals. The trick is simple: grains of space are transformed into grains of time, and conversely. This loss of space grains equals the process of dematerialization.

Recent experiments have shown that it is possible to slow down the speed of light and even stop it by the refraction of a wave group that prevents excitation of a hyperfine energy level (two excitation waves canceled by destructive interference [electromagnetically induced

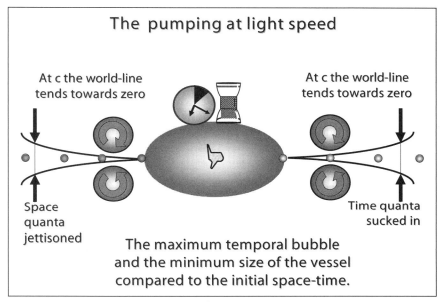

Figure 70

transparency]), either by a Bose-Einstein condensate (more efficiently separated resonance frequency), or by a crystal, such as a ruby, bombarded with two laser beams resonating as a result of "coherent population oscillation." These experiments render the resultant frequency transparent with regard to the unexcited atoms absorbing it. In short, the temporal quanta are "imprisoned" in the system without being transferred to space quanta. As a consequence, the inverted process (constructive interference) allows the dematerialization to take place by "freeing" time quanta. That explains the presence of superconductors and crystals in UFOs.

It is extremely difficult to visualize something that cannot be visualized: time. It can only be felt. It cannot be geometrized, because geometry is a property of space by definition. Therefore, any attempt to understand time must be made outside geometry, contrary to the large majority of current theories. The doubling theory, for instance, is first and foremost a geometrical theory. Whereas this theory says that time accelerates, I am saying that quantum time increases. An increase of time is counterintuitive for a civilization that has based its understanding of the world on the spatial instrument par excellence: our eyes. However, there exists a physical magnitude that describes time: energy!

We are trapped into believing that the energy we measure is complete because we live in accordance with a time flow intrinsic to our physical system. Energy conservation is real only for a partially enclosed physical system. Therefore, there is accessible and inaccessible energy in every system, the latter also being the energy of the vacuum in quantum mechanics. However, is not the vacuum nothing other than imperceptible spatio-temporal fractals? The vacuum is never empty and infinites do not exist. All that we can perceive is the "trace" of spatio-temporal fractals. That should be a relief.

Let us go back to the notion of temporal density. It is a specific time flow. For us, a second lasts as long as the second hand indicates. In a higher time density, this same second only lasts, for example, a tenth of a second from our macroscopic point of view. However, for the person living that second the duration is still one second. At least, that is how it feels. This could be called conversion if the temporal density was always stable, but that is not the case. This change is caused by motion, or internal and kinetic energy. However, internal energy only applies if there is no dynamic interaction with objects and other systems, but the universe is all about interaction.

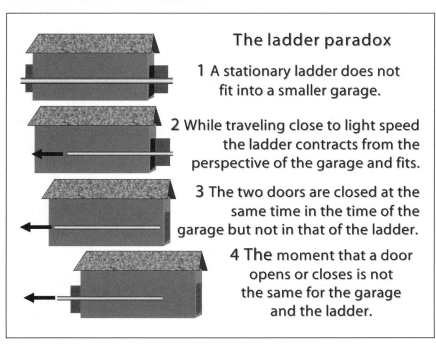

The ladder paradox

1 A stationary ladder does not fit into a smaller garage.

2 While traveling close to light speed the ladder contracts from the perspective of the garage and fits.

3 The two doors are closed at the same time in the time of the garage but not in that of the ladder.

4 The moment that a door opens or closes is not the same for the garage and the ladder.

Figure 71

I think the intrinsic meaning of energy has never been understood, because it has numerous expressions depending on the scale of the objects to which it is applied. Energy can be mechanical, biological, chemical, electromagnetic, quantum, it can exist in the vacuum, etc. The meaning is time! More than just an effort is required to understand it more completely. Our mind has to take a quantum leap and disregard centuries of mistakes: the physical time of our watch does not exist. It is but a pale copy of the profound meaning of time, of which psychological time describes the quintessence.

Einstein argued that simultaneity is an illusion, particularly through the ladder paradox showing that a long ladder traveling horizontally at almost the speed of light undergoes a length contraction and is made to fit into a smaller garage. This allows us to close the entrance and exit doors at the same time. This is true if we are part of the reference frame of the garage, but not in that of the ladder. In other words, an event can be part of the present, the past and the future, depending on the reference frame in which it is located.

There is a problem with size in the explanation given by Einstein, who said that the perspective of the garage is equivalent to that of the ladder. The temporal asymmetry of the systems proved to be subject to the perspective of consciousness. The time difference between

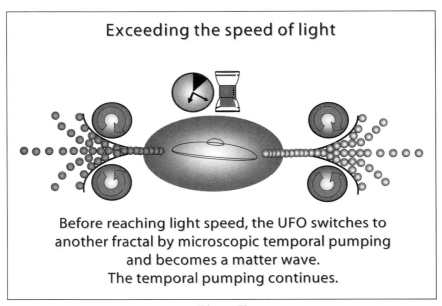

Exceeding the speed of light

Before reaching light speed, the UFO switches to another fractal by microscopic temporal pumping and becomes a matter wave.
The temporal pumping continues.

Figure 72

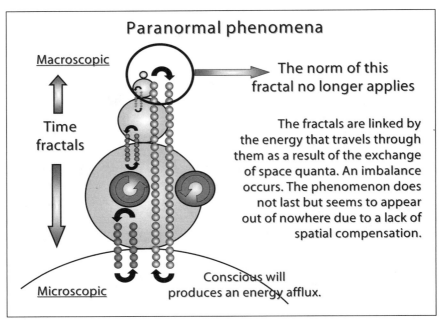

Figure 73

present (in the most common sense of the word) and past or future (i.e., distant in any sense) becomes more important as the temporal density increases.

The same applies to UFOs that possess a sometimes quite different temporal field. They could be small enough to enter your house and still be the size of a hangar on the inside. This explains why abductees indicate that vessels are much larger inside. This temporal field concept is essential to the understanding of phenomena and eyewitness accounts related to UFOs.

Eyewitnesses of the paranormal can describe situations with more or less significant temporal differences,[91] depending on whether or not their consciousness and therefore their perception has accessed high temporal densities.

General relativity describes gravity as a ST curve. It uses only geometry. However, as I already pointed out, the nature of time cannot be described in terms of geometry, even if it is tempting to do so for our materialist mind that is on an eternal quest for the answer to "where is everything," while we should be asking "when do the facts exist." It requires a much more powerful mind to think in terms of non-geometry instead of geometry, which is spatial by definition and accessible to our "lower" senses. This superiority of the intelligence of time may not be recognized immediately, because it comes from a perception that excludes the use of our eyes to see the world.

Classical physicists are least likely to understand reality because they have been trained according to the principles of geometry, which is several thousands of years old, whereas chronometry is millions of years older. At best, we can draw some interesting and even indispensable parallels between time and space. However, the content of a box (time) is not the same as the box itself (space), just as the frequency of a radio station is not indicative of what the DJ says in the microphone. We can line up all the equations in the world, but they will tell us only what our consciousness sees when it accesses their meaning. The world is subject to the individual. So let us ignore fanatical skeptics. Not feeling is a handicap instead of a sign of realism. Let us not pity those who feel, but those who do not feel.

Scientists increasingly see the universe as a superposition of STs, i.e., layers of fractal systems (self-similarity of a form due to the scale change), where space and time have specific values, and not as a single great whole called ST, in which space and time are relative as Einstein believed.[92] This is the study of the new discipline of quantum cosmology.

In general relativity, it is not the mass that increases along with velocity, but the inertia. We have been speaking of inertial reference frames ever since Galileo. The apparent increase of mass is caused by a geometrical effect. Mass seems to increase, but actually remains constant. In absolute relativity, mass is determined by the ST. It does not have any meaning as such, because it only produces effects as a result of a geometrical change. As a consequence, velocity does not behave as the resultant of Minkowski space-time, as general relativity dictates, but as the resultant of a geometrical rotation compared to the ST from which it is observed. The application of a force aimed at increasing the speed of an object gradually diminishes the axis of motion as the object picks up speed. Imagine you push a train car to make it accelerate. Our direction remains constant, but that of the car changes. You start to push it along the rail axis, but as it picks up speed, you will be forced to push it to the side at a simultaneously increasing angle. Once it reaches approximately ninety degrees, it will require a tremendous amount of energy to gain a few millimeters per second. This is the meaning of the required infinite energy of which general relativity speaks as light speed is approached.

However, in absolute relativity — unlike general relativity where the force is applied from the perspective of a specific ST — both the source ST (the one that pushes the train car) and the ST that receives

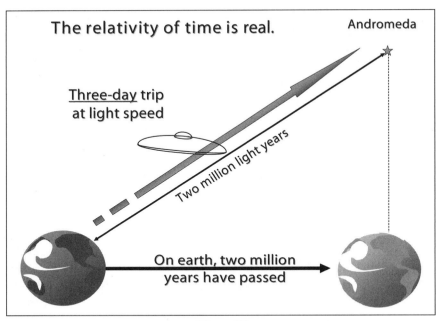

Figure 74

the energy (the car) shift, i.e., a translation of spatio-temporal differential. The doubling theory would say that the subsequent horizons of Ω_0 and Ω_6 are simply moved. If horizon Ω_0 is that of a vessel on our scale, it becomes that of a molecule on our scale. Therefore, the speed of light is not a boundary. It is only because it represents the maximum difference between two interacting STs. Absolute relativity suggests rotating the source ST and the receiving ST at the same time so that the required energy is always available. This explains why vessels change the state of matter by transforming it into matter waves. Astronomic distances are quickly reduced to ridiculously small numbers and the entire universe is within reach. A vessel traveling at light speed (space contracts) can reach Andromeda, approximately two million light years away from our perspective, in three days. In other words, going back and forth takes six days, but on Earth four million years will have passed.

Let me address an extremely important notion for a moment: the conversion of time. The aforementioned figure describes the traditional conception of special relativity. Scientists indicate that as the speed of light is approached, time dilates or…slows down. If time dilates, we have the right to apply the principle of time density explained in the previous pages: space quanta transform into time quanta. This makes quantum time algebraically superior. In this sense, time dilates, i.e., increases numerically.

However, time slows down. In other words, it must quantitatively decrease compared to the temporal flow that is millions of years old on Earth, but only equals a few days inside a space vessel. Where does this contradiction come from? It is caused by the intervals between time quanta that do not have the same ray. It is also caused by the fact that we persist in our inertial way of thinking. Indeed, the conversion of quantum time is not entirely dedicated to the kinematics of the object that approaches light speed. It is actually most of all Einstein's error, for whom this conversion took place in extenso. In absolute relativity, quantum time goes from a kinematical use to an informational use, and vice versa. What does this mean?

What is seen in a given ST as a kinematical phenomenon is seen as an accumulation of information in a higher ST. Please note that the vibratory state of a body is in itself a ST. Hence, there are two different situations: one where the motion takes place in, or is seen from a ST of lower temporal density and one where the motion takes place in the ST considered common to the vibratory state. However, in this case, the motion is related to the irruption of a higher temporal density. Therefore, it will not be seen as such! In other words, the temporal quanta disappear in terms of time flow and gradually transform into simultaneous information, but are translated into motion in the lower space-time. This happens to high-atmosphere muons that seem to live longer. These muons are heavy electrons that are therefore part of a high time density, different from ours. In the other case, extratemporal quanta appear in the ST in question, where the movement is not felt as such — we feel what seems to be a longer duration. Nevertheless, the increase does not last because the number of space quanta decreases. Therefore, the very idea of motion is no longer of consequence.

As we have seen in "Time for reflection," our most important mistake is that we associate time with the feeling of temporality and therefore with the passage of time. Remember that in Einstein's thought experiment nothing happened to the momentum of the photon. From the perspective of absolute relativity, all the time quanta linked to the motion are "consumed" by superimposed quanta and then transformed into pure information. It has been proven that time can be superimposed, particularly in Bose-Einstein condensates. This superimposed time is expressed by simultaneous information. It is all the more important because the temporal density is high. In other words, the greater the increase of the temporal density, the smaller the number of quanta that can be transformed into motion. We have also seen that the temporality of time as we perceive it is actually the absence of time (or time quanta), since the feeling of temporal flow comes from the intervals between temporal quanta forming the structure of the entropy.

Figures 42 and 43 show that the feeling of time flow increases along with the temporal density. Therefore, we are approaching what mystics call eternity. This applies as long as we remain immobile compared to lower STs in the temporal density in question, i.e., in a given vibratory state. Of course, this "immobility" is more stable as the space quanta disappear, thus preventing our consciousness from "moving." This is how dreams work. They seem to last for hours, but only seconds have elapsed in Earth time. In the case of a displacement close to light speed, some of the temporal quanta are assigned to this displacement. However, these quanta no longer exist as "entropic time" (= duration) for the ST of the object (or consciousness) in displacement, but as simultaneous information. Absolute relativity, with fractal, discrete and 3D time, thus associates the speed of light with the speed of thought!

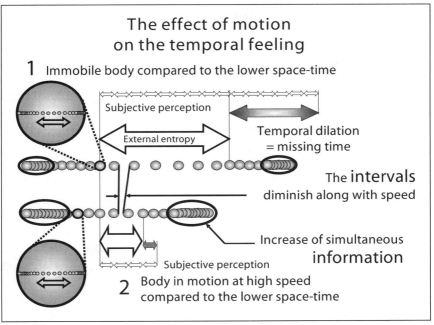

Figure 75

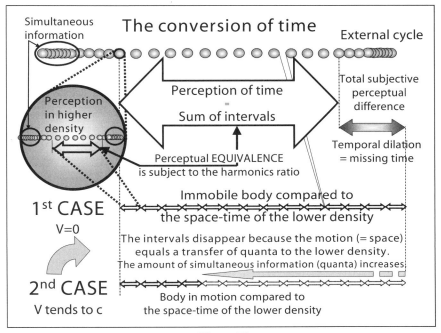

Figure 76

This displacement exists only for a lower ST. To visualize this phenomenon, imagine a vehicle traveling at high speed. In reality, you do not see the scenery that seems to be traveling just as fast, only in the opposite direction (Einstein's conception of inertia). You accumulate more and more information about this scenery as you accelerate. At the same time, you increase your stock of simultaneous information. As a result, the temporal quanta are moving closer together, reducing the intervals between them and therefore the feeling that time is passing. This is called a blueshift, where the intervals between these moving quanta are gradually eliminated. In other words, instead of feeling a longer duration as a result of vibratory change, we experience a shorter duration as a result of spatial change.

Figures 75 and 76 explain the capital notion of temporal conversion that breaks with the traditional conception. Please note that the compression of time quanta will be considered energy by lower STs, which is in line with general relativity.

This wonderfully explains why, in psychic experiments, displacements seem instantaneous, as the perception of the duration is reduced to its simplest expression, or instantaneity! Consciousness is indeed always in a vibratory state that is higher than the surrounding "scenery."

Since this scenery is made up of lower-density objects, we see it as immobile as the physical world around us. You need to understand that the motion of an entity (or object) exists only for a lower ST, but not for the entity (consciousness) itself.

In a way, and ironically, time quanta are lost as we go faster! However, this constitutes a loss of temporality (time flow) and not of time itself (cyclical time). It therefore follows that the increase of time due to motion causes us to lose the feeling that time has passed, because some of the time quanta are assigned to the displacement (= information in the ST in question). Many abductees have described space travel in an extraterrestrial vessel as extremely fast considering the distance covered. In other words, time slows down as we go faster because this "fastness" applies only to a lower ST.

Nonetheless, in general, the seeming paradox of UFOs is caused by the fact that quantum time is converted from a kinematical mode (rotor) to an informational mode, where time merely constitutes simultaneous information. This conversion is caused by a changed vibratory reference frame rather than a changed inertial reference frame. Not only has space contracted, it has partially disappeared. Quantum time has replaced space by information, in other words, by memory. Astral travelers describe it as covering a 360-degree field of view. They are part of a vibratory state that cannot be compared to the physical state, where time flows differently. In their ST, ETs therefore hardly see their own movements, but we see them in ours. They see only an increasing amount of superimposed information, which has allowed their vision (larger eyes) and psychism (larger encephalon) to adapt over time. The law of evolution is always valid in the high time densities. Since travelers may experience duration as unpleasant, ETs first increase the number of time quanta by a vibratory change (on site) and then by spatio-temporal conversion (motion). We do not notice this phasing because thousands of conversions take place every second.

If our creators are indeed ET voyagers,[93] our evolution has understandably taken only a few days from their perspective, which may explain why ET sightings have been rare on Earth for many millennia. Considering the increased frequency of sightings in the past fifty years, they seem to have walked among us constantly since the last world war.

We need to make a short esoteric digression. It is easy to imagine that our life seems but a brief moment in time when it is converted to a higher temporal density after death. In the next life, we only retain a blurry memory of the mistakes and progress we made. We cannot remember past lives, for that knowledge can be accessed only from higher densities (through hypnosis or meditation). Images of these lives are compressed to fit into our daily life (physical temporal flow), to the point of becoming a sublife. These compiled moments disregard specific circumstances, but provide an evolving soul with a general framework. The compacted reincarnation disguises as a cyclical progressive motion leading to the intuitive self-realization of our consciousness. It is important we become aware of these mechanisms.

Planck, one of the founding fathers of quantum mechanics, laid down the principle that energy exchange between matter and radiation takes place in packets of specific quantities; hence the name "quantum" (pl. quanta) attributed to each elementary packet.

By definition, quantum physics is not the study of the infinitely small, but of wave packets. It seems to include the boundary that exists between the microscopic and the macroscopic, considering the extremely small size of Planck's constant. This is a strong indication of the fractality of nature. In other words, there is a scale problem linked directly to our knowledge and control of the wave packets! Controlling the flow of temporal quanta in a given geographical zone means having total power over matter. This is exactly what ET technology is all about.

In quantum mechanics, the superposition of states caused the (false) paradox of Schrödinger's cat, which is easily explained with 3D time. Schrödinger's cat is placed into a sealed steel chamber containing a lethal mechanism that is triggered depending on the condition of a proton. This cat can therefore be both dead and alive at the same time. In absolute relativity, and therefore in 3D time, several time densities pass simultaneously in a system as long as the measurement has not been performed. This means that variable t can take several values on which x, the position of a point, depends. The probability of its position is in fact determined only by the quantity of emerging temporal grains (quanta) at the moment of measurement. The microscopic world may seem completely autonomous, which is actually the case as long as we do not observe it. Since time appears twice (t and c) in the expression t-x/c, the position and moment of a particle are subject to the relative viscosity of time observed during the experiment. Quantum probability is simply the expression of an exchange average between grains of time and grains of space. The measuring instrument imposes its macroscopic time flow upon the particle, just as our physical body imposes its flow upon our perceptions. The wave function collapses and the lens of Young's double-slit experiment, or double-slit interference, "photographs" the combination of two temporal flows and the wave behavior of "quantum entities" is generated only by the fact that two spatial fractals meet.

We usually see matter in terms of space, since we see objects in 3D space. Regardless of the size of these objects (large, small, minuscule), we tend to reproduce and apply our thought pattern to the infinitely small, like Aristotle and, in more recent times, Rutherford did. In fact, it is incorrect to speak of infinitely small or infinitely large. The principle of 3D time marks the end of infinites, because we change fractals every time we approach infinity until quantum entanglement allows us to reach the unity of all. In a way, it conceals the presence of limited microscopic observation leading to the idea of the continuity of principles, regardless of the observed scale. However, the presence of quantum electrodynamics cutoffs, for example, is a strong indication of discontinuity.

Nothing in our current knowledge allows us to disprove the idea that we may have to take a leap to bridge the gap between the principles of quantum mechanics and the content of immeasurably smaller scales, of very high temporal densities. Let us return to Smolin's theory. All things considered, the differences could be just as big as the ones that exist between classical physics and quantum physics. This could be called metaphysics, i.e., global physics, or even knowledge of the first principles. I think these causes are non-causes because of quantum entanglement, i.e., the intervention of sheer will originated in the unity of the nature of particles that we separate both conceptually and sensorily (spatial scale shift). We can either undergo or choose the causal fate.

These principles are provided by absolute relativity. Addressing these principles means we also need to address the study of the EPR paradox.

In 1935, Einstein, Rosen and Podolski (EPR) introduced a thought experiment arguing that quantum mechanics is not a complete physical theory. It is still considered one of the greatest paradoxes in the history of science, similar to the wave-corpuscule duality in more general terms. They considered a two-particle system after interaction and separation, depicted as a single wave function. In other words, if the velocity or position of one of the two particles is measured, the velocity or position of the other is automatically known.

The authors concluded that the velocity and position of both particles were well defined prior to measurement based on the reality principle. In quantum physics, the velocities and positions are undetermined before measurement and it is the actual measurement performed on the first particle that concretizes the velocity and position of the two quantons simultaneously. Einstein was puzzled by the fact that measuring the first particle determined the velocity and position of the second. The three scientists therefore believed there were hidden variables exposing quantum physics' incompleteness.

The quantum physicist argued that the measurement creates the behavior of both particles at the same time. However, how is that possible? The problem of the choice of variables of velocity and position as observable parameters does not allow us to choose between the classical physicist, who said that the disintegration caused by the matching system forced the particles to move in the opposite direction, and the quantum physicist, who said that we did not know what happened in an "ignorance zone" prior to measurement. In other words, they used the spin measurement, which is much more subject to chance. John Bell subsequently established his theorem of inequality[94] that violates the quantum theory, but not the classical probability principle.

In 1982, Alain Aspect conducted an experiment on protons and photons. A vacuum chamber was used to inject calcium atoms excited by two lasers. The excitation emits photons, after which the atoms return to their fundamental state. It is extremely important to note that the quantum entanglement generates photons, rather than laser photons, after returning from this excited state! This return corresponds to a coordinate of the "present of 3D time." Quantum mechanics cannot explain this situation. Aspect found a value of 2.7, while it should have been lower than or equal to 2. The two photons had an additional polarization value, despite the fact that everything humanly possible was done to ensure that neither photon would have information about the other prior to and during measurement. So there were no hidden variables.

However, how do these two photons communicate while traveling at light speed known as the final frontier? Can information turn back the hands of time? Another experiment conducted by Antoine Suarez took place in Geneva in the year 2000, using a very different principle of a half-silvered mirror, where each of the two photons could either pass or be reflected. They showed the same behavior each time. To ascertain whether or not information could turn back time the photons were shielded completely from the experimentation mechanisms.

Could there be a "programmed" correlation (common cause in the past) or a "telephone" correlation (existence of a signal between the two)? Neither argument proved applicable under the strict conditions of the experiment. The explanation given was that the correlation occurred without any time passing. That is partially true as the

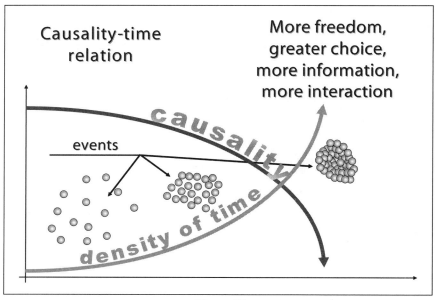

Figure 77

quantum entanglement occurs "behind" a temporal portal, a non-observation stage of a faster temporal passage. The quantum theory points to the existence of a quantum entanglement phenomenon connecting the fate of two particles without providing an explanation! This means that the dogma of the light speed boundary contradicts another dogma, that of strict causality. The causal function, the pillar of absolute relativity, will be addressed later.

In absolute relativity, the explanation is much simpler and even obvious considering the presence of superimposed STs: there is only one photon while we see two![95] (This well-known entangled cause-effect concept will be discussed later.) We see two separate photons because we see them from another ST!

Einstein and the quantum physicists had it all wrong. There is no hidden variable other than 3D time applied in the framework of absolute relativity, i.e., spatio-temporal prisms. The only meaning of wave functions is the "spatio-temporal optical distortion" created by a difference between two STs. It is this optical distortion (caused by our consciousness) that creates the causality sought after by physicists.

Causality is therefore conditional. However, it is not the same as time! It is caused by a different perception of space-time. The link between time and causality remains an extremely persistent tautology.

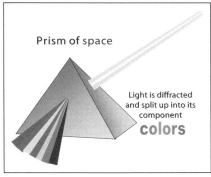

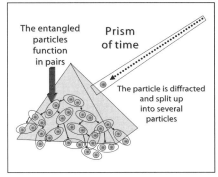

Figure 78   *Figure 79*

Quantum entanglement is a diffraction, just as rainbows are a diffraction of light!

The two are logically related, for the light enters a specific ST, that of traversed matter. We need to see it as the study of interactions between STs.

Virtually every quantum phenomenon is caused by a correlation, or quantum entanglement. Therefore, all matter is merely the expression of previous correlations, in other words, of the same identity that we see divided by a relativistic effect in the sense of absolute relativity — seen from a lower ST — and where the unfolding of history is made possible by the unfolding of space. That is an extraordinary revolution. In scientific terms, it means that we are separated only because we see ourselves from a ST that differs from our source ST! Science thus proves the existence of consciousness! In this day and age, science without consciousness only triggers its own destruction.

All of this has huge repercussions on the concept of causality. Causality is subject to the ST from which it is considered. If we were in the ST of the allegedly doubled photon, we would see only one because the larger scales do not exist on this scale, but that still does not mean that time has disappeared. On the contrary, this time possesses all the information of the lower STs, just as we see the stars without being aware of the relative gravitational differences. In addition, the amount of information of the "entangled photon" is higher. This is the principle followed by intermediary qbits in quantum computers. This specific photon determines the history of all photons and other similar particles, which I qualify as primordial particles, not in the sense of the Big Bang model that I am disproving, but in the sense of a primordial (original) ST for the separate photons that we see.

ET vessels show the same behavior and return to the source particles (dematerialization) after having developed daughter particles (materialization). We may therefore see the light doubling or even multiplying, resulting in a much larger number. The reason is simple: the variable density of the vessel's temporal bubble adjusts to the particle time flow. The quantum phenomenon of large-scale (macroscopic) correlation therefore remains imperceptible, the so-called matter waves in the BEC[96] experiment.

I should add that communicating with after-life STs of a high time density is always difficult. Just as we cannot see our dead in their invisible state, they cannot see us in our physical form either. They merely tune into the highest aspects. They view us as a memory structure, as structured thoughts and emotions, identifiable as a personality and as embodied individuals evolving in society. Since they "live" in a time slightly shifted towards our future, they are capable of guiding us, of warning us about possible events. The probability of these events occurring is subject to our ability to choose. This ability is also subject to the time density we attain in our meditations. That is actually the reason why some incarnated wise beings have powers immeasurably superior to those possessed by deceased entities. Therefore, we should not systematically turn to the dead. It is important to verify the nature of their cooperation depending on their former attitude in life.

Please remember that we are made of particles and that our consciousness is subject to observations, whether these regard very large horizons such as everyday objects, or much smaller horizons. Every family of horizons, or range of frequencies, corresponds to a means of observation such as sight, hearing or intention. However, we can use these senses only if we develop them and keep them developed, allowing us to perceive the activity of particles through the effects they have on our consciousness.

Every primordial particle originates from a higher ST (spatially smaller from our perspective) and thus from a mother particle. As I pointed out, a particle is a punctual ST. The entire history of the universe exists all at the same time, on every floor, in mother particles and in daughter particles (this genealogy is created only by the history written by lower STs). As a result, indeterminism creates determinism as we descend into lower STs (space expands from our physical point of view). Our consciousness needs this determinism to evolve in the first stages of its awakening. However, it is possible, under so-called paranormal conditions, for indeterminism to affect lower STs (our scale). These conditions prove the existence of neguentropy, i.e., the organization of information, probably in pairs as suggested by quantum entanglement[97] experiments, super conduction mechanisms (paired electrons) and, more in general, by bosons. In other words, resultant waves unfold perfect harmonics (the present of time) without energy loss (coherent waves).

In special relativity, electromagnetism is explained by the fact that a magnetic field is an electric field in a somewhat disguised form. The faster an electron travels in a laboratory reference frame, the more intense its radial magnetic field. However, from the perspective of the circulating charge, the density of the opposite charge increases leading to a build-up of the equally radial electric field as a result of the contraction of space that subjects it to its speed. In terms of absolute relativity, this electric field describes the fractal distance between two STs, that of the circulating charge and that of the environment in which it circulates. As these two STs translate into a larger number of temporal quanta, the source ST (Ω_0 before translation in the formalism of the doubling theory) shows a considerable visible magnetic field, even if the electric field inside the system (Ω_0 to Ω_6 after shifting scales) remains constant. This magnetic field in the source space-time generates an electromotor force capable of producing the upward motion of the vessel. This magnetic field is even larger, because the electrical resistivity of materials is zero, as in super conduction. This explains why ET vessels use superconductors, i.e., crystalline structures.

We know that measurements create temporal irreversibility, which is not part of the Schrödinger equation (wave function). Hence the idea that causality is brought about only by an interaction between adjacent and superimposed STs. In other words, UFOs control the causality of the physical world, because they control the source of this causality. That is why they can behave in such an amazing manner.

From the perspective of absolute relativity, an atom consists of a nucleus ensuring that the number of space quanta remains limited. To compensate for this limitation in the whole called atomic structure, space quanta are projected towards the outside of the nucleus represented by the electrons as a proportional amount of time and therefore of energy. Opposite signs are caused by the resistance of space and time, to provide some kind of counterbalance. The well-known resistance to radiation serves the same purpose. In other words, an electric charge with a conventional sign symbolizes a time or space charge, thus forming opposite signs. As a consequence, a proton for an electron in all atoms to ensure invariance.

Let me add that the hydrogen bond in DNA — weak electronic coupling (allowing us to manipulate genomes) — is a determining factor in the inability of our physical body to travel into higher temporal densities (the so-called ascension) and dematerialize naturally. It requires us to add other helices in order to increase the capacity of the information flow in terms of connectivity, which is synonymous with temporal density. However, let us take another look at quantum entanglement, the key to grasping the true nature of time.

Superconductors are macroscopic objects showing quantum behavior, in this case the indiscernibility of quantons (electrons in superconductivity). Imagine a ripple in the water crossing another. The ripple is not the water, but its motion. This characteristic resembles quantum entanglement. It should be clear by now that paired photons are actually a single photon. Super conduction speaks of paired electrons (equal state of pulsation = coherent behavior). Therefore, you will understand that there is no resistivity in the super conduction phase, because there is no energy loss, as occurs during collision. The collision does not occur because although we see two, there is only one electron. The electron cannot collide with itself!

They are the same object. It is as if the fingers of a hand become the hand. Coherence is obtained by extreme cooling (suppression of specific motions), by using a resonance mechanism without excitation or by maintaining the excitation at a stable level (without photonic emission). Forcing two particles into resonance is the same technology used to travel from one fractal to another. It is the axis of the present dimension of 3D time and explains why two atoms can coexist at the same location! They are a single atom constituting a temporal portal. It means that at least one spatio-temporal prism is deleted. Let me give you another description to prove this cohesion. The temperature of absolute zero equals zero kinetic energy, the "sub-sub-atomic" scale (smaller than electrons). It is the famous fractal of "condensed causes and effects," where we enter the realm of spirit and divine will!

Quantum entanglement is responsible for the holographic nature of the universe. We see a multitude that exists only for us, macroscopic beings, because space is unfolding. On a much smaller scale this division is not at all real. One could say that the universe is in a constant state of Big Bang, the fundamental principle of which is the expansion of space, but most of all it is subjective.

According to absolute relativity, the temporal flow of a quantum experiment is determined when the macroscopic temporal flow merges with that of the particle (that explains why materialists are so fond of determinism). The quantum theory tells us that when two isolated systems (measured particle and measuring instrument) start interacting, they become a single system described by a single wave function that contains all the possibilities of the two systems. The separate history of two entities becomes a single history. In absolute relativity, two separate STs merge and form a new hybrid ST, in between the microscopic and the macroscopic.

However, when the global system divides into two separate subsystems again, it is impossible to describe each subsystem by means of an independent wave function, but there is always a global wave function for the two as a whole. Note that this particular wave function is temporarily autonomous from other wave functions! It is a totally unlinked piece of history. Let us return to our famous genealogy.

Recent experiments proved the so-called teleportation of atoms. The properties of one of them are "transferred" because of the indivisibility imposed by quantum entanglement, i.e., without a causal link. The wave function remains global, for it is the same object seen from another ST (ours) when the number of space quanta is increased. There is indeed an observation problem, but for different reasons than those suggested by idealistic physicists.

In our case (absolute relativity), the observer sees the creation of a new ST, or rather of a new sequence of history that is added to the sum of partially independent histories of the universe (see the causal function below). It is possible to add a specific history to the general history without being part of it, which is known as space travel. This interaction occurs in addition to those already happening, whereas we can "step outside" thanks to the weakness of the causal links. The equation is simple: high time density (or large fractal intervals) = weak causal links. The technology used by ET vessels derives its power from the fact that it taps into these collective histories of the material universe at will, even if it leaves behind tangible, but very local traces.

You will now understand why our quantum mechanics experiments multiply our incursions in extratemporal STs. They are therefore rightfully concerned about the consequences of such unconscious invasions. The invaders are not necessarily the ones we should believe, in this case the humans. So it is not surprising that these invaders (us) suffer a few after-effects. Perhaps the "abductions" should be considered collateral damage caused by cyclotrons and other colliders that produce earthquakes in the ET realm.

The decoherence theory takes the idea of superimposed states one step further. It argues that matter is non-material in a configuration that represents a coherent system in the electromagnetic sense of the term. This means that matter is not material as long as the wave packet is not reduced (absence of macroscopic interaction). This theory explains how objects can materialize or dematerialize. A recent scientific article[98] was headed: "The largest quantum objects ever concocted." The introduction states the following. "A biological molecule with 18 atoms and a molecule with 108 atoms have been observed dematerializing for the first time!" In fact, such experiments have been conducted since 1999, but never before with such a significant number of atoms. In this case, fullerene[99] and fluorofullerene macromolecules were subjected to the experiment.

Dematerialization resembles a folded fan that preserves the memory of the shape that unfolds, or materializes, when the fan is opened. Shapes are preserved in the high temporal densities, just like fractal shapes, on every scale. That is the fundamental meaning of a holographic universe. A shape simply represents an information structure that can be compressed by our computers without any significant loss. Unlike materialists, we should not confuse shapes and objects. In both cases, it is a simple problem of information undergoing a homothetic translation. You must understand that every structure (or being) is already a specific fractal, more or less ideal system, for which the changing grains of space and time follow a particular causal logic. As a consequence, every object or living creature possesses its own "imprint" in the high temporal densities, which explains psychometry or a family's heredity through reincarnation, for instance.

ET vessels are able to dematerialize because the parameters of the shape are stored, like software, and the spatial scale diminishes as quantum time increases, allowing the vessels a range of motion that is unhindered by the shackles of inertial thinking.

CHAPTER 44

The secret life of atoms

IN THE PREVIOUS FIGURES, I used quantum time to describe waves. In the past fifty years, up to the early twentieth century, the scientific community was convinced of the existence of some intangible ether in which all waves propagate. They need some kind of medium, they argued, just as waves disperse on the water. That ether could only be absolute time and space. Of course, Einstein's special relativity disproved this argument. He pointed out that nothing could exceed the speed of light in the vacuum, which explained the importance of the Lorentz transformation.[100] However, did he define the vacuum? No! Is it the absence of matter? No, because matter does not exist as such. So what does the vacuum stand for? Once we find the right answer, the physical world will need a complete overhaul.

One clue is that the vacuum contains hundreds, even thousands of times more photons than any other particle. We are thus faced with an inadequately defined boundary. Waves propagate at the speed of light, but what is the actual meaning of propagation under these conditions? To find the answer, we must look into the microscope and find out what we really see. First come the cells, then the molecules, then the atoms, then the nucleus, then the electrons, then the quarks, then the…? We have reached the limits of our perception. However, do we really see atoms or electrons or quarks? Not entirely. We model them. We see them with the help of computer visualizations.

In ancient times, people thought that nature was made of indivisible particles called atoms. In the very beginning of the quantum adventure, Rutherford introduced the idea of "playing with marbles," arguing that the atom was composed of small balls or spheres with a central nucleus

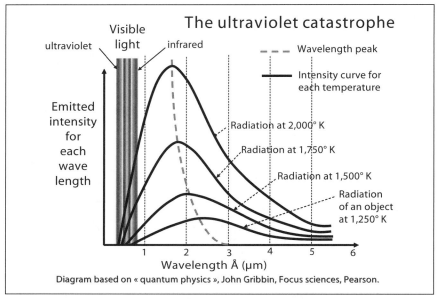

Figure 80

containing a cluster of balls (protons and neutrons[101]) orbited by another type of balls (electrons). That was the view of classical mechanics. However, the "ultraviolet catastrophe" occurred and utterly confused the classical physicists. Quanta were born. It is important to understand what this ultraviolet catastrophe was all about.

When an object is heated (strangely called a black body), its color changes. As the temperature rises, its color increasingly turns from infrared to ultraviolet. These colors are just different frequencies, ultraviolet being the highest frequency of light. Therefore, the yellow-orange color of the sun is caused by its surface temperature (6,000 K).

Experiments have shown that the electromagnetic spectrum of black bodies possesses a peak, where the radiation intensity reaches its maximum. On either side of this peak the emitted radiation is very weak.

Mass spectrometry contradicts the principles of classical physics. According to the law formulated by Wilhelm Wien, the radiation intensity should be proportional to the frequency. To be more precise, there is an inverse relationship between the wavelength of the peak of the emission of a black body and its temperature. John Rayleigh complemented the law by arguing that the radiation intensity is proportional to the absorption temperature and inversely proportional to the square of the wavelength. Basically, the hotter an object is, the shorter the wavelength at which it will emit radiation. However, it means that

Rayleigh's formula can no longer be applied to the blue and, more in particular, to the ultraviolet. The values should be almost infinite. Energy levels drop back down on each side of the measured peaks. Paul Ehrenfest would call this contradiction the ultraviolet catastrophe. This clearly shows the same flagrant mistake in contemporary science as the ones made with gravity.

Planck solved this enigma by arguing that light is made of small "packets" (quanta). The vibrations manifesting the heat of a body do not spread in accordance with every possible value, but obey a specific law. He laid down the formula that links energy E with frequency f — $E = h.f$ — where h is Planck's constant and E/f is always h or 2h or 3h or another multiple integer of h. Planck's discovery thus marked the beginning of the era of discontinuity. That is why, contrary to a widespread incorrect idea, quantum physics is not the study of the infinitely small, but of wave packets. Each atom can emit electromagnetic radiation in the form of quanta. Excited atoms change their quantum level and immediately return to their original state while emitting light. The color of this light depends on the atom in question, allowing us to determine the atomic spectrum by studying the type of light it emits during excitation. The frequency of this light equals the energy difference between excited state and fundamental state divided by h: $(E_1-E_0)/h$.

It therefore requires a great deal of energy to emit a quantum at high frequencies, which is why particle accelerators increasingly demand energy to generate particles that do not exist in a natural state on our spatio-temporal scale. Since atoms are more or less energetic, we choose atoms capable of generating such particles for their high potential intrinsic energy. At large wavelengths, it is easier to emit quanta, for they demand less energy. However, these quanta do not contribute much to the spectrum. In other words, there are large numbers of atoms with average energy values (our classical material world) emitting large numbers of quanta. Hence the peak in the curve of a black body.

We have seen three categories of objects sorted by degree of difficulty in generating and observing quanta and therefore by frequency range. However, the colliders used to discover high-energy particles all have one aspect in common: particle collision occurs when added particles are increasingly accelerated to up the collision force. Energy is generated by accelerating projected particles.

There is however, a less violent way: a gradual frequency change. Some exotic materials can be naturally transmuted by a change in frequency or amplitude as a result of constructive interferences. This is the function of the central oscillator present in UFOs. The light quanta produced by these combined technologies are high in energy but do not produce heat. Currently, cold laser applications use the resonance frequency of the atom. The light emitted in this process is much more powerful than traditional black-body radiation, which explains the brilliant luminence of UFOs mentioned by so many eyewitnesses.

It is vital to understand what an atom is really made of. Remember that Planck himself did not perceive quanta as full-fledged particles. He viewed them as an internal mechanism of atoms, allowing them to emit these packets of light, which he continued to see as waves. In absolute relativity, the excitation corresponds to the exchange of time quanta for space quanta on the microscopic scale. The excess excitation energy then constitutes the opposite process. Particle shock interactions also show such transfers. Each shock is an exchange of space quanta for time quanta that do no belong to the ST of the system (in the case of atoms). The time quanta are then restored to their original condition (space quanta) by thermal radiation.

Therefore, UFOs cannot possibly be using a hot plasma. Plasmas are unstructured and cannot prove the conditions of the neguentropy. High temperatures are synonymous with significant intervals between STs. The possibility of interaction disappears as they move farther apart, causing loss of "temporal flight" control due to the constant and random leak of temporal quanta. Excitations can be controlled via a resonance stage that limits particle collision. It was proven long ago that the quantum behavior of corpuscles becoming waves go through the stage of macromolecular evolution.[102] The laws of thermodynamics are somehow violated as a result. Without these laws there is no causality. UFOs are thus using some kind of structured cold plasma. This means that the notion of speed does not make any sense in a universe of coherence (dematerialization), because space disappears! In other words, UFOs do not travel in the traditional sense of the word and do not traverse space.

Einstein's findings proved the existence of the photoelectric effect (solar panels). The corpuscular nature of light was the only possible explanation, considering that photons collide with the electrons of subsequently ionized atoms to produce an electric current. However, this corpuscular nature may be more fragile than it seems.

Have you noticed that electrons are stationary waves (conjugation of an emitted wave and an incidental wave [in the opposite direction])? Imagine throwing a pebble and a hoop into the water at the same time. The pebble creates a wave moving away from the center;

the hoop creates a wave moving towards the center. The crossing of the two wave trains is a stationary wave. Electrons are therefore stationary three-dimensional waves. Quarks are also stationary waves, but their "geographical" boundary is like one section of an orange. Three quarks make up one orange, i.e., a proton or a neutron. More precisely, a stationary wave is the result of a function that is subject only to time divided by another that is only subject to space. Amazingly, the velocity is zero at the node of these waves. If it is zero when time goes by, the space quanta a priori tend towards zero and the time quanta tend towards infinity.

In the course of the twentieth century, we discovered that these small solid spheres (called particles, i.e., indivisible parts of matter) showed either corpuscular or wave behavior, but not both at the same time. If particles first resemble a solid sphere and then a wave without being either one, then what are they? They are quantum entities! We still have not made much progress.

In absolute relativity, an atom is a fractal space-time unity. As strange as it may seem, an atom is an indivisible entity! It is not made of matter but of time and space intertwined within well-defined bounds! The layout of this space and this time defines the properties of an atom. This is a major conceptual leap.

The more there is space, the less there is time, and vice versa. That is the fundamental principle of absolute relativity. This means time may even appear superimposed, as the previous figures have shown. How can time be superimposed? It may seem inconceivable, but that is the way it is. Let us see why. We are used to thinking of objects in terms of motion and separation. In a rectilinear and consistent motion, we have to select the duration depending on a given velocity to find out the distance covered by a body. The shorter the chosen time, the shorter the resultant distance. The act of measurement is based on the thought that time decreases over distance.

Special relativity added the thought that time dilates as the object goes faster, in particular when it approaches the speed of light, in which case time diminishes much less fast. The distance diminishes correlatively.

When physicians present a theory, they start by saying something like: "either a mass of particle m and…, etc." They have already separated reality by designating the particle a separate being! The principle of absolute relativity, arguing that time increases when space diminishes, whether there is motion or not, is amply justified by the fact that we must always consider the presence of structured natural wholes, rather than place ourselves in a theoretical conceptual realm of imagination that does not relate to any experimental references. The danger of mathematics is that, although it is able to detach from the facts and perceive the underlying mechanisms, it creates an ever increasing confusion between the expression of reality and the conceptual means used to understand it.

For example, imaginary numbers are instruments that avoid the problems that come with formalism. Although they do not exist naturally, electrical engineers use them on a daily basis. However, if we lack discernment, we may easily be seduced by the allure of such mix-ups and carry the superposition of the concept and the way in which it is expressed too far. The complexity of topology is a good example in this respect. When it is no longer possible to visualize, we over conceptualize. However, we have completely forgotten to attend to our feelings!

Time can be superimposed because we divide up parts originally joined by a spatio-temporal link. Therefore, the nucleus and the electrons of a given atom are forever linked by their original structure forming a single whole that I am calling "homeostasis with dynamic flexibility." This actually explains why a nucleon always consists of three quarks.

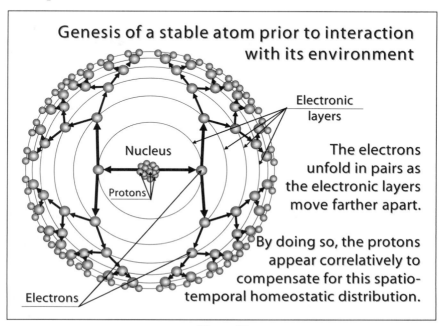

Figure 81

What does this mean? Homeostasis is the ability possessed by living beings to maintain or reestablish certain physiological constants regardless of their outer environment.

This tendency applies to every constituted body. It is the key to understanding absolute relativity. Atoms are unitary entities that are able to adapt to any environment. Electrons, which seem unconnected to the nucleus, are merely the spatio-temporal expression of the nucleons forming the nucleus. To really understand our mistake, we must begin by studying the genesis of an atom prior to interaction. The dynamic flexibility lies in the number of electronic layers that allow for the sharing (or freeing) of peripheral electrons.

Although we may obtain tangible results, we simply do not understand quantum mechanics, because we do not have the proper definitions. That is why there are so many positively unsettling quantum phenomena confusing our physicists. Imagine your arm being torn off because: "either an arm of mass m and..., etc." Your arm is nothing without you. It loses its ontological meaning when it is no longer attached. It is no longer part of your body's structural outline. The information stored in your brain no longer includes its presence, but preserves its memory. In reality, this arm or particle contains the holographic information of its structure, such as the DNA or the spatio-temporal atomic equilibrium. Atoms thus store the memory of their "absence" and can subsequently join others to create molecules and complete incomplete electronic layers, while doing all they can to restore themselves. Therefore, in absolute relativity, an atom has memory. Water memory, described by the Frenchman Jacques Benvéniste, is based on reality, on an essential atomic property. There are however, atoms with more memory than others.

In general, the most complete electronic layers — independent of external assistance (link with other atoms) — have the longest memory retention, because the original signal remains intact, pure and undispersed. In other words, the atom that has been least affected by interactions, is most capable of preserving the memory (the software) used in the dematerialization. One of the most efficient methods is the protection of an electromagnetic field that rejects the material environment. That explains the effects shown in UFOs.

In water, the memory is stored by the naturally weak hydrogen bond that keeps a specific form of memory integrity. Homeopathy is entirely based on this atomic property. Refuting this therapeutic procedure for the commercial reasons mentioned by the medical lobby is denying the existence of already existing quantum computers that

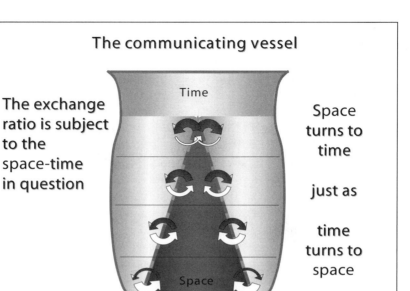

Figure 82

keep information stored by minimizing interactions. In addition, homeopathy has already demonstrated its usefulness.

The first notable indication of this atomic homeostasis is the presence of the same number of protons (positive charges) and electrons (negative charges), except, of course, for positive or negative ions that lack either electrons or protons. An ion is an incomplete atom. Physicists are quite right to argue that this equivalence phenomenon corresponds to an electric balance. However, what does electric charge fundamentally stand for? The right answer is energy.

What is energy really? The traditional answer will just keep changing until it contains a circular argument and equations.

In absolute relativity, energy is essentially a distribution of differential time in a specific temporal reference frame (see "Towards a new formalism"). In absolute relativity, a fractal is a spatio-temporal balance. The distribution of differential time is the very nature of electromagnetic waves of which the frequency in fact translates as a relation between variable time (sinusoid) and another (conventional or fractal time). The fractality of the latter is confirmed by the quantum, or discontinuous, nature of matter on the small scale (hence the ultraviolet catastrophe), which explains the frequency modulations on a carrier wave. The higher the peak, the greater the "pressure" of the time quanta emerging in the temporal fractal in question.

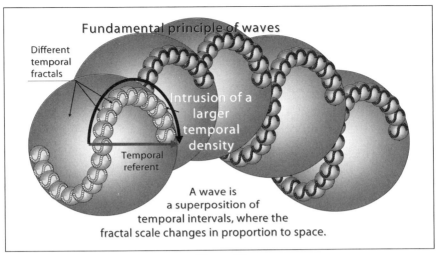

Figure 83

Rather than speak of conventional and arbitrary time, the reality of energy lies in a relation between two temporal densities.

The second indication of size can be found in the model of the atom laid down by the Danish physicist Niels Bohr. It clearly shows that the difference in energy between the electronic layers increases as the

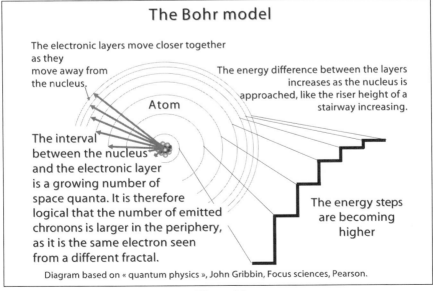

Figure 84

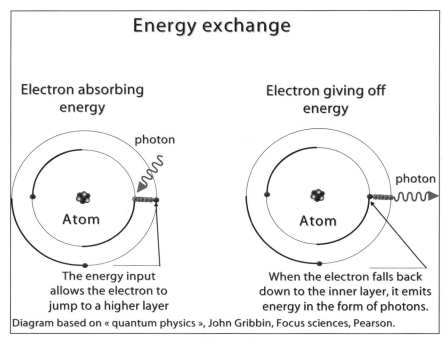

Figure 85

nucleus is approached, the energy gradually radiating away while converging towards the center around which the electrons gravitate. In addition, the layers move closer together as they move away from the atomic nucleus.

The electrons can jump to any higher, incomplete layer by absorbing an energy quantum. Photons are emitted as they return to the lower layer.

In our case, the electromagnetic interaction between electrons and nucleons is reduced to a spatio-temporal relation, where the nucleus is the center of strong interaction that brings the nucleons together by blocking the charge interaction with the same sign (protons), bouncing off naturally. This interaction is actually the gluonic force that connects quarks and is transmitted from one nucleon to another by the color charge of the quarks inside, thus ensuring that the neutrons, although they have a neutral charge, cannot escape from the nucleus. The asymptotic freedom of the quarks shows the extreme temporal vitality that exists below spatial scales that mark the boundaries of our knowledge. The closer they are, the more freedom they possess. This freedom, discovered in 1973, quickly became the field of research of

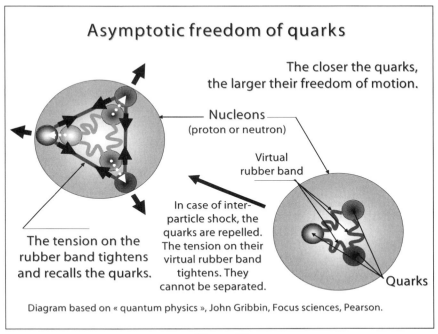

Figure 86

quantum chromodynamics and bears a strong resemblance to a new fractal with less space and more time (compared to the atomic scale). The nuclear force is therefore the manifestation of a resistance to the transformation from time into space, as some kind of anti-return valve. Hence the stability of matter.

By breaking this force (fusion, fission), a time flow is transformed into spatial expansion through compression (the same procedure used in nuclear bombs). Breaking a nucleus destroys the spatio-temporal equilibrium of fractals. Nuclear weapons therefore shake up the fractal worlds of ETs considerably, due to the temporal collapses they produce. The ground may literally disappear from under their feet. That explains why ETs keep a close watch on Earth and, more in particular, on our strategic nuclear sites.

The third indication is the superposition of quantum states, allowing a particle to exist in different places at the same time in the absence of macroscopic interactions. How is that possible? These potential places exist only for us, who belong to a different spatio-temporal fractal, not for the particle that is part of the initial unitary system. The particle is in fact a spatio-temporal congruity to the whole called atom.

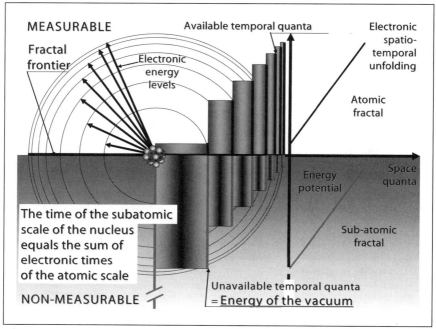

Figure 87

To fully grasp the nature of an atom, the figure above presents the distribution of chronons (temporal quanta) beyond and below the atomic fractal limit. Everything below this dividing line constitutes the quantum vacuum (spatio-temporal fractal), from which the energy of the vacuum can be drawn.

Every electron consists of several photons (another spatio-temporal fractal) of which the equilibrium is lost due to energy level changes. That explains why an electron can absorb a photon (when it lacks one) or emit one (when it is too full). Not surprisingly, Japanese scientists from the Hitachi research laboratories proved that photons behave just like the electrons in Young's double-slit interferometry experiment conducted in the 1980s.

It also explains why Feynman diagrams foresee simultaneous photon emission and absorption by an electron in quantum electrodynamics (in fact, in absolute relativity, they are neither emitted, nor absorbed). I should also point out that anti-photons do not exist. Please remember that the calculation of an electron's magnetic moment requires adding four invisible photons to obtain the precise experimental value to within one ten-millionth! That considerably supports my approach to time.

I cannot insist enough on the fact that the intense light is sheltered from our physical perception by the vacuum (high temporal density). Those who understand this vision can solve a considerable number of mysteries related to the journey into the afterlife and to several luminous psychic experiences. The spiritual worlds are not just luminous as a figure of speech, but they literally are seen as such by the mind!

Temperature exists only in a lower fractal. More specifically, temperature exists only in a specific horizon, or it would not go down in proportion to distance. The agitation of atoms or molecules (particle shock) can be considered intrusions of chronons into microscopic space, because space is "compressed" when the shock occurs. The higher the temperature, the greater the fractal difference between the source and the object. The absolute zero corresponds to the highest fractal we can reach from our physical ST, for a magnitude is only absolute in a relative whole (Ω_0 to Ω_6). The same applies to light speed. At absolute zero, the speed of light is in fact zero. However, there is no absolute speed limit, for two particles are one, regardless of the distance between them. They are separate on our scale, not on theirs. The distance is just a problem of fractal perspective. Thus, on their scale, all the photons of the stars are extremely close together. The speed is then similar to a non-locality.

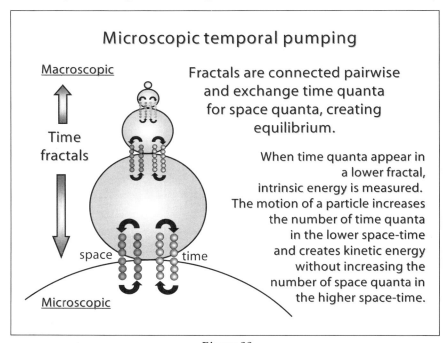

Figure 88

Every Bose-Einstein condensate is the mechanism used to correlate particles by reducing the temperature difference between the source fractal and the fractal at the receiving end. Every condensate is a sign of the universal oneness! That is why black holes cannot emit photons. They are an expression of a sub-sub-atomic fractal. Black holes are a quantum vacuum. They hide their photons in the same way they hide the magnetic moment of an electron. Black holes will be addressed a little later.

A temporal pumping phenomenon of time quanta takes place from the higher fractal to the lower ST. The space/time ratio increases and quanta move from the denominator to the numerator. The temporal pumping can take place in both directions. It brings about causality, which is therefore variable depending on the pumping pressure. All pumping from the higher to the lower draws up the latter in a temporal balance phenomenon (asymmetry of thermodynamics: from hot to cold). This pumping is therefore subject to space (distance). The conservation of energy is explained perfectly by this law of pairwise fractal exchange, in which fractals seek permanent balance. The intrusion of energy in a given horizon is translated into a new exchange between this horizon and the spatially superior horizon. Hence the second law of thermodynamics.

This increasingly allows us to interpret the interactions of nature (strong interaction, weak interaction, electromagnetic interaction and gravity) as simple spatio-temporal exchanges that occur in different fractals.

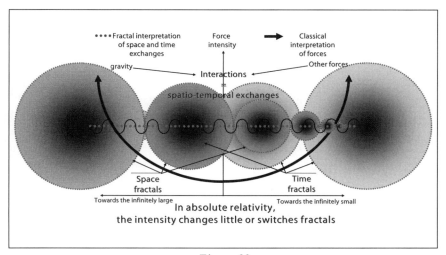

Figure 89

Interactions are the effects produced by a space/time ratio that triggers the interaction mechanism and translates the existence of a force into a system.

As a result, interactions are simple mathematical rules, but only if mass is expressed in terms of space and time, as shown in "Towards a new formalism." I argued that mass did not actually have a real dimension, despite its physical magnitude "kilogram," attributed by science as a result of inertial logic.

CHAPTER 45

The soft sciences: weightier than billions of suns

IN ABSOLUTE RELATIVITY, time is three-dimensional, fractal and discrete. In general relativity, it is one-dimensional and continuous. This means that in absolute relativity time is virtually non-existent between celestial bodies. The fact that the "chronal charge" of the cosmic vacuum is so weak causes the suppression of all energy forms. This is predicted by the classical models of the universe, as the wavelength of photons follows the universal beam dimensions in the theory of universal expansion. From that perspective, the energy of photons decreases[103] while mass is conserved. The energy of the universe is therefore not constant as mass is conserved. That causes problems. The difficulty with this standard model is that galaxies, galactic clusters and superclusters should dilate along with the universe! However, that does not happen! They behave like confetti stuck to a balloon that is being inflated. Only the vacuum follows that expansion. We are thus faced with a considerable logic problem. Fractal time solves this problem, for every stellar or galactic system is a fractal whole in itself. Surprisingly, however, mass cannot remain constant in proportion to distance. The Compton wavelength in quantum mechanics clearly shows that mass diminishes as the distance[104] grows. To really grasp the concept of fractal STs, it is therefore important to distinguish between the interstellar vacuum and the quantum vacuum. They are opposites. The first possesses very little energy; the second has massive amounts of it that cannot even be measured given the current state of our technological abilities. In other words, determining the age of the universe does not make sense, because it should be seen as a series of sheets of partially separated STs, with specific metrics of type log p/log q and a

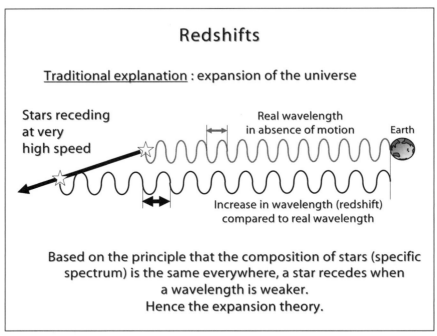

Figure 90

constant primordial unitary homeostatic relation. It is being born and it has always existed at the same time. Everything between present and eternity is just a problem of spatio-temporal perspective.

As we have seen, redshifts are one of the pillars of present cosmology, caused by the recession velocity of stars moving away from us. This is the framework of the universal expansion and, in a broader sense, of the Big Bang.

The light of more-distant galaxies shows an even greater redshift in the light spectrum. However, I should specify that the theoretical composition of stars follows a simple rule. A denser star produces larger amounts of heavy atoms in its core, where the presence of iron allegedly marks the outer edge. This production triggered by gravity is compensated by the degeneracy levels (emission outside the star of particles produced in collisions). Such emissions are similar to a water leak that is getting bigger as the pressure builds in the water pipes, allowing stars to remain stable for a very long time.

This frequency change can also be explained by the most important law of absolute relativity, i.e., the more there is space, the less there is time, and vice versa. As a consequence, the greater the distance between us and a star, the less time pass. In other words, since the frequency is directly linked to fractal and discrete time, distance is the actual source of redshifts without causing a Doppler effect.

The Hubble constant, a supposedly fixed value, is expressed in kilometers per second per megaparsec ($3,061.0^{19}$ kilometers). Astronomers do not know the exact value. It presumably lies between fifty and one hundred, probably around sixty-five. The rate at which a star is moving away from Earth (or recessional velocity) is calculated by using the following equation:

$$v = H.d$$

where v is the recession velocity, H is the Hubble constant and d is the star's distance. As H is constant, the recession velocity of more-distant stars increases. Please note that the distance of stars (d) is measured based on the estimated distances of nearby stars, which are also based on approximations. The age of the universe is thus determined by a continuous series of estimates based on this constant's estimate, which has been adjusted constantly to make sure that the oldest bodies are also included in the predicted age, currently estimated at 13.5 billion years. However, does the universe really have an age?

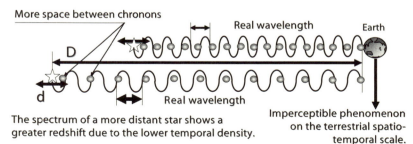

New redshifts

Version in absolute relativity : fractal static universe

The possible recession (d) of a star is much less quantified by a redshift than distance (D), which separates it from Earth.

More space between chronons

Real wavelength

Earth

D

Real wavelength

d

The spectrum of a more distant star shows a greater redshift due to the lower temporal density.

Imperceptible phenomenon on the terrestrial spatio-temporal scale.

The more there is space, the less there is time

Figure 91

Rather than interpret the redshift as the recessional velocity of celestial bodies that increases in proportion to the distance (the foundation of universal expansion), the amount of time decreases as we probe deeper into space.

In fact, this loss of time occurs in leaps and bounds, for every galactic (and even stellar) system possesses its own passing time. The universe is also static in absolute relativity, but for reasons that are unrelated to simple stellar dynamics. Einstein, who later abandoned this hypothesis, was right, but for quite different reasons. As a matter of fact, we no longer need a cosmological constant (he was wrong).

It is remarkable that Halton C. Arp's Atlas of peculiar galaxies mentions countless cosmological incoherences in the standard model. Contrary to Hubble's law, in some galaxy pairs the closest galaxy has a higher recession velocity than its more-distant neighbor. This suggests that the temporal flow between these two galaxies influences our perception of it because they are almost collinear (the visible angle being weak).

Too large an angle would annul the cumulative effect of the temporal density of the interval between these two galaxies.

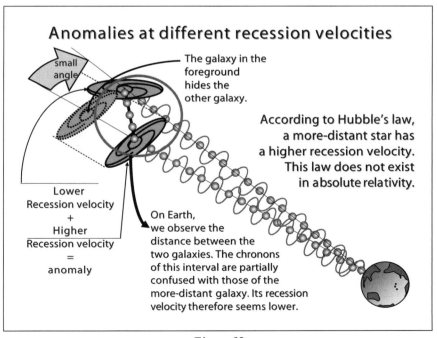

Anomalies at different recession velocities

small angle

The galaxy in the foreground hides the other galaxy.

According to Hubble's law, a more-distant star has a higher recession velocity. This law does not exist in absolute relativity.

Lower
Recession velocity
+
Higher
Recession velocity
=
anomaly

On Earth, we observe the distance between the two galaxies. The chronons of this interval are partially confused with those of the more-distant galaxy. Its recession velocity therefore seems lower.

Figure 92

This also suggests that the two galaxies are relatively close together compared to the distance between them and us. The superposition of temporal flows of the space intervals does not equal the flow of every single distance. These temporal flows are probably additive in nature.

The danger of interpreting cosmic events based on our weak macroscopic scale is that the spatio-temporal fractals are disregarded by telescopes.

We have all heard of the so-called missing mass of the universe. Our magazines overflow with this unpredictable type of mass. We do not lack some, but almost all of it. Why is this mass so low? Two essential forces are known to exist in the universe. The forces of expansion that tend to move mass further away from us — the centrifugal force of galaxies being one of these forces — and gravity, which tends to pull in mass. We are inclined to believe that these forces are neutralized when a system is stable, like our Milky Way. On the one hand, we have defined and categorized the composition of every single mass in the galaxy by spectral analysis (every atom possess its own spectrum). On the other, we know the expansion forces of rotating celestial bodies depending on their mass. Unfortunately, the calculations have shown that the mass of these bodies was quite insufficient to justify this equilibrium between centrifugal force and gravity. Logically speaking the law of universal gravitation, shared by every observatory on Earth, should not prevent galaxies from flying into pieces. So what holds galaxies and other clusters or superclusters together?

In line with my equations, I should a priori add mass to this collection: it is the missing mass (or dark mass) that we still have not seen despite the progress made in measuring instruments (Hubble space telescope).

Astrophysicists therefore picture two scenarios. It is either 'dark mass', i.e., matter that does not radiate light, or "shadow mass," i.e., the matter of an invisible mirror universe.

The problem with the first scenario is to justify that an imperceptibly low density of matter is still capable of compensating for the seventy to ninety percent of missing mass! When this proved impossible, a repelling dark energy was invented, the existence of which had never been proven under laboratory circumstances! Laboratories may be neither a panacea, nor a reference (even less in absolute relativity), but the idea that two parts of the universe can push away from each other clashes with our rational intellect. This is a huge dilemma, because numerous enigmas persist despite this explanation. Recent studies have now unexpectedly led to its abandonment. We never cease to correct the cosmological constant, which was reinstated after an intellectual quarantine, and change the local expansion rates as often as we change shoes. In addition, the universe is flat in the sense of four-dimensional ST geometry, which is supported by the initial conditions prescribed by theorists. A flat universe is neither in infinite expansion, nor in future potential contraction. In short, a world walking the razor's edge! The "coincidence" of the initial conditions seems a little bit too good to be true and makes me wonder if it exists at all. It resembles a die with a thousand faces (in reality there are more) showing the required number on the very first attempt to create a deterministic world! Would coincidence create the absence of coincidence?

In the other scenario, we have to deal with a shadow mass that allegedly exists in a twin universe made of antimatter and that can only communicate with our world through gravity. Not a single photon can pass! That is actually one of the justifications for the existence of superstrings digging the ten-dimensional tunnels (universe with ten spatial dimensions) through which this force apparently moves. The minor problem with this twin universe theory is that it requires the Big Bang to create an antimatter world. In addition, this anti-world, taking into account the parameters needed for its existence (no star reaches stability), cannot sustain life!

It is sad to see an omnipotent creator fail (there always has to be one, even and particularly in case of the Big Bang), or as they put it in the movie *Contact*: "Seems like an awful waste of space!" It would mean that the other half of the universe always remains inaccessible, from either side! In less than a century man has conquered his planet without having created it, but The Creator of the universe allegedly allowed half of His territory to turn into no-man's land. The divine choices between repression (dark matter) and arrogance (shadow matter) hardly seem appealing.

In reality, we are not missing anything! I am proposing the fastest, most spectacular materialistic slimming treatment of all time: trillions of billions of billions of megatons less on the scale. This is an offer you cannot refuse. It is quite possible that soft (social) science will come to the rescue of hard (natural) science. The emergency aid has only just begun. Indeed, understanding the nature of time, of which psychological time describes the essence, quickly allows us to see that absolute relativity could solve this matter in the blink of an eye. As time changes in inverse proportion to space (according to the fractals), the greater the latter, the less we feel the effects of time. But still.

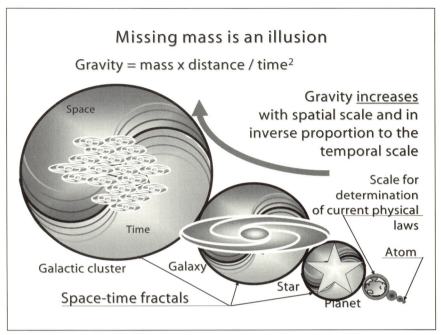

Figure 93

Gravity is a force. Force equals mass times acceleration. Acceleration is distance per time squared. Decreasing the denominator (time) while increasing the numerator (space) gives us a rapidly increasing number. For instance, twenty divided by four (= 5) is higher than ten divided by five (= 2). When we multiply this number by another (mass) and the latter decreases less rapidly than the denominator (in absolute relativity, weighty mass diminishes when space increases), then the outcome will be significant enough to create a divergence between fractals.

Here is our missing mass! Gravity on large scales has been highly underrated!

The funny thing is that gravity (relatively) increases with distance. This is strictly in line with what we have observed. Indeed, the factor of missing mass for a galaxy is between three and five compared to the estimated missing mass. However, it is ten or more for a galactic cluster! This means that space fractals (system scales) are linked to time fractals. In other words, the fractal changes in the time flow determine the gravitational potential.

In a nutshell — and without taking into account the mass that attracts you — if you weigh 70 kg on the Earth scale, you will weigh

300 kg on the galactic scale and one ton on the scale of a large galactic cluster. Scary, isn't it? Do not worry. On the atomic scale you will feel as light as a feather. However, you are still the same person. In absolute relativity, the more there is space, the less there is time. Therefore, the vaster the spatial scale, the stronger the gravitational pull.

On the other hand, according to absolute relativity, the smaller the scale, the weaker it should be. It is strange (considering the role of coincidence) that gravitational interaction is the weakest force of nature… on the microscopic scale! It is 10^{36} times (one plus thirty-six zeros!) weaker than the nuclear force.

It is not surprising that physicists have crawled through every nook and cranny to find it, but in vain. It has disappeared! Would you like to know how antigravity works? Take the mechanisms of the infinitely small and apply them to a larger scale! This fractal law can be violated, just like the causality subject to this scale.

Fussy readers could point out that the definition of this force should also be applied to the other fundamental forces, which would cause them to increase with distance, just like gravity. However, what distinguishes traditionally defined force from an interaction is the existence

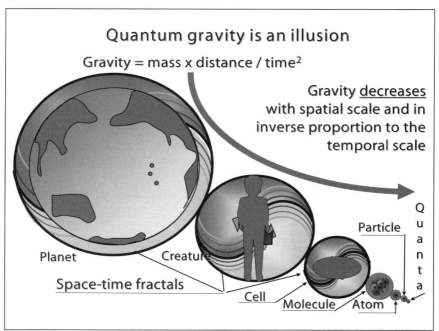

Figure 94

of a point of origin. The quantum theory, however, presents interactions as emissions of virtual particles. Therefore, gravity originates on a given scale (the point of origin must be material, i.e., strictly corpuscular), but most of all in a decreasing quantum time flow. In fact, we have seen that a distinction must be made between inertial mass and so-called weighty mass that varies depending on time and space ratios.

Let us return to our telescope. In addition to the missing mass preventing the dislocation of galaxies, another enigma, related to the first, causes our scientists many sleepless nights: gravitational lensing.

This process takes place when a galaxy is exactly behind another. Traditionally, the effect is caused by the mass of the closest galaxy that "reroutes" the photons of the farthest galaxy. The closest galaxy indeed distorts, or warps, the ST around it, causing the path of the photons to be curved, like an optic lens bends light. As a result, the background galaxy may appear to be located to the side of the one that hides it, instead of behind it.

Calculations have shown that the mass of this galactic lens should be much greater in order to produce the effects observed (double-imaged quasars or an arch-shaped gravitational mirage). The explanation of this

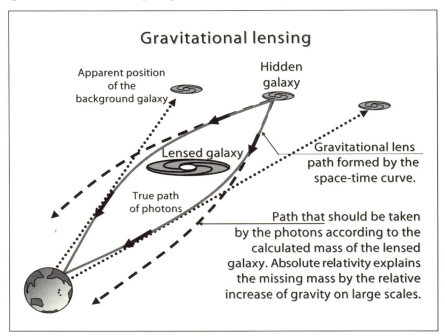

Figure 95

difference is once again that nothing is missing; gravity (or the ST curve) is underestimated. This galactic fractal acts as a much stronger magnifying glass than Einstein's simple gravity — who saw time as one-dimensional — and therefore validates the three-dimensional, fractal and discrete nature of time. You now understand that where Einstein saw a ST curve, I see adjacent sheets of ST fractals where time and space increase and decrease in inverse proportion to each other.

A galaxy is a disk that rotates around itself, like the rotor of an extraterrestrial vessel. However, the greatest mass (the so-called density of matter) of the galaxy is clustered together near its center. Because of the kinetic moment of the rotation, everything in the center must spin much faster than in the peripheral zones. Curiously, the circular orbit curve measured from the center of the galaxy to the periphery shows velocities that are very similar between the axis and the crown! The observations of orbital velocity in a galaxy therefore reveal an excessively high peripheral velocity! Almost as high as in the center. The outer stars go into hyperspeed. No one has ever explained this phenomenon (except for some ad hoc acrobatic tricks performed in the two theories of dark matter and shadow matter). With 3D time, the universe does not only

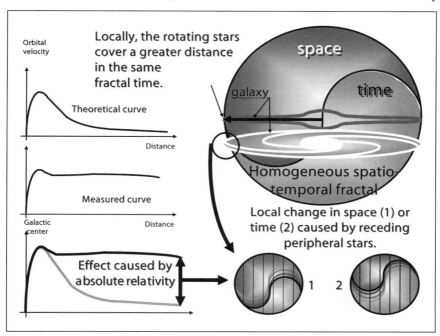

Figure 96

become more elegant, but also simple and logical! A galaxy is a quasi-homogeneous fractal whole, in which the time flow is relatively stable. However, taking into account the gradual recession of stars compared to the center, these stars are forced to cover a greater distance in the same fractal time. As a consequence, they travel much faster than our terrestrial laws dictate.

We can also interpret this outcome somewhat differently by arguing that the peripheral bodies engage in a much more significant macroscopic temporal pumping (taking in extra chronons), which increases as they move further away from the center. This temporal pumping is an effect of absolute relativity, causing every rotating body to absorb a much larger amount of temporal quanta (chronons) than an isolated body in rectilinear motion, shielded from all systems. In fact, this can be compared with the relativistic effects of special relativity.

Since the stars in a galaxy are connected to each other by a gravitational center, they constitute a single whole. However, this whole is sufficiently elastic to allow for different relative velocities. In fact, a galaxy is homogeneous on the structural plane, but inhomogeneous on the kinematical plane. The temporal pumping consists in taking in more chronons in front of the star. As the rotation takes place on a certain plane, the available "stock" of chronons is larger on a rotation plane (two dimensions) than on the rectilinear path (one dimension) of an isolated body. As a body absorbs more chronons, its velocity increases (due to the correlative distance) and eventually reaches a state of equilibrium, that of the spatial fractal this time.

Let me end this part by saying that the solution to the mysterious flatness (and rotation) of (most) galaxies can also be found in absolute relativity. Most astronomers think the answer lies outside the stellar wholes due to the effect of so-called primordial fluctuations; some kind of particle plasma. According to the standard model, these huge matter fluctuations formed after the Big Bang due to the gravitational pull.

Needless to say the explanations for this flatness are abstruse and flimsy at best. Why did we not simply find spheres of matter in an initial homogeneous whole, instead of our beautiful galaxies that twirl like ballerinas? An embarrassing question. One of the fundamental principles of absolute relativity is that while moving from one spatio-temporal fractal to another on the microscopic scale, space expands and unfolds in three dimensions, whereas it only had two before. Remember that particle spin is based on the rotation of that same particle around itself. This rotation means that only two dimensions are

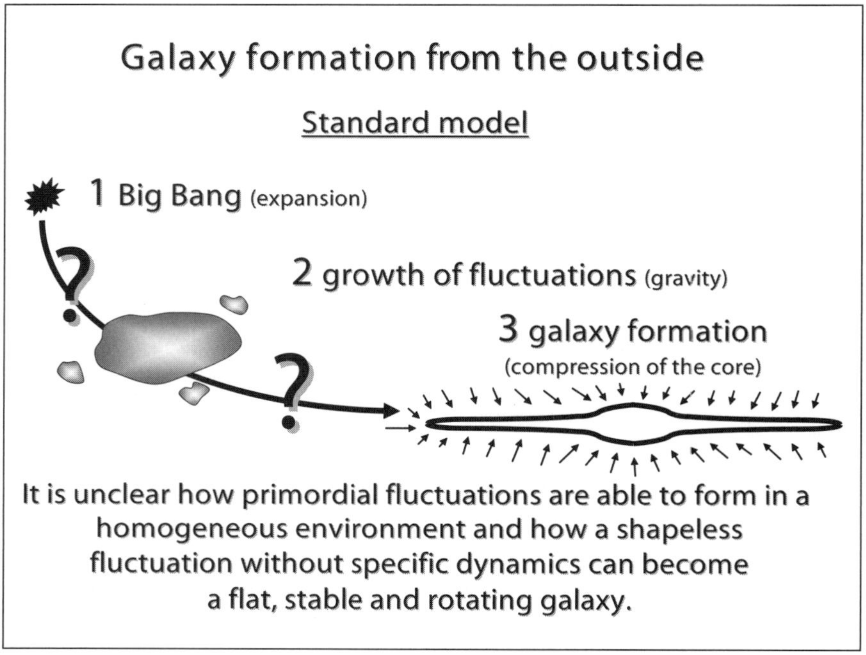

Figure 97

active. The galaxy is formed on the subatomic rotation plane of its core. In other words, each galactic structure has its own gradual Big Bang!

The galaxy is formed from a ST fractal adjusting to the vacuum of a Bose-Einstein condensate (the central black hole of a galaxy). This vacuum is actually an imperceptible ST fractal, for time passes too fast from our perspective. This fractal is the source of considerable, but non-measurable energy that transmits some of itself to its environment.

Therefore, we see the world turned upside down. Matter is not compressed by gravity to create a core. It is the vacuity of the core that unfolds to create a galaxy and to create gravity. The cosmic dynamics has to be adjusted to absolute relativity. We should thank all the anomalies that undermine the standard cosmological model, such as a universe that is younger than the stars in it.[105] More in general, the fractality of the universe becomes more tangible as space and time scales, both in the infinitely small and the infinitely large, are farther away from ours. This means that these first clues will compel scientists to completely review their equations and the interpretation they give to their observations. The sharpest readers will immediately grasp the

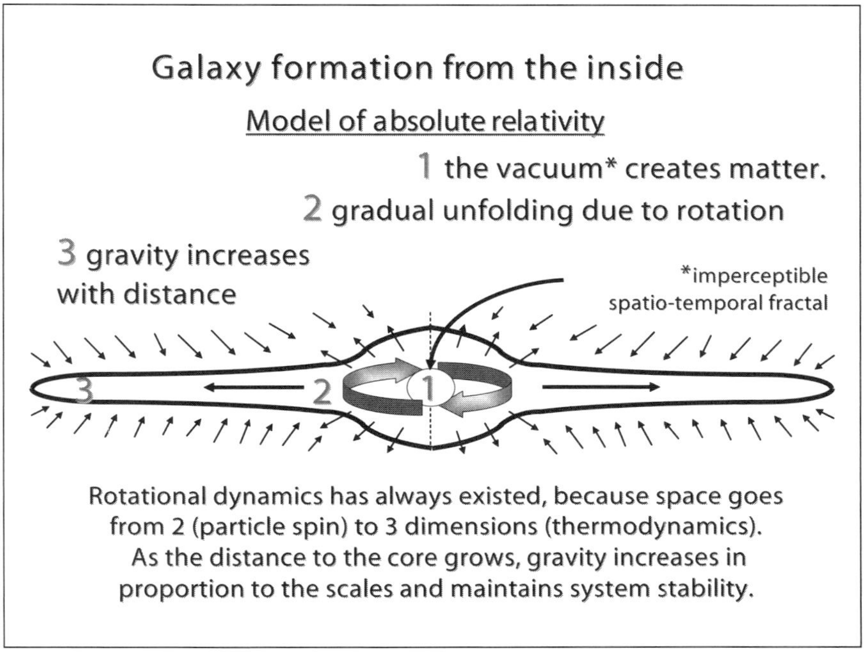

Galaxy formation from the inside

Model of absolute relativity

1 the vacuum* creates matter.

2 gradual unfolding due to rotation

3 gravity increases
with distance

*imperceptible
spatio-temporal fractal

Rotational dynamics has always existed, because space goes
from 2 (particle spin) to 3 dimensions (thermodynamics).
As the distance to the core grows, gravity increases in
proportion to the scales and maintains system stability.

Figure 98

scope of the upcoming change. Our metric is relative, well beyond Einstein's relativity. It is a Copernican revolution that precedes a new, springlike, scientific vitality like a breath of fresh air! That is what the cosmos and its inhabitants have to offer.

A proper overview would not be complete without mentioning the universe's entropy, which has a huge surprise in store for us.

The physical interpretation of entropy, which describes the relation between heat and the work of each particle performed during transformation, remains rather vague in thermodynamics. Its meaning only becomes clear with the help of statistical mechanics (which means we are moving further away from causality!), showing us that S (entropy) increases as Ω (number of combinations of states for the same equilibrium) grows.

S measures our current lack of information about the microscopic nature of the system we observe. That explains why quantum mechanics experiments are complex, because their objective is to reduce as many of the thirty plus uncontrollable parameters as possible, until obtaining S=0, i.e., $\Omega=1$. Thus, the effects obtained are valid under conditions that have nothing to do with our everyday reality. We even manage to produce effects (Casimir, Compton, Hall, etc.) that do not exist naturally. Even your microwave oven produces waves that do not appear in nature's catalogue. Science does not describe reality, but redirects it and discovers what drives the universal mind.

It is sometimes said that entropy is a measure of the disorder of the system. This imagery, which tries to use the evocative power of the word "disorder" to give us an intuitive understanding of the notion of entropy, is dangerous, for the word is too ambiguous and often causes grave errors. We should not try to give it any other meaning than this "lack of information" about the microscopic state implied by the Boltzmann[106] equation. Actually, the fluctuations of time and space quanta are too fast from our perspective beyond this limit. In fact, they are not fast, but fractally distant from our density. This digression seemed important to appreciate the great importance of an article[107] written by Jacob Bekenstein[108] about the holographic universe. Remember that a hologram is an object representing three-dimensional information, whereas it only has two. "All the information describing the three-dimensional scene is encoded into the pattern of light and dark areas on the two-dimensional piece of film. A three-dimensional holographic scene cannot contain more details than the roll of film of the hologram in which it is engraved," Bekenstein reminds us. In addition, when we break a hologram, every piece holds the information of the whole. This means that a holographic universe implies the existence of larger amounts of information than those we can access, because we do not see the whole of which the scene is a part.

CHAPTER 46

The holographic universe or the reality of dreams

IN HIS INTRODUCTION, HE ARGUED: "more than half a century of research has taught us that the fabric of dreams and the fabric of reality are not so different: information is just as crucial an ingredient to the physical world as matter and energy....Information is a crucial player in physical systems and processes. Indeed, a current trend initiated by John Archibald Wheeler of Princeton University is to regard the physical world as made of information, with energy and matter as incidentals." This is in perfect alignment with absolute relativity: a dream is not a figment of our imagination!

In absolute relativity, information brings structure to the ST, and vice versa. Let me point out that Wolfram Research, famous for its powerful and popular software program *Mathematica,* recently published a huge book (more than one thousand pages) on a new kind of science, dealing with the creation and the functioning of the universe by information up to the smallest possible scales.

May I remind you that the entropy of a physical system is subject to the number of microscopic states the system can be in without affecting its macroscopic state. The entropy therefore increases with time. The notion of entropy is interesting in the sense that our macroscopic world does not know what goes on in the center of the world. The illusion of our reality is very real. That also characterizes the behavior of UFOs.

At the same time, in 1948, the formal information theory was founded by mathematician Claude Shannon, who "invented" the bits, or binary digits (0 or 1). Please note that this definition of information does not enlighten us about the value of information, which is as dependent on context (of the software) as a telepathic message. Shannon immediately understood that his definition is the same as Boltzmann's: the number of combinations counted by Boltzmann's entropy reflects the amount of information in the numeric sense considered necessary to implement any particular arrangement. I should add that the quantum computers of the future will not settle for 0 and 1 — corresponding to the lowest energy level of an electron and the next excitation level up respectively — but also include all the intermediate levels in between. Qubits will therefore contain more information.

However, even if we make the right choice of units, Bekenstein said, the values of these two forms of entropy (thermodynamic, used in chemistry and binary, used in informatics) in the same system differ vastly in magnitude. For instance, a classical electronic chip has an entropy of 10^{10} bits, but a thermodynamic entropy of about 10^{23}. The thermodynamic entropy is subject to the state of billions of atoms that make up each transistor. Knowing that a degree of freedom is any quantity that can vary, such as a coordinate specifying a particle's location, the two entropies are equal when they are both calculated for the same degrees of freedom.

According to Bekenstein, there could be more levels of structure than we can imagine. We can finally shed light on the spiritual world of which the edges are blurry. We now know the fundamental constituents at the deepest level of structure[109] of an entropy, which, as we have seen, becomes sheer unlimited information. It is only logical to assume that the materiality of information has long since gone up in smoke.

The Israeli argued: "It is impossible to determine what is inside a black hole, of which the horizon is a sphere. No detailed information can emerge across the horizon and escape into the outside world." This sentence is essential, because it suggests a boundary between the physical information and other types of information. This boundary seems to be that of the quantum vacuum identified by absolute relativity as a ST of which the temporal density only leaves traces through particle shock or the Casimir effect, for instance.

Let me say a few words about black holes. They are a so-called singularity. When a human vessel wants to break free of the Earth's gravitational pull, it needs to reach a certain speed called the escape velocity. On Earth that speed is 11 km/s. It depends on the mass from which we want to break free. The greater this mass, the higher the escape velocity. A black hole is therefore a pointlike object in space, of which the matching escape velocity is higher than the speed of light. Therefore, not even light can escape. The Schwarzschild radius (Rs) is then the horizon below which the photons cannot be freed due to the excessive gravity of the black hole object. This is the simplified conventional presentation of facts. Black holes seem to follow the conservation laws in terms of energy and the kinetic moment, but they can be measured based on their effects on the surrounding space-time. However, this is still a tautology. How can we define a phenomenon when it is approached from a different reference frame than its own?

In absolute relativity, black holes are much more than a gravity surplus. We have seen that gravity increased relatively with distance, but that mass increased simultaneously when distance diminished. We have seen that mass is in fact a relation between fractal time and space ratios. The Schwarzschild event horizon therefore corresponds to a translation of the group of seven iterations of light speed, which is also a relation between fractal space and time ratios. Therefore, the variable e_n (see "Towards a new formalism") undergoes a homothetic translation.

Black holes seem to violate a fundamental law, namely the second law of thermodynamics. "This law summarizes the familiar observation that most processes in nature are irreversible," Bekenstein's article reads, which is similar to saying: "We can see the sun because it is daytime." The habitual tautology of time between causality and temporal irreversibility seems to be tightly linked, because these affirmations come straight out of a — renowned — scientific magazine. This irreversibility lays the foundation for the law of cause and effect, which is such an intricate part of our understanding of the physical world.

The fundamental principle of black holes applies to alien vessels. In astrophysics, large black holes must be huge singularities, because we believe we can already prove the existence of micro black holes[110] on the microscopic scale in the LHC[111] project performed at CERN.[112]

Rafael Sorkin (Syracuse University) argued that, since the event horizon of the black hole is an impassable boundary, the information that falls into it no longer affects the universe outside. This may imply yet another tautology. Is this boundary not simply that of a temporal flow? Amazingly, the commonality between black holes and quantum mechanics is the existence of photons that are invisible to us. On the one hand, there is gravity; on the other, there are various aspects of the diffusion matrix, such as electron self-energy. We pretend that the same phenomenon is at work and that the boundary is temporal rather than spatial. We definitely have the right to ask what a black hole really is. A fundamental entropy? Leonard Susskind (Stanford University) defined the holographic entropy bound as the maximal entropy of matter and energy contained in a given volume of space. This shows us once again that what we see is limited by the spatial matrix.

The professor from Jerusalem said: "The second law of thermodynamics forbids such inverse processes....As first emphasized by J. A. Wheeler, when matter disappears into a black hole, its entropy is gone for good, and the second law seems to be transcended, made irrelevant. Perhaps the universe has somehow managed to spontaneously become/turn into a self-organizing system by sweeping disorder under an event horizon from which it cannot escape." This question curiously reminds me of structured (neguentropic) dematerialization phenomena. Jacob Bekenstein added an interesting argument: "...The increase in black hole entropy always compensates or overcompensates for the 'lost' entropy of the matter. More generally, the sum of black hole entropies and the ordinary entropy outside the black holes cannot decrease. This is the generalized second law — GSL for short." Bekenstein is saying in his own words what I am arguing here: the quantity of information, and therefore of time quanta, increases in the invisibly and infinitely small!

Remember[113] that two American physicists, Emil Mottola of the Los Alamos National Laboratory and Pawel Mazur of the University of South Carolina, have established a theory on so-called gravastars,[114] in which, beyond a certain limit, matter resembles a Bose-Einstein condensate, i.e. vacuum bubbles! Their claim is backed by the Frenchman Eric Gourgoulhon from the Meudon Observatory. In other words, the vacuum, in reality the absence of all corpuscular behavior, is allegedly full of entropy and therefore of information!

More specifically, the immaterial possesses more information than the material! In absolute relativity, both time and information increase during non-observation intervals. Understanding the above means understanding abductions, dreams, imagination and all sorts of spiritual experiences. All these experiences are "more-than-real," because they possess more information than the physical world. Do I even need to emphasize this point? Do we need to tell neurobiologists about the origin of information perceived by the brain, or psychiatrists about the origin of mental experiences? If the entropy of chemistry (10^{23} bits) is considerably higher than that of informatics (10^{10} bits), the entropy of a black hole, made of vacuum, cannot be compared with the aforementioned because it measures approximately 10^{66} bits! Of course, this digression on black holes is not directly related to the illustration of my argument. The moral of the story: invisible worlds possess superior knowledge!

In reality the vacuum is full, much fuller than our physical world. We can now begin to envision the powerful reality of the vacuum and the information that can be found in high temporal densities — when our consciousness travels, for instance — and the translation limits of mental structures to which our waking mind is subjected. Indeed, the fact that there is much more information in non-matter than in matter means there are types of information that we cannot possibly retranscribe.

As the physical envelope (surface) grows smaller, the entropy therefore increases! Picture the "fuselage" of UFOs as being this envelope: it grows smaller as the amount of information grows. That is the exact same definition given by absolute relativity of the time quanta–space quanta ratio. Curiously, I am saying exactly the same with the argument that in higher time densities, UFOs (and their occupants) can tap into more information (psychic information, for example) and more degrees of freedom! Vessels also increase their interior volume,[115] while we see them growing smaller from our ST. Likewise, a star collapses as its entropy increases.

The fact that the physical surface grows smaller as the entropy increases is however, not the most outstanding aspect, Bekenstein pointed out, even if absolute relativity scores points here. The most astonishing aspect is that this holographic bound does not depend on the volume of space in question, but on the surface of its boundary (UFO fuselage). This explains why the ideal vessel possesses the largest possible surface and why the ideal and therefore most efficient shape is a disk or a sphere. Hence their superior observation capability.

The holographic bound corresponds to the overcapacity of information in a black hole. This argument applies to the entire universe: we see a holographic universe of which the entire history is stored in the higher time densities, without the whole of time and space quanta being stored in the visible universe. This holographic vision of entropy is in line with the quantization of time. Before showing how ET vessels and paranormal phenomena interpret the three-dimensional time structure and absolute relativity, I would like to elaborate on the principles of the latter. It is important to understand that there is no fundamental difference between physical and mental information. They are both the result of an interaction with consciousness.

CHAPTER 47

ST or divine millefeuilles

INFORMATION BRINGS STRUCTURE to the ST, just like the ST brings structure to information. The more there is space, the less there is time, and vice versa. We could be fooled into thinking that we grow increasingly smaller ourselves as the density of time increases. In fact, we become smaller to those who stay in a lower time density, but not to ourselves. We need to remember that the universe is fractal. Every fractal possesses a scale boundary. When we are transferred to a specific fractal, our consciousness immediately adapts to the new space/time ratio. The journey from one fractal to another is hardly noticeable, because it is quasi-instantaneous. We still feel that the volume remains constant and that is also the case, because space and time are both subject to the same problem of perspective. We may even feel more voluminous because the entropy increases. This is what happens during astral projection, for instance. Our consciousness aligns itself with the space-time references of the astral plane as long as it remains there sufficiently "long." To access the astral plane, there is therefore no conscious continuity compared to our physical world. Imagine you want to go from one room to another, larger room without going through the door.

The access to an information system exposes our consciousness to this information, even if it is just temporary. There is no such thing as an absence of consciousness. We can only speak of forgetting the conscious information of a given system, once our consciousness has returned to a lower ST. There is always much more information in the higher time densities (in the sense of the cosmic entropy), part of which cannot be recovered once we are back in our normal ST. We simply do

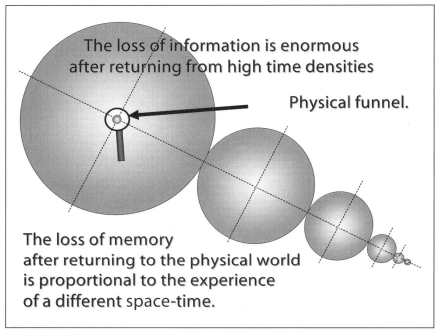

Figure 99

not remember every dream detail because we return to the temporal density of our body that influences our perception of time in the sense of the reduction of the wave packet and, more precisely, the time flow we are able to incorporate in terms of information.

This absence, or oversight, is caused by the distance between two systems separated by a very different time flow. Therefore, the loss of information depends on how high we ascend into the time densities. A mystical experience is indescribable, for the quality and amount of information of this experience do not have any equivalent in our habitual temporal density. Let us return to the analogy. Picture the physical body on its own spatial scale as a glass collecting rainwater. Of course, not all the rain will fall into the glass. When this same physical body is studied under a microscope, but considered in its entirety, it will resemble a water tower. The same body on the quark scale will look like a lake receiving a rain shower of information. Finally, on the scale of the vacuum, your being will resemble an ocean "stuffed" with information from the skies.

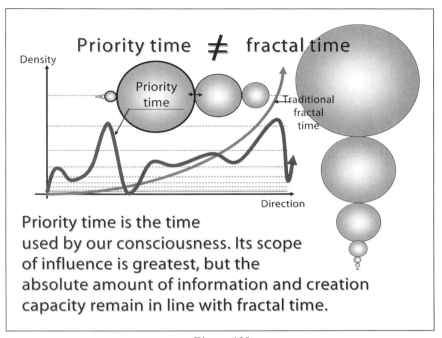

Figure 100

We are constantly being influenced by the prevailing time flow, called priority time.

In the waking state, our priority time is that of the material world. For dead Earth-bound spirits, it is the astral plane. To escape its influence, we must detach ourselves from the physical world. Through sleep or meditation in a fixed posture we disassociate ourselves from the influence of the time flow of the physical body.

The memorization consists in connecting with other STs. Consciousness is therefore spread out over several STs. This means that parapsychological abilities manifest themselves as this ability to reconnect. Our common goal is to ascend into temporal densities that are both encyclopedic and cooperative.

Please remember that there are only three space dimensions and three time dimensions. The universe is a spatio-temporal interaction matrix. Potential energy increases with distance (space) and is in inverse proportion to the density of time. The kinetic energy increases with the density of time (space therefore diminishes). The opposite approach to absolute relativity is that of contemporary science, which fails to include space and time in its equations. Nonetheless, time can increase or decrease independent of space fluctuations. The opposite also applies. As it decreases in terms of temporal quanta, it spreads out producing history and causality. In time travel, a date therefore only has meaning in a specific ST. The production is caused by the unfolding of space.

In other words, absolute relativity is the theory that allows every phenomenon to be reduced and interpreted by a differential of the algebraic space/time quotient. An ST is defined by an interval of quantum values in the sense of spatio-temporal granularity. The quanta of space and time can be chosen arbitrarily, for they have reality only through a relation. When we know the physical values of Planck time and the Planck length, we can take any very low value.

The equation of God is: infinite space/infinite time = 1. God is therefore definitely the unit. This means that time and space only exist through a system. Every phenomenon occurring in the ST of the considered system will move farther from or closer to this divine ratio, in the positive and the negative sense. A unitary ratio corresponds to the total absence of motion, phenomena and energy. It is essential to remember that:

- energy is the expression of granular time.
- (Potential gravitational) mass is the expression of granular space.

More precisely, energy and mass are two aspects of the same thing. The information is then equivalent to the granular ST. It defines or is defined by the ST it traverses. The information tends to go from more time towards more space (top-down), i.e., the second law of thermodynamics. The evolution of consciousness tends to go from more space towards more time (bottom-up). The temporal asymmetry (causality) is the resultant of an encounter between consciousness and information in several STs at the same time. The interaction between two adjacent STs causes asymmetry.

Lower STs also have lower time/space ratios. In this respect, relativity is absolute. The cosmic wave function describes the superposition of STs, just as the quantum wave function describes the superposition of states. This is why general relativity implies the "equality" between time and space, i.e., between energy and mass. The quantum state function uses a term related to space (position) and time (energy). The space/time ratio thus combines the two important theories of science. The generalized symmetry discussed before is expressed by the fact that temporal quanta appear as space quanta disappear. In case of accelerated motion, we witness the distribution of quanta in accordance with the axis of the motion, until they disappear from this dimension. This explains why quantum entanglement functions in pairs that evolve in a plane (one particle compared to another). However, the motion aligns itself with the temporal pumping. This means that both energy and time are vectorial in nature, but the vector is jolted by the fractals they traverse, which explains the exponential growth.

CHAPTER 48

Consciousness creates the world

IN THIS BOOK I AM ARGUING that consciousness needs space and time to exist. However, as it exists it understands that it can do without. Thus is the movement of consciousness from absence towards its own presence. It builds the ST only to tear it down again. It needs the journey to create the destination, which is nothing other than the absence of the journey, because it is its own creation.

Consciousness manifests itself in the quantity and quality of the information it receives. The quality of the information is the same as the actual system (the software). Consciousness is therefore part of a system. The most-complex systems contain the largest quantity of information. We live in a complex system called the body. However, it is not the only one. The "I" entity is also a system, and even more complex. However, "I" should not be mistaken for consciousness itself. When "I" takes the upper hand in what consciousness conveys, "I" becomes ego. When "I" travels within consciousness (successive levels of information), it chooses its identity, allowing us to detach ourselves from ego. The quantity of information creates quality of information through the system it can produce. Thus, the more granular time there is, the greater the consciousness of all. Consciousness therefore travels from the personal towards the universal. That explains why the identity of consciousness depends on the quantity of information. We are not who we think we are. It is up to us to choose who we want to be!

The question "who are we?" can be answered by saying that the sense of identity of our consciousness is transformed depending on the quantity and quality of information present in STs. However, the question "where are we going?" can be answered by saying "here and now," i.e., focused on higher STs where oneness and freedom exist. The term "where" in this question suggests that we are separated "geographically" from a point of departure, while we are actually "temporally" separated. You will therefore understand that the importance of identity evolves from survival (= retaining existing information) towards cooperation (exchange of available information). This sharing enhances its freedom to take on other identity forms. Spiritually evolved ETs do not have any identity as we know it and can even shape-shift! However, that still requires an act of willpower. Imagine our psychology if we had the ability to change our face at will. When we understand that, we will begin to understand the ET psyche. We are often wrong about our own ability to say what we really want. Escaping a dangerous situation in a lucid dream is not for everyone. It is this weakness that is often exploited by hostile ETs. Tell yourself often that you really want to liberate yourself from fear. Ask and you shall receive, but wanting requires a great deal of energy and an ad hoc technique (the affirmation "May this or that come true!").

This freedom helps you turn your own personal identity into another one that is higher — in terms of quality — than the sum of identities of your (present) reincarnation. Thus, the influence of "wanting" grows as "I" is transformed. All quantitative and qualitative information systems will interact with each other. The higher-quality consciousness can then release or bring in any system, as shown by paranormal phenomena.

When ETs "play" with humans, they play with the fear engendered by the identity in which we believe. Those who cling to their identity also trigger the manifestation of their fears. Reincarnation is a strictly unnecessary belief if the one who believes it does not move towards an inner detachment from who he believes he is. It is essential to comprehend the link between constant adaptation and the eternity of the soul. That brings us a little closer to the extratemporality exhibited by the extraterrestrial beings that visit us. These beings can be recognized by their varying degrees of adaptation and eternity.

The difference between a negative and a positive attitude comes from adopting an evolution process or an involution process. We either focus on controlling lower STs — which means totally subjecting the beings in these STs to our will because we believe theirs is flawed — or on controlling higher STs and adapting to a new, larger and cooperative identity. Negative and positive entities can thus be identified by the focus of their consciousness. Note that the term "negative" does not necessarily have a moral connotation. We are often ambivalent and take two different directions at the same time. We choose importance (survival) and gratitude (cooperation). In other words, we cannot choose between materialism and spiritualism.

CHAPTER 49

All is one and one is all

THERE IS A MARVELOUS scientific and direct measuring instrument within each one of us that makes us aware of all-that-is: our emotions. Every feeling belongs to either magnetic pole. That explains why true joy exists only when the two come together.

This oneness is universal consciousness seem from within. The energy can be broken down into a multitude of energies that grow less intense as the relative quantity of time decreases. That division is the only proof that we are moving towards the Unity (God) ST from a different ST. This unity exists thanks to the existence of superimposed (read: fractal) space and infinite (fractal) time, each at the extreme opposite of the other in the fractal scales. At the same time, these infinites seem incompatible. That is why God is "The Unknowable": He cannot be described, for any description is equivalent to separation (by describing God, we point at what we are not). However, He expresses himself everywhere and His expression can be described, but is incomplete by definition. To give you an idea, one might say that the correlation of microscopic particles, viewed as pointlike STs, is universal. They correspond to a single particle (or metaphysical entity) seen from at least one ST down.

Congratulations on a job well done! You have made it this far! I have given you a general idea of what fundamental physics is all about. We have been surfing a huge tidal wave. However, there is so much more to it. We have hardly scratched the surface! It is now time to find an explanation for the behavior shown by ET vessels and to take a mental break.

CHAPTER 50

No, it is not a dream

UFOs CERTAINLY CANNOT be summarized just as material manifestations. Quite the contrary! We have been conditioned to imagine space ships as metallic carcasses[116] covering astronomically large distances between different stars. That vision should be abandoned. Why would we cross the Pacific Ocean in a small boat if we can take a plane? We can fly over the water below us without ever touching it. We usually search for UFOs and extraterrestrials among the stars at night. Ironically, conditioned as we are by the preeminence of space in our mental structure, we think of travel in terms of covering a certain distance, but we actually need to replace it by time (the less space there is, the more time there is). In other words, extraterrestrials are extratemporals. They do not travel, they "transfer" themselves. Therefore, they are infinitely closer to us than we can imagine.

The "flight area" of most vessels is non-material. It would show great progress if ufologists were to acknowledge that fact. We are taking a bottom-up approach, whereas we need to start from the top and work our way down when studying the concepts and laws applied by ETs. Basically, they are more ultraterrestrial than extraterrestrial, just as we are ultramaritime in our jumbo jet flying over the Pacific. The reason is very simple: the degree of freedom and therefore of maneuvering is much higher in higher time densities. The difference is so significant that it is almost like comparing our abilities to those of a car or an airplane. The height adds an extra dimension for the aviator. It is true that from time to time, airplanes land and steer like ground vehicles, which is what ET vessels do when they become visible. An airplane is designed to fly, not to drive. A space vessel — including its occupants — is designed to ascend into higher temporal densities. Ask a pilot where he feels most at ease and he will answer "in the air"! Ask an extratemporal where he feels freest and he will say "in time"! To answer the famous question "why do they rarely show themselves?" we merely need to understand that, unlike airplanes that refuel on the ground, extraterrestrial vessels have an infinite energy supply, particularly when they are invisible, for time is energy in high temporal densities. The invisible realm is also the mental "flight area."

Many psychiatrists fail to recognize the physical laws that apply to human beings. These laws superimpose those of fundamental physics, in which matter is immaterial! The magic storage closet called the realm of imagination shows the inability of man to incorporate a new regime. Once we start the work of self-realization, through deep introspection, we gain control of our identity and gradually travel into the higher time densities. In fact, this happens every day: we are in a different time density in our dreams. Though short, they may still be quite detailed!

However, we hardly control or clearly remember these experiences. They reflect our uncontrollable desires and fears. Dreams are often our own creations; a curious mélange of collective archetypal symbols and personal concerns. Please note that this dream overlap between private space and collective space is the overwhelming proof of the limitations of free will, which we believe gives us the right not to care about the implications collective space may have for our ability to decide. Unconsciously, our decisions always affect others. In dreams we therefore resemble a drunk driver on a badly lit road. Those who have already experimented with lucid dreaming know that we are getting better at controlling them! There comes a time when our organized and consciously transmitted thoughts will stand before us.

Lucid dreams occur in a time density that is higher than the traditional astral plane, where the essence of our emotions resides. Alice (the soul) in fractal land could not see any continuity as she was jolted through the STs in which she traveled. That explains why she seemed disoriented. She believed that she was traveling, but in reality it was the world around her that traveled at the speed of her thoughts.

CHAPTER 51

The ones we call ETs

AFTER ALL THAT IS SAID you will understand why ETs are in reality ExtraTemporals. In French the term extranéens is sometimes used, a combination of extraneous — meaning alien, strange, foreign — and the French néant — meaning nothing. This is true in part if you consider time a spatial non-geometry or a nowhere. In a way, one could say that UFO phenomena are about embodiment at will. When Fermi stated his paradox wondering why he could not see the ETs that are allegedly present throughout the entire universe, he limited himself to a strictly materialistic logic. He asked: "If they

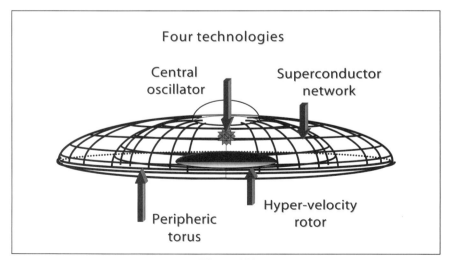

Figure 101

317

exist, then why haven't we seen them?". The answer is simple: ETs and their vessels are not materialized!

Several mechanisms provide the technological basis for this dematerialization:

a double high-speed hyper-rotor, a (crystal) oscillator, a superconductor network and a ring encircling the rotor or even the entire craft (in the case of discoid shapes).

The following diagrams show these technologies in detail.

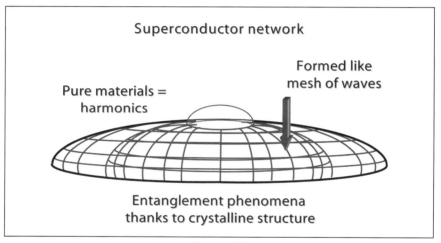

Figure 102

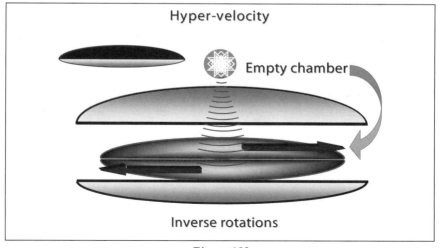

Figure 103

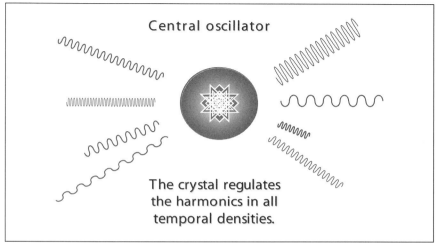

Figure 104

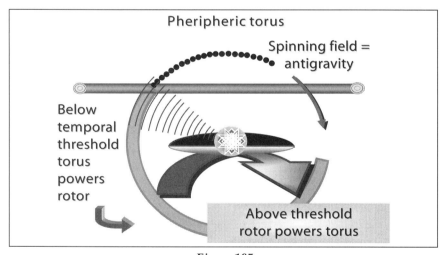

Figure 105

Subsequently, four states of matter can be established: the stable state (known matter, our reality), the unstable state (vibratory increase), the luminescent state (state of pseudo-transparency, but still visible) and finally the invisible state.

The mutation may occur slowly, but usually proceeds very rapidly. The transition from the luminescent to the invisible state takes place upon the emission of a very specific sound — a break frequency of some kind: a very sharp crystalline tone that is probably of an unparalleled purity. It is crucial for ufologists to understand that all these four states can occur within UFO craft simultaneously, which explains their apparent form changes. These vessels do not travel in space but across superimposed (or overlapping) STs. Such voyages come with dozens of phenomena and may upset our common sense notions that are based on the experience of our physical world and our traditional temporal referent (we all travel at the same speed, that of the Earth). ETs can be called extraterrestrials because they are unaffected by physical Earth time. This may help to explain countless apparent oddities. The explanations you are about to discover constitute the basic structure central to understanding UFO phenomena. Often, complementary aspects related to known physical mechanisms need to be included, but they will seem secondary compared to what is presented here. The emission of a specific spectrum by UFOs, microwaves for example, will have consequences already recognized by our physicists. On the other hand, they do not know all the effects generated by these emissions, particularly on organisms. Let us not lose sight of the fact that the intensity of space-time exchanges largely determines the intensity of these very phenomena. In addition, vessel specifications differ slightly from one model to another, while they are all based on the same fundamental principles. This is how absolute relativity explains UFO phenomena.

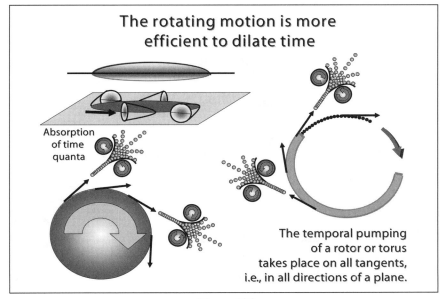

Figure 106

UFO vessels do not violate the law of gravity. They obey it entirely. Gravitation is determined by a force, i.e., mass times acceleration. Acceleration is distance per time squared (t^2 is in the denominator). By dilating time (increasing time quanta by the torus and superconductor rotor in an electromagnetic field), gravity decreases very rapidly, just like the dilation square, until it is negligible.

The theory of rotating fields laid down by Ning Li from the University of Alabama particularly anticipates a gravity-change effect, just like a controversial experiment conducted by Podkletnov in Finland showed.

It is recognized by many that the controversy is caused by a deliberate attempt to conceal technological progress that is incompatible with strategic interests. This superconductor specialist reported a two percent drop in the weight of objects placed over a device made up of a superconducting ceramic disk of thirty centimeters in diameter rotating at five thousand rpm suspended over a magnetic field produced by three electric coils enclosed in a cryostat. The key to antigravity and manipulation of time is a rotating field that generates temporal quanta (like any other sufficiently fast motion). N. A. Kozyrev's experiments already gave us a general idea.

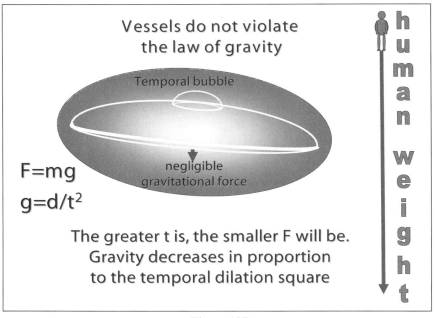

Figure 107

The spinning motion (macroscopic temporal pumping) combined with electromagnetic rotating fields (microscopic temporal pumping) gather sufficient amounts of chronons to allow the system to "tip" from one fractal into another. During the interval, Earth's gravity will have been considerably decreased.

Vessels can move like falling leaves. This pendulum motion of UFOs sometimes observed is caused by the deceleration differential between the two inverse-rotation rotors that produces a slight precession phenomenon, thus creating this falling leaf motion.

The fluttering or tipping of UFOs always precedes an arrival or departure maneuver (rotor acceleration or deceleration). The center of gravity of circular vessels is located above or underneath the double concentric rotor. The application axis of gravity crosses almost exactly the center of the vessel. Hence the "wobble on axis" effects caused by a slight rolling. This effect disappears when the rotors are realigned. In general, a vessel changes its inclination by temporarily using a rotating differential between the two rotors to achieve realignment. The chosen inclination does not obey the laws of aerodynamics or magneto-hydro-dynamics (MHD) in any way, but is connected to the width of the field of view selected by the pilot.

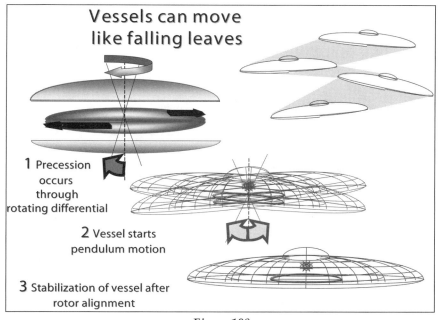

Vessels can move like falling leaves

1 Precession occurs through rotating differential

2 Vessel starts pendulum motion

3 Stabilization of vessel after rotor alignment

Figure 108

Photographs of UFOs are blurred. This usually occurs because the shutter speed of a camera is too slow to adjust to the density of the temporal field of the vessel.

This is similar to photographing a fast-moving object, except that a vessel can remain perfectly stationary as we photograph what is in the foreground: its temporal bubble. The more the temporal density in this field is high, the more the photo will be blurred.

When a UFO flies over a vehicle, the engine seems to stall and the lights to go out. This is a matter of perspective. The engine failures and extinguished lights are caused by the ST continuum change affecting the vehicle. Both the vehicle and its passengers (and any witnesses in the vicinity) will "experience" part or all of it as missing time! They start moving at a much faster pace than the pistons. The sound frequencies collapse in infrasound (or rather the witnesses live at a pace at least equally as fast) and no further noise reaches the vehicle. The beams of the headlights (as well as the light indicators on the dashboard) move much more slowly compared to our density. Their visual effect on the surroundings may weaken to the point of disappearing. In fact, everything functions normally in our ST, but to the driver the events will have slowed down to such an extent that both the engine

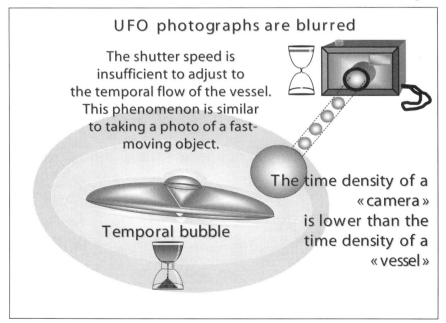

Figure 109

and the lights seem dead on another time scale, that of the temporal bubble of the UFO, whether the latter has materialized or not. Of course we stopped actually feeling the mechanical vibrations of lower frequencies normally experienced by the body long ago. As soon as this temporal bubble stops affecting us, time resumes its normal course and our perception of events corresponds to material reality again. This explains why witnesses claim their vehicle restarted all by itself whereas it never really stopped functioning in the first place. In the case of diesel engines that do not seem to stall, the explanation could be found in the harmonics of the low frequencies specific to diesel traveling through the body, thus keeping intact the kinesthetic sense of a normal functioning of the engine during the experience.

Any actions or attempts made by the witness[117] (if he is not paralyzed) to restart the car and/or reset the controls actually leads to the opposite result: total system failure. Hence the confusion about the cause of these breakdowns. If the temporal bubble influences a moving vehicle only for a short time it will stop functioning after a few meters. In our reality it will keep on moving. If the influence continues for a more extensive period of time, vehicle and passengers can

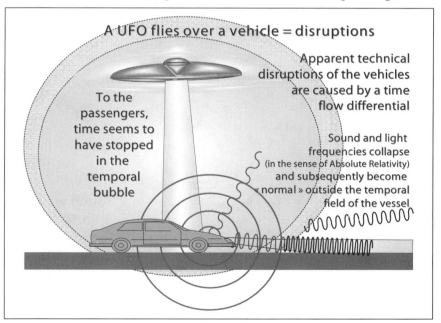

Figure 110

reappear in an unexpected location after disappearing from our reality, depending on the movement of the vehicle at the moment of the continuum shift, on the degravitational influence exercised by the vessel and on its trajectory. It is not unusual that vehicles literally hover above the ground. In addition, an energetic (temporal) pumping takes place near high-voltage power lines being absorbed by the temporal bubble of the vessel. Hence the occurrence of electric malfunctions, real ones this time. We should keep in mind that in absolute relativity, voltage is related to a fractal differential between a circulating charge and the environment in which it circulates. When it finds an identical temporal environment the potential difference disappears. That is what causes the great urban blackouts.

UFOs are silent. Everyone has heard of the sonic boom. It occurs when the speed of sound is exceeded. This shockwave cannot pass unnoticed. Fighter jets that exceed Mach 1 all cross this barrier. The expression supersonic boom is based on this term.

Everyone also knows that UFOs accelerate at astoundingly high speeds and inevitably exceed the speed that corresponds to this sound barrier. However, they remain silent. How is that possible?

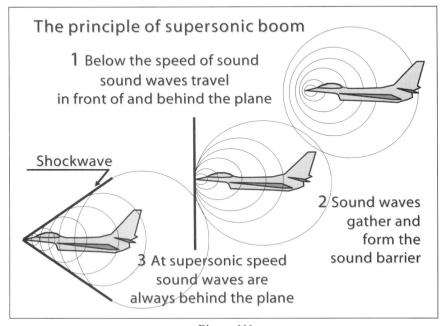

Figure 111

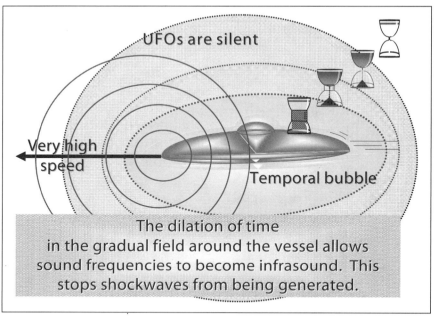

Figure 112

While in a materialized state and moving at high speed, UFOs do not produce a supersonic boom because time is contracted around the vessel and the air gradually slows down as it reaches the hull. There is no shockwave because the relative velocity of the vessel is low compared to the ambient air inside the temporal bubble! However, as the craft accelerate, their corpuscular appearance will take a vibratory form, in which case the aerodynamic load disappears. Before dematerializing the acceleration equals an increase of time density that compensates the growing pressure correlative to the acceleration.

UFOs are also silent in the materialized state, because the frequency of the sound emitted by the vessel — which is in fact a shockwave that travels through the atmospheric gas — has slowed down to such an extent ("redshifted") that it becomes infrasound. What is heard in the extensive spectrum of frequencies generated by UFOs is an almost imperceptible sigh (a few kilohertz). Under certain non-material conditions this could be ultrasound.

This explains why animals sense their arrival without seeing them, because unlike people they are endowed with ad hoc means of perception.

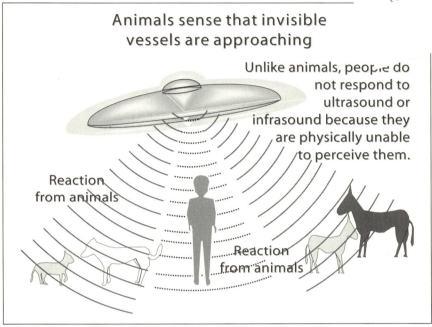

Animals sense that invisible vessels are approaching

Unlike animals, people do not respond to ultrasound or infrasound because they are physically unable to perceive them.

Reaction from animals

Reaction from animals

Figure 113

Depending on the atmospheric pressure, sounds may be heard corresponding to the usually very short time spectrum of sound frequencies generated by an arrival maneuver (materialization) or departure maneuver (dematerialization). Contrary to what is sometimes read, it is absolutely impossible to distinguish between good and bad ETs (if that makes sense at all) based on the existence or non-existence of sound emissions, as these are determined by atmospheric pressure. Such sounds often resemble that of a blown fuse marking the electromagnetic interaction between vessel and atmosphere. In some cases, a loud noise is heard generated by a rapid change of time quanta, a rather sudden braking caused by the materialization process.

In general, witnesses mention either a buzzing or whistling sound when vessels are not silent. These frequency ranges correspond exactly to the sound barriers of infrasound and ultrasound respectively. Most UFOs are silent. It is one of the major reasons why sightings are rare. We often only look at the sky when a sound attracts our attention.

Vessels may hide in the clouds. In high temporal densities, temperature differences can be reduced as a result of the proximity between the source ST and the ST where energy flows (after a sufficiently long time). The thermodynamic effects are quite weak because the Bose-Einstein effect (matter-wave) minimizes the kinetic energy of the particles. This minimization is synonymous with a temperature drop.

Both the vessel and its temporal bubble are cold compared to the surrounding air. Depending on humidity and pressure rates, this low temperature brings about the formation of water vapor condensation in the ambient atmosphere. A cloud (or mist) may form around the non-materialized vessel in a stabilized position, thus hiding it from our view once it has materialized.

The appearance of mist in paranormal phenomena can be explained in the same way. This mist often takes anyone entering it into the past or the future, which can be accessed from the high densities. We should also take into account that the (light) contrails noticed behind some vessels are nothing other than this condensation mixed with a local temporal density change, which explains why they are luminous (the light is the very proof of the high time density). Of course, retinal persistence also takes part in the residual observation of this contrail.

Vessels can change their shape and size. The apparent shape can be changed, from invisible to visible, by manipulating the frequencies of each of its parts, thus showing all or part of the structure. A discoid

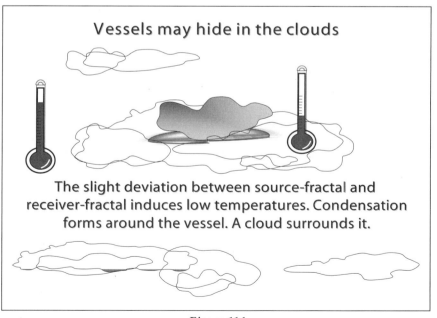

Vessels may hide in the clouds

The slight deviation between source-fractal and receiver-fractal induces low temperatures. Condensation forms around the vessel. A cloud surrounds it.

Figure 114

vessel can look like a boomerang, for instance, or a ring. In addition, the movement of a disk can make it appear like an oval balloon by using visual compression in terms of special relativity. However, to touch down on terra firma it will have to materialize completely and its real shape will usually appear (aside from exceptions caused by an intermediate state). Certain external frequencies (radar or otherwise) contribute to their total or partial invisibility by constructive or destructive wave interference.

Depending on the beliefs of the witness, the shape of the vessel can be induced by telepathic means. We should not forget that there is no fundamental difference between physical and mental information. The consciousness of the witnesses is scanned in the high temporal densities and their thought forms are amplified and reemitted by the oscillator, like a deforming mirror. The multi-frequency oscillator of the forced non-linear type (see Ari Lehto) would act like radar emitting electronic decoys and receiving the signals of our consciousness and unconscious mind, which is what it is only because we cannot reach this temporal density in the waking state. However, it can be achieved by the power of the mind in the contracted time of ETs. Witnesses will see first and foremost the created mental image traveling through high

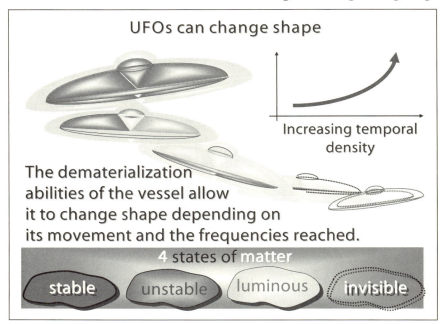

Figure 115

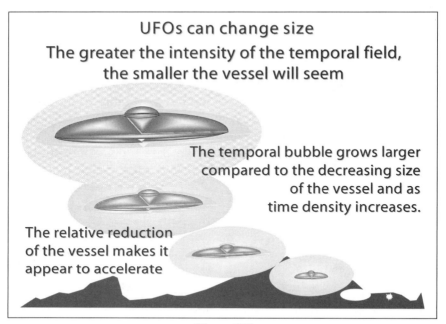

Figure 116

temporal densities, which is superimposed on the real image of lower time densities.

This is why UFOs and ETs can take on utterly incongruous shapes. ETs may do so to remain anonymous, to show a sense of humor or simply to respect the local and historic beliefs. The size of the vessels and their maneuvers are quite relative and are determined by the materialization stage. In accordance with absolute relativity, a small fifteen-meter vessel may transform into a five hundred-meter vessel or in a dot of light depending on the time density attained.

Since the internal temporal density of a vessel is higher (closer to the rotor), it is always larger on the inside than on the outside. This has been reported by numerous abductees.

Some crop circles are made by UFOs. Crop circles are among the most spectacular phenomena in ufology. These geometric shapes are left behind in farmland where the stems of the crop have been flattened. The differences in height between vertical and horizontal stems constitute a crop circle. Viewed from above they are even more spectacular. The geometry is not always circular. Some of these cereal shapes are huge, several hundreds of meters in diameter. This phenomenon occurs almost on a worldwide scale. While the first contemporary circles were found in England — well known for its humid climate — they quickly multiplied in appearance in Europe and on the American continent. At the moment there is insufficient data from other parts of the world. The film *Signs* starring Mel Gibson that came out in 2003 centered on this phenomenon. It is perhaps unfortunate that the producer's version of the truth was actually way off. These crop circles[118] are the most tangible sign left behind by ETs. They are measurable, sustainable, repetitive (annual), didactic and macroscopic. That is why it is important to examine them more closely.

Some crop circles are man-made. They are the work of discrete artists or university students who, unlike most, do not sign their work, or very rarely. This form of modesty may seem virtuous, but is actually just another misinformation method. As some kind of hoax, or in a deliberate attempt to cover cosmological tracks, crop makers such as Dave and Doug, two English septuagenarians nicknamed the "grandpa hoaxers," are the typical agents of anti-UFO propaganda. Their instrument is simple: a sufficiently heavy plank pulled by ropes to flatten the wheat. Needless to say, although this method is silent, it still takes considerable time to cover the area of some of the achievements that are out there. Have you ever been in the middle of a field of wheat ready to be harvested? You will be at least hip-deep in wheat. You will have to crush all the stems in your path to achieve an artistic pattern. This inevitably leaves behind tracks that cannot be seen in numerous real formations. While you are on the ground, instead of at a certain altitude, your mental projection of the complex shape to draw will lead to countless inaccuracies and inevitable angular deviations. Many crop circles occur at night. You will have to use spotlights to work, thus reducing the odds of remaining anonymous, unless you wear night vision infrared goggles. In that case you may risk permanent eye damage if the tenfold intensity of blindingly bright headlights of a vehicle passing in the early morning happens to hit the rods of your retina.

Even for a group of people it is impossible to create a crop circle in a time span as short as measured in some cases, in no more than a few minutes. In addition, what about the complex pattern of stems woven in counter flow to each other found in genuine crop circles? It is impossible to copy such patterns with a simple plank. Because of the tools used, the human artworks can be distinguished from authentic crop circles by the inaccuracy of the measurements, the absence of microwave radiation and the absence of entanglements, of anomalies to the nodes of the stems or of abnormal growth of the seed heads.

Some have tried to explain these agroglyphs[119] by the intervention of highly sophisticated military technologies. Indeed, the hypothesis of the plank with ropes is dispelled in some farmlands, and in some cultured minds. Microwave laser-type technologies would be loaded upon stratospheric balloons for testing. Aside from the insurmountable difficulties of stabilizing these balloons at high altitudes (some jet streams may reach up to four hundred kph) and the inherent inaccuracy, the major question is why such tests would be conducted in civilian fields! What is to gain by realizing complex figures at the risk of no one seeing them? Why bother peaceful farmers in several dozens of countries, rather than use the vast militarized zones where wheat would grow just as well? Everyone knows that discretion is paramount when it comes to military tests. However, in these extraordinary cases it is the exact opposite. In addition, even at a distance of several meters from the stems, it requires incredible accuracy to "light up" and target with a laser beam the first joint or node of the seed head that bends the stem when it yields. This growth is close to the ground and therefore masked by the denseness of the field. So imagine doing this at a distance of twenty thousand meters! Aiming at a target you cannot see and hitting it in the first attempt…that is what the military hypothesis suggests. Like the truth, the light of the microwaves comes from "elsewhere."

We have arrived at the ET hypothesis, the version of absolute relativity. A considerable number of these geometric representations has been realized by vessels or (sometimes invisible) probes located in very high temporal densities, to the point of being mere minuscule luminescent dots of light. Eyewitness accounts, as well as videos (!), include large luminosities moving at a dizzying speed at no more than a few meters above agroglyphs being formed!

The properties of genuine crop circles were identified years ago by expert biologists and botanists, in particular by Professor Levengood, and includes the mystery of the first node of the flattened stem mentioned above, which is characterized by abnormal thickening or a clean and simple break. However, another node in a similar state can be found a bit higher on the stem. It seems as if the seed heads have been saturated with water and boiled by microwave radiation. Another astonishing factor is the amazingly fast ripening of the seeds (dozens of times faster than in laboratory samples). Thirdly, countless witnesses experienced nausea after prolonged exposure to the circles. In short, there are far too many mysterious phenomena to justify human origins. How can they be explained then? If they are not man-made they must be extraterrestrial, we are told. Still, how do they proceed?

Once again, absolute relativity provides us with the answer! The first factor to be considered is condensation, which is more common at night than during the day. When the outside temperature drops, it approaches dew point, i.e., the temperature at which invisible water vapor changes into fine microscopic droplets. This is how mist is formed. Crop circles particularly form at night, when the circumstances for humidity are more favorable. Great Britain also possesses this hygrometric peculiarity making it a perfect location.

Moreover, we have seen that when the dematerialized vessel is stationary, a spatio-temporal differential caused by its temporal bubble produces condensation (caused by temperature reduction, linked to a slight Brownian movement of the vessel particles). Before creating a crop circle, the still invisible UFO will hover over the field in a stationary position long enough to saturate it with humidity. No one will notice. One could even wonder why a sudden fog has appeared. However, what is more natural than meteorological oddities, especially in England? Let me add that, as we will see, the night is not dark in high time densities. It is often as bright as daylight.

In the second stage the vessel descends to a lower temporal density and becomes luminous. It also emits in the microwave spectrum, just below infrared. These emissions immediately affect the seed heads in two ways.

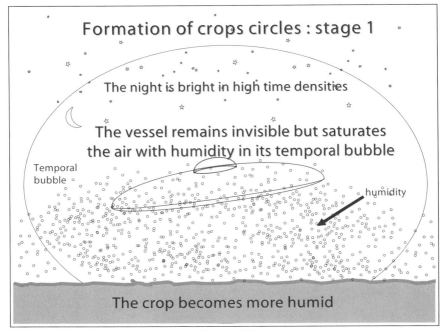

Figure 117

The radiation ionizes the air and the water. As the wheat is being coated in humidity, it immediately absorbs this water and softens for several minutes due to a slight microwave boiling.

Moreover, the wheat plants themselves are turned into weak magnets because they are ionized by the water they contain.[120] They can therefore be easily bent during the third stage. This is the creative period. It is short from our point of view, but sufficiently long for an ET artist inside a high temporal density. Our seconds equal their minutes.

In the third stage, the vessel (sometimes several) covers an extremely precise trajectory for two reasons. The first is that, in absolute relativity, what the passenger sees outside his vessel is proportionally larger than our standard. A wheat seed head can resemble an electric pole if it is inside the temporal bubble. In addition, the vessel is assisted by calculating means that approach the colossal possibilities of a quantum computer. A high time density signifies an infinite entropy (amount of information). Like an airplane calculates its navigation, the trajectory of the vessel is thus programmed to realize the desired geometric shape. The most complex shapes become child's play. However, what happens to the wheat?

In a way, the wheat is partially "abducted" or taken! Unlike isolated human beings that are not tied down to the land, the wheat field is rooted into the soil. When we see ETs going down from their vessels to extract plants it is exactly because that is the only way they can do it.

This is where absolute relativity makes its most fascinating contribution. The part that is firmly rooted into the ground is kept in the ST of Earth. This part will therefore not be subject to the contraction of space and the dilation of time in the same way as the part located beyond the first node. In a way, this node is the weakest link. As the vessel luminosity goes by, everything located above the node contracts. By contracting in both directions (of the length), from the bottom to the top and vice versa, the upper part of the seed head pulls up the part connected to the soil almost mechanically. The lower part resists. It remains in the Earth fractal. The first node dislocates so fast because it has absorbed a large quantity of humidity during the first stage. It is a bit like tearing off the leaves from an herb in an upward motion. The weakest spot yields. As the node has become more fragile the upper part easily bends.

Since gravity is low inside the bubble, it is, however, only after the passage thereof that the wheat will begin to fall down, thus causing the lower part to fall down as well. While this spatio-temporal mechanism is not as violent as the human hand, it is still sufficiently strong to explain widely reported distortions, one of which is the accelerated germination of the seed heads. The very brief exposure to a high temporal density has caused them to go through a temporal growth spur (time goes by more quickly). Observant readers will understand that reforestation and abundant energetic crop cultivation could replace the current ecological and nutrition imbalances if science was the least bit interested in absolute relativity. Is this not also one of the messages conveyed by crop circles?

Finally, the fourth stage is that of the actual artistic effect. The ionized seed heads behave like magnets and follow the magnetic field of the vessel! As they shrink (increase of molecular density), they become even more ionized. Since they are still soft and the vessel flies over them sufficiently fast, they simply lie down one on top of the other to follow the movement of this magnetic "aspirator."

Moreover, the trajectory of the vessel partially goes over an already flattened zone again, a bit like going over several lines with a highlighter pen. The imprint will be darker on the intersection of two linear surfaces. The magnetic field of the UFO, while slightly out of phase compared to the previous passage, once again attracts already flattened stems lifting them slightly, this time from the side. It weaves

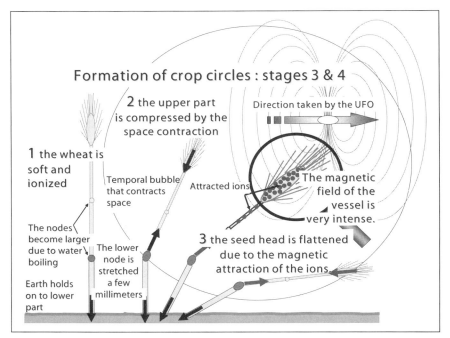

Figure 118

them with the adjacent stems when the latter bend down. Like the intersection of two highlighted lines, there are thus zones of woven patterns inside crop circles. Take into account that this is a very rapid process because, even though the ionization of the wheat is moderate, the magnetic field of the vessel is enormous, several teslas large. The stems therefore respond immediately without actually being torn off.

The fifth stage is the drying phase. Like food prepared in a microwave oven, but at a relatively low intensity, the wheat progressively loses part of its humidity due to the residual microwave radiation. It remains edible. Its premature growth even renders it ready for consumption in less time. Since it is still connected to the Earth it continues to grow. Ethically speaking, no food is wasted. Their temporal youth bath causes the affected wheat plants to keep a high energy level.

As a consequence, witnesses on site are also affected. The nausea experienced is caused by a slightly different temporal flow in the center of the crop circle, less mixed with the traditional Earth temporal density than on the outskirts. This difference disappears....over time. Before that happens it would be useful to conduct mental experiments in the center of these formations for those who have the ability. Perhaps crop circles are quite simply a telepathic means of communication between them and us...We just admire them on photographs without actually going there. Maybe that is why we do not understand their purpose.

Finally, specialists may observe a thickening of the nodes that were humidified, stretched and boiled. However, the stems return to their original size when they return to normal time flow. The contraction and expansion of the stems therefore goes by unnoticed. The meaning of the geometries of crop circles is a whole different discussion. Let me just say in general that the frequently observed fractal shapes constitute technical information directly related to the scientific clues of the fractal nature of space and time described in this book. It is also how the ETs, who admire our artistic sense, show us their artwork. In their time scale, crop circles last for centuries.

Discrepancies between eyewitness accounts do not always mean that the stories are made up. If two witnesses are at different distances from a vessel (even if the difference is small), they may have a very different perception of the craft, both in shape, in size or in the nature of the sighting; they may see a mere light or the shape of the vessel.

If two witnesses are located at very different distances, this deviation may even range between nothing and everything. Apparitions of the Virgin Mary[121] stem from the same phenomenon, depending on the

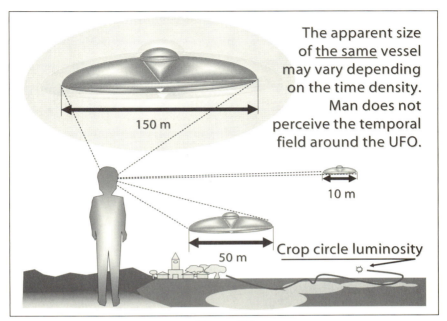

The apparent size of the same vessel may vary depending on the time density. Man does not perceive the temporal field around the UFO.

150 m

10 m

50 m

Crop circle luminosity

Figure 119

mental ability of each person and/or the influence of the temporal bubble of the entity.

According to absolute relativity, a temporary temperature increase shows the sudden presence of an unusual temporal field differentiation (the temporal bubble). This explains the burns sustained by some witnesses caused by microwaves. These microwaves are nothing other than the expression of a superior time density. However, it is possible that after an adjustment time, this temperature drops to a great cold, as seen in paranormal phenomena, because there is mutual resonance between the STs (temporal bubble and visited location).

Whether or not witnesses feel a temperature change depends essentially on how fast or how slow the temporal effects occur. When a UFO hovers in the same position sufficiently long and progressively changes its temporal field it may seem as if the temperature has not changed. Reports of sightings may also include slight time slips (see missing time). The descriptions are therefore largely determined by the given situation and the abilities of each person (which makes these phenomena so difficult to grasp).

The density of time decreases as it moves farther away from the vessel. Hence the order given by the American administration not to go near it. The temporal field is a barrier in itself: one can have the perception of

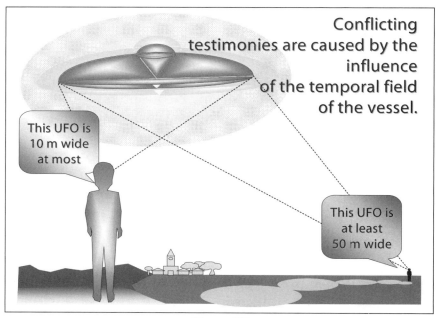

Figure 120

being paralyzed as soon as it is approached (vital sign changes). For example, when a human body dives into the water its movements are slowed down significantly. In the same way, paralysis is not in itself a sign of hostility, but an imponderable linked to the laws of physics.

Sleep paralysis affects numerous witnesses. The traditional explanations explain absolutely nothing. They replace the true experience by words. In absolute relativity, sleep paralysis is caused by a temporal flow deviation between the physical body and the local surroundings. The latter may be the result of two situations.

In the first, the consciousness is localized in the astral body only, of which the temporal flow is then the individual's preferred time. In other words, he will feel as if his physical body no longer responds. This paralysis may cause the individual to panic. To protect ourselves against it, it is first of all necessary to understand this mechanism of temporal differentiation. It is necessary to wait patiently until the reintegration in the body is complete. This can be done by visualization.

In the second situation, the most commonly known type of sleep paralysis is caused by the presence of an entity in the room. The symptoms are always the same: sensing a strange presence (sometimes visible), a heightened state of consciousness, the inability to command muscles to move, the impression of being crushed, feeling cold, feeling at the mercy of the entity, growing fear. Like witnesses of ETs close to the vessel, paralyzed by their proximity or by a beam of high temporal density, those who go through such a sleep paralysis experience a time flow differentiation. Taking into account that human organs possess their own vital signs and vibratory level, the denser ones will no longer be in temporal connection with that part of the brain responsible for motor control. In terms of connectivity, we should remember that the brain is the most suitable organ to adjust and elevate to superior time densities. The more "primitive" organs are unable to do so.

Between these two extremes, certain functions remain operational, including the eyes, the lungs and the blood circulation. These functions and organs seem to have a fractal structure or arborescence. Please note that the nervous system itself is not paralyzed because its offshoots unfold in fractals (like the branches of a tree). Witnesses are therefore able to receive information from their body such as the temperature, the weight of the covers, physical noises, etc. Only the "primitive" organs stay below the threshold of the required temporal density. The vital signs of the body are therefore not jeopardized. There is no mortal risk, except for a lethal fear that may cause a cardiac arrest in extreme cases (a very rare occurrence, often related to black magic). It is not easy to control such situations without training. Once again,

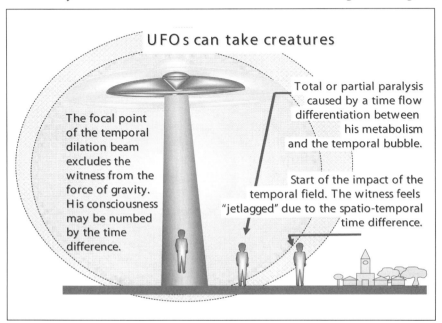

Figure 121

understanding this mechanism will facilitate the experience. Neverthe-less, the best defense is to address the creature, reminding him that it is you who makes the decisions.

Vessels can take objects, animals or people. The temporal field behaves like an electromagnetic field. It can therefore be focused on and directed at a specific point. Considering the fact that the force of gravity is determined by the flow of time, the weight (which is a force) disappears where the beam is directed, this being the focal point of temporal dilation.

Note that the truncated light beams perceived by some witnesses can be simply explained by the boundary of the temporal bubble above which the frequency of the projected light changes (time change) and renders it invisible.

Vessels may multiply. Permanent "pump priming" is ensured by two rotors with inverted rotation transformed in some kind of highly ener-getic undulatory cold plasma (on our physical plane) with a variable fre-quency in an empty chamber, which itself is included in other less and less empty chambers like Russian nesting dolls (depending on the model of the vessels). This pump primer is the core of an extremely dense tem-poral field on which the whole of the vessel and its surroundings

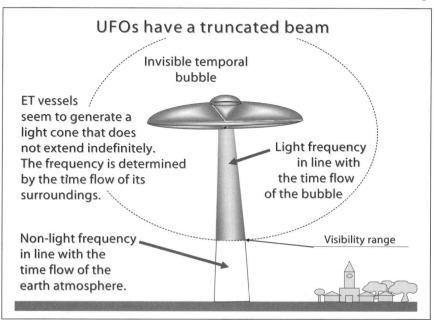

Figure 122

depend. Before materialization, a vessel is an enormous matter wave (tuned to several frequencies) that may be doubled as many times as needed, because this is the same wave function projected into space, like paired photons in quantum entanglement. All frequencies are inter-linked to a (crystal) oscillator located above or below the pump primer to vibrate the entire content of the vessel at harmonic frequencies. This requires pure materials tuned to a very specific spectrum. However, as long as the light vessels remain non-materialized, they can remerge into the same wave function in a higher temporal density.

This is why seemingly separate lights may be observed that join to form a single one. In fact, they were always one and the same appari-tion to begin with, stretching out in a ST by "corpuscular diffraction." Logically speaking, these multiplications do not occur when UFOs are already materialized.

UFOs can be detected by the proper means, even if they are invisi-ble. Such means can be physical or mental. Let us first talk about radar.

Radar emits on wavelengths that can be much lower than radio waves and higher than light waves. Every type of radar emits and receives in a specific spectrum (frequency range or band). The principle of radar is to send waves in all directions that material bodies, either

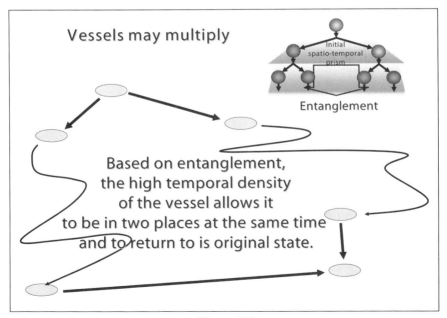

Figure 123

moving or stationary, reflect. Solid objects send back only a small part of the waves towards the detection module, like a mirror reflects the light. This weak signal is amplified manifold and subsequently translated on a screen in the form of a luminous plot. The latter moves on the screen in the same way as the detected object, depending on the selected distance scale. This is called primary detection (real signal).

Modern aircraft are equipped with a transponder emitting an identification code. This secondary detection, combined with kinematical data calculated by the device, provides an important amount of information (flight number, speed, flight level, rate of descent, etc.). The difference between military and civilian air traffic controllers is that the first always work with primary detection, whereas the latter use only secondary detection.

Materialized UFOs can therefore in theory be detected by radar. This has actually been reported by numerous stations, both military and civilian. However, there are countless cases in which the controllers did not detect any tangible signs. This absence of detection contradicts eyewitness accounts. It is said that UFOs have a stealth mode, just like certain modern military craft. This technique is essentially based on the dispersion of incidental waves generated by the angular contour or, on the contrary, a very round contour of the craft, which renders the radar incapable of amplifying even the slightest signal. Materialized UFOs are often flattened disks that offer an ideal detection surface for air traffic controllers. How can they slip by unnoticed and escape the sophisticated technology of military radar? It is suggested that they are made of graphite, which is known for its ability to absorb electromagnetic waves, or even that they ionize the surrounding air, creating a protective cloak. We can notice the partial ionization of the atmosphere by the smell of "ozone" often reported in close contact. Nevertheless, this explanation does not suffice.

The answer is still based on the same principle of the temporal bubble. The frequency of radar waves entering the temporal bubble of a vessel is inevitably changed. If this change is too significant and even if the vessel is materialized, the incidental frequency is no longer compatible with the radar spectrum but exceeds it. It is thus possible to see a vessel with the naked eye, even when it is not picked up by radar.

Its stealthiness, which is inevitably variable depending on the time density attained in the bubble, consists of modifying the detection frequency itself instead of changing the trajectory (principle of our own stealth planes).

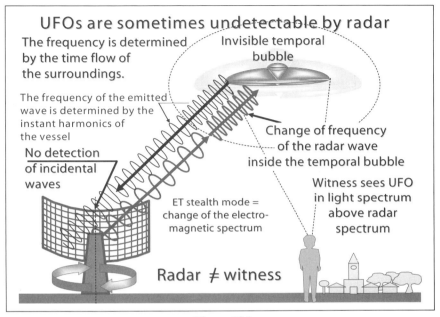

Figure 124

Prior to materialization a vessel is an enormous matter wave (tuned to various frequencies) emitting harmonics, including lower frequencies. A materializing vessel — by decreasing its temporal density — emits increasingly lower frequencies (redshift), such as microwaves (below the spectrum of light, which it hardly ever leaves to remain in stealth mode). Therefore, a craft can be detected by using a microwave detector or even an X-ray scan emitting large amounts of energy. The difficulty is to look in the right place and to sufficiently amplify the signal.

Considering the rapid displacement of vessels, the detection has to cover a large range simultaneously. To do so, a "faceted atmospheric mirror" must be created to reflect the high-frequency waves back at detection stations. In nature, the ionosphere reflects large radio waves in the same way. This is one of the objectives of the HAARP weapon system.[122] The different colored light beams observed on UFOs are in fact analysis beams of which only part of the spectral rays is perceived. Their purpose is to identify any form of emission that may compromise the integrity of the vessel on several wavelengths. Every destructive external frequency is analyzed as either a threat or a potential opportunity.

Another way to interfere with the navigation of vessels is to send out high-energy and high-frequency longitudinal waves, equivalent to

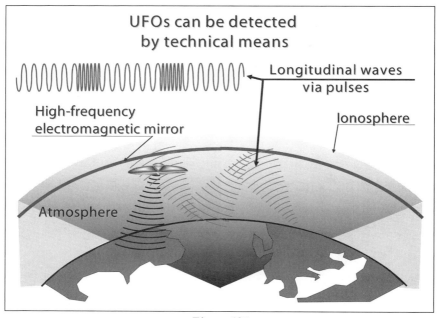

Figure 125

highly energetic ions that subsequently disrupt the control of the craft. The HAARP system emits such waves.

Microwave radiation is often found at landing sites. It is evidence of materialization. If we had the necessary means, we could measure X-rays and gamma rays in light apparitions, i.e., physical traces depending on the stage of materialization.

Mental means of detection also exist. Witnesses who report feeling watched by a UFO, whether it has materialized or not, are affected by a partial change of temporal density causing an increased mental perceptiveness. They have become part of the temporal field of the vessel and approach the time flow of the psychic function. In other words, this psychic perceptiveness is "simply" determined by the unusually small temporal difference between the (alien) emitter source and the (human) receptor source. It is then possible to set up a dialogue by exchanging mental images (thought forms). Teams of remote viewers can detect the presence of invisible vessels.

In remote viewing, our consciousness projects itself at specific locations or beings. Scientific Remote Viewing (SRV), used by the military and American secret services, was born during the Cold War. SRV would have been used by the CIA for espionage purposes in the framework of the Grillflame and Stargate projects. Two institutes participated: the Stanford Research Institute of Technology and the Monroe Institute. Harold Puthoff, the author of *Mind Research* written in 1977 together with Russel Targ, was extremely interested. It was also Puthoff who proposed one of the world's most sophisticated UFO propulsion modes. The following description pretty much covers it. Between 1970 and 1990, a sum of twenty million dollars was allegedly spent on developing a remote viewing program. Curiously, and against the expectations of the espionage services, the remote viewers brought back information provided by ETs and about UFOs! It is often ignored that such projections may be subject to a considerable time difference, which may have led the CIA to abandon its research efforts, or in the very least with regard to its prime objective, i.e., research on human enemy sites.

The crystal (oscillator) of the vessel also serves as a mental relay between all living creatures, both human and animal. An entire range of feelings may be emitted towards a particular creature — of reassurance or fright — without the emitter himself actually being the source of the emitted feeling. Benevolent ETs can project feelings of fear, according to the witnesses concerned (war pilots for instance), to protect themselves. On the other hand, negative entities cannot send positive feelings because their vibration is incompatible.

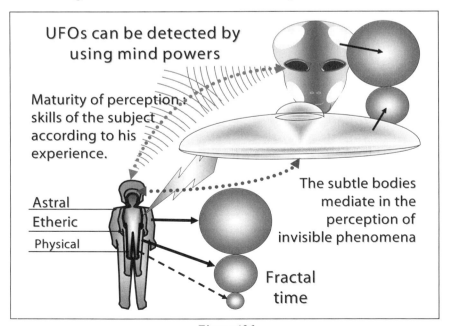

Figure 126

ETs can choose the witnesses: a mental broadcast inhibits perceptions and vice versa.

The vessels are piloted mentally. The vessels are controlled by means of a high-quality mental link (easy in high temporal densities) and/or sensory link (by hand) via the crystal that sends back the temporal navigation order to the pump primer, i.e., the inverted rotors. The vessel becomes a living being piloted by another one. A focused mind is imperative to piloting a vessel. Please note that the primer adjusts to the local temporal density changes controlled by the crystal, spreading through the vessel by harmonic contamination.

Missing time cannot be explained as mere memory loss. Missing time is a space-time continuum rift caused by the transport of an individual into a temporal field that is not his own (where time goes by more quickly compared to our material plane).

The feeling of being abducted is strongly connected to the paralysis of the physical body which this transfer renders obligatory, unless it has an altered, more-complex DNA that can adapt to high frequencies. The individual feels incapable of responding. This impression is real for the physical body, but does not apply to the bodies or organs of a higher temporal density (etheric, astral, mental, spiritual). This explains why

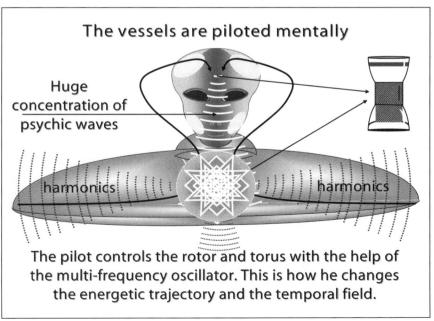

The vessels are piloted mentally

Huge concentration of psychic waves

harmonics   harmonics

The pilot controls the rotor and torus with the help of the multi-frequency oscillator. This is how he changes the energetic trajectory and the temporal field.

Figure 127

paralyzed witnesses can still move their eyes[123] (otherwise they would not be witnesses) and remain conscious of what they see.

Most of the time, however, abductees become aware of their abduction only after noticing the missing time on their watch. They do not remember what happened or if anything happened due to a consistent loss of information after returning from the experience, as if waking from a dream (cf. immaterial entropy). This is a return from a higher temporal density than in the aforementioned case (conscious witness).

It can be explained by the fact that higher time densities contain larger amounts of information. Based on the generalized second law of entropy stating that the immaterial possesses more information than the material, every experience, incorrectly called imaginary, is in fact the essence of an entropy — in terms of information — greater than the events of the physical world. After returning to the physical time flow, this information disappears because it cannot be retained (there are fewer time quanta). I should add that vessels travel in time. By going back into the past, even a little — prior to an abduction, for example, or prior to a crucial moment of the experience — it may seem as if the situation never took place. The abductee whose unconscious mind cannot comprehend the disappearance of a causal relation in physical time feels as if nothing ever happened.

When psychologists speak of creating false memories, which sometimes occurs in the waking state when it is not in line with a higher entropy, they utterly disregard the bases of fundamental physics. Of course, that is not their field of expertise. The excessive use of statistics does not even begin to explain the real mechanisms. Most individuals do not have the perceptual maturity required to screen the information they receive to distinguish between the emission of waves (creation) and their reception (real perception) during telepathic experiences. The discipline of human sciences reduces the importance of the "reception" element in the creative part. The problem of debates is that ignorance has declared itself the truth.

It is almost impossible to ascertain the nature of the experience with the help of a mechanism used to return to the temporal densities where the experience took place. A conscious effort allows those who regularly meditate or who make an effort to remember their dreams (both using the same mechanism) to recall all or part of this experience. Sleep, meditation, remote viewing and hypnosis all trigger a similar process. We detach ourselves from the physical time flow by reducing

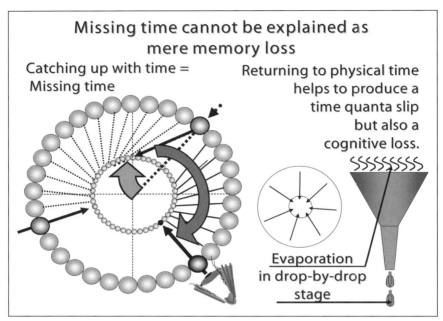

Figure 128

the temporal influence of the body as much as possible, or at least partially, in a fixed posture. The mind cannot access other, currently inaccessible temporal densities when the physical body is in motion, except in exceptional cases.

Countless witnesses claim they possess new parapsychological talents as a result of an abduction experience. This makes total sense. Without verbalizing it, they assimilated the mechanism of temporal ascension after the experience, which proves that some "abductions" are a source of development. Finally, I should state that we can increase our perceptiveness in non-mental ways, by being inside a space shuttle (macroscopic temporal pumping) and/or inside a high-speed rotation device generating spinning electromagnetic fields (macroscopic and microscopic temporal pumping), for instance. Such experiences should not last too long to avoid any harmful side effects.

Witnesses say that vessels do not have a source of light on the inside. Many abductees mention the fact that the illumination on board does not seem to come from a specific source.

In accordance with 3D time, time elapses more slowly during electronic phenomena, which makes it much easier to see the energy emanating from atomic stimulations (emission of photons) that cause only

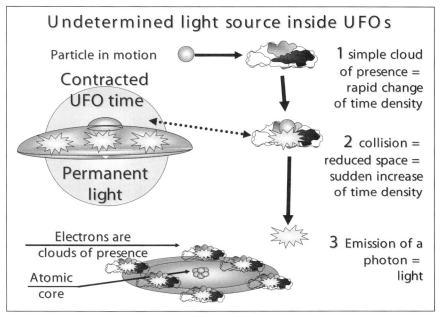

Figure 129

partial appearance of these phenomena in our world. Our conscious-ness receives a much larger number of these stimulations in high tem-poral densities because of the dominant local entropy.

As for electron self-energy, vacuum polarization and so-called "dressed" vertices, please note that the Feynman diagrams foresee the existence of photons that are born and disappear without us being able to ever notice them because they do not travel at the atomic scale. Feynman described the photon-absorbed-electron-emitted phenome-non, in which incoming photons are immediately emitted and absorbed by an electron, explaining the deviations between theoretical calculus and experimental values of the magnetic moment of an elec-tron. There was only one ten-millionth of a difference between theory and experiment for four incoming, unobservable (so-called virtual) photons, which become invisible to a photon that is visible to the macroscopic world. These four photons are, however, perfectly visible in high time densities. Here the most dominant energy of the sur-roundings is determined. Light comes from everywhere because it is everywhere. Therefore, it also makes sense that the sky at night is in fact bright during a temporal UFO flight. In general, there are one thousand photons for one particle in the interstellar void!

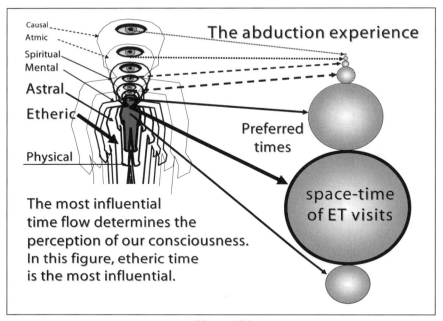

Figure 130

Abductions are not always a sign of aggressiveness of those who commit them. Abductions are either effective kidnappings (in the traditional sense) for the purpose of medical-mental experiments conducted against the will of individuals or emergency mental care, as practiced by medical professionals on the physical body (after sustaining traumas, falling ill, etc.), in which case the intervention is positive. Sometimes they simply make contact with an individual in preparation of an upcoming collective interracial rapprochement.

It is difficult for human beings to retain knowledge of all the consciously chosen personal experiences that occur in high time densities. This reality cannot be brought back into our physical world due to a loss of temporal quanta. In other words, our unconscious mind is a reservoir of information located in the high temporal densities that can only be accessed consciously by regular meditation and visualization. This does require sufficient self-knowledge. What we are and do in the high densities often has nothing to do with our incarnated personality. The inscription at the temple of Delphi expresses it well: "man, know thyself and you will know the universe and the Gods." Our identity is therefore a matter of perspective. Our identity is relative, as are the events that concern us.

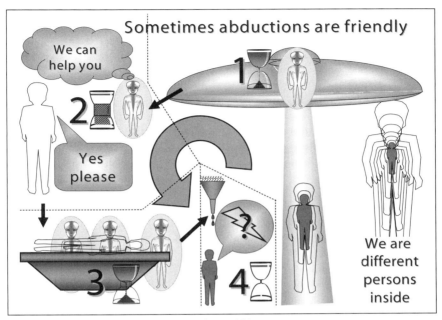

Figure 131

Knowledge of self and of our true choices requires us to study ourselves like an object. In that sense, we can take offense by an event that takes place against our will but we speak in fact of our will as a lesser physical human being and not as an evolved telepathic human being. Just imagine, in our dreams we do things we would never dare to do in the waking state. When it comes to abductions, we compare incomparable choices: the ones made in the waking state and the ones made in the state of superconsciousness. So we can either disregard what takes place in high temporal densities, where we use our waking analysis ability unwisely, or access it as often as possible, by meditation for example, and discover its true nature without making poorly adapted "deductive inferences." In other words, the term abduction is sometimes inappropriate. It is a mental experience similar to being taken, but from which we emerge matured, even transformed and feeling better about ourselves. It is a deliberate choice to "play the game." Affirming our personality allows us to gain more knowledge about whom we are dealing with in the high time densities. However, all abductions are not friendly. It also allows us to defend ourselves adequately against potential aggressions. We must know the definition of "I" to know what "I" really wants.

Vessels travel in time. At first sight, time travel poses difficulties once described in a book as the paradox of the grandfather (past) and knowledge (future).

Barjavel wrote a science fiction novel in which a careless traveler went back in time and changed it. He inadvertently killed his grandfather before the mother of the traveler was born. This means he could not have been born, or have made this voyage, or have killed his grandfather for that matter. Hence the paradox.

A book (could it be this one?) about future knowledge was dictated by a time traveler from the future to a man from the present. He had it edited. This knowledge thus became part of the present, in which case it was no longer part of the future. So who was the real author of this information?

The real problem lies in the causality of such phenomena. A correct definition of "travel" and "time" is indispensable to understanding time travel. A concise answer could be that time travel does not exist and that it is therefore futile to even consider it. It would be superfluous to challenge the concept of causality because it is the very foundation of science born under Descartes. It is impossible to travel a road that does not exist! The issue of time travel is not a simple matter of imagination that we will be able to concretize some day, because it actually boils down to rejecting the basis of science: reproducibility! If strict causality is the attribute of the essence of phenomena, everything is reproducible, as scientists love to think. It is then enough to create the conditions of a cause to produce an expected and measurable effect. However, we have seen that reality is changed by how we look at it.

Discussing time travel leads us to some rather curious questions: what is traveling really, under which conditions, and why? That last question is hardly ever asked. However, it constitutes the heart of the problem. In fact, it seems to be brought up by the very word. If this mystery seems inaccessible to us, is it not because we are not ready? Is it not because the wishes underlying our questions change their meaning and render them inadequate? Just as watching one single thing changes it and makes it appear (quantum mechanics), so could wishing for something very well close the path to it or, quite the opposite, make it happen.

It is often said that a large part of consciousness is perception. However, would there not be a higher degree of consciousness that consists of wishful thinking? Apparently, this wish is not only related to future things, but also to things in the past. In other words, does not the cause called intent play a role in the game of cause and effect? If the intent is to change causes for a trip to the past, whereas it is a cause itself, there is an incompatibility that cancels out the perceptual function of our consciousness, the effect of which can only be proportional to what is readily accessible, such as punctual and isolated experiments of quantum mechanics. May I remind you that a quantum mechanics experiment requires the definition of some thirty parameters, which comes down to isolating the effects on the surroundings as much as possible and keeping the course of collective events intact. In short, time travel is possible only when we know what to expect. The elegance of this approach lies in the fact that the so dreaded paradoxes are dissolved thanks to the means that enables time travel: neutral, non-destructive intent! The quality of the witness determines the quality of this neutrality. The notion of time travel is difficult to define. Therefore, the figures below try to represent the mechanism called "travel" as accurately as possible.

As long as we are sealed in our material time density, or rather in the ST to which the speed of the Earth subjects us, we cannot possibly verify whether or not such travel exists. We are not in the right vehicle. Other vehicles exist also: the etheric body, the astral body, the mental body, the spiritual body, etc.

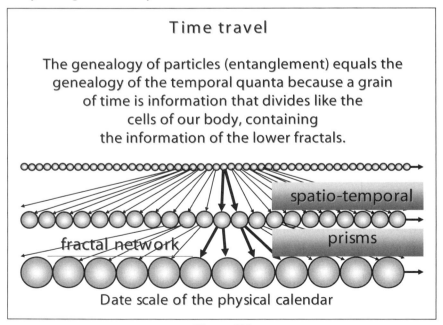

Figure 132

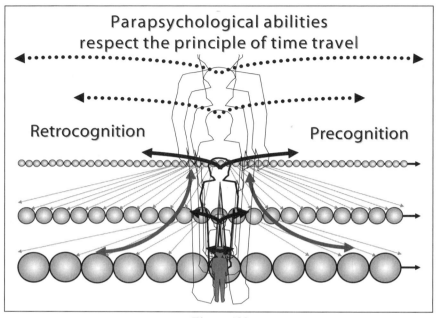

Figure 133

Each of these vehicles corresponds to a specific temporal density where time is more or less easily manipulated and malleable. Time can be manipulated by quantum entanglement, allowing history to unfold through the expansion of space. This property favors time travel and thus retrocognition, precognition and prophecies. Our natural tendency is such that some students of esotericism have tried hard to consider only the bodies cited above rather than the bath in which they are dipped. These baths are exactly the STs of which we speak. In scientific terms, they are electromagnetic waves tuned to fractals! Slowly but surely, we are beginning to see that time travel means altering a vibratory level, i.e., a frequency. A UFO is thus a "fabricated" body bathing in an ST. Science consists of examining and manipulating the container, i.e., physical magnitudes (the signifiers), whereas consciousness consists in examining and manipulating the content, i.e., symbolism (the signified)! This has a remarkable consequence: a vessel is always inhabited by the consciousness that directs it, even if we do not see it, because it must be aware of its temporal trajectory.

We have seen that space and time do not exist in an intrinsic manner, but that our intellect needed them to "construct" that in which the phenomena take place. In fact, only our consciousness is left to receive and emit.

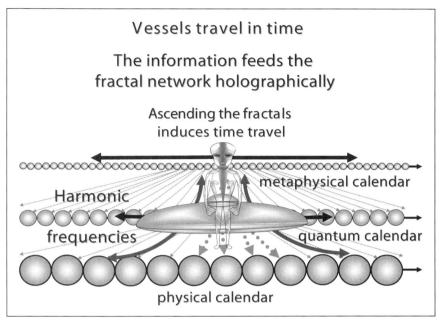

Figure 134

The only purpose of this detour is to concretely feel that materialization and dematerialization are required stations in time travel. This transfer works around the paradoxes that are essentially based on our incorrect ideas about time travel. We need to bear in mind that an ST is first and foremost an amount of available information. By materializing ourselves we lose a huge part of this information, particularly about the past and the future. What is to gain by going back to a material past that inhibits our freedom? In addition, the concept of free will does not make any sense if we can get away with changing the physical past and our past choices can be contradicted, which is contrary to nature and the love of the deity within us. Neither causality by determinism, nor causality by freedom thus has any basis. In reality, we can relive the past without being able to change the choices made by our past selves (in a previous life or otherwise).

We remain spectators, except when we take over a physical body that is not ours. This happens when someone is possessed, the most manifest form of disrespect for the divine laws in time travel. The price to pay will then be very high for the one who risks such an endeavor. Please note that our Internal Master is no other than our future self; in other words our self in the highest temporal densities (i.e., our destination!). By listening to it, by allowing it to become the better part of us, we accelerate our liberation. This decision is in itself a choice made in our present, in our current living state! The Internal Master, who is closest to God (= very high temporal densities), is in fact the quest of future religions in the etymological sense of the word (*religare:* to connect).

It is amusing to ask which advice we would take from ourselves if we had to talk to our past self. This captures all the constraints of the so-called free will. However, whose free will? Of the ignoramus or of the wise man within us? It is easy to understand that this depends on experience, on knowledge. Such knowledge of time travel is accessible once we have understood the modalities of these 'reflective interferences'.

Another "detail" could easily be overlooked. Returning to the material state means we are subject to the laws of aging and risk the trials and tribulations of physical pain. Those who are accustomed to living in a very high energetic state (high temporal density) will hardly be interested in aging rapidly and even less in losing awareness again (loss of temporal quanta). This is one of the reasons why ETs and their vessels rarely materialize! They have achieved immortality.

If we had to change the past, we could actually supply information only to someone already willing to embrace it. Try to convince stubborn or illiterate people. Attempt to explain to a man from the Middle Ages that your contemporaries have walked upon the moon. What has become of the millions of witnesses of paranormal phenomena? Have they radically changed their lives? Is not their testimony ridiculed, demonized or ignored? Those who accept these paranormal phenomena have already acquired the knowledge they need. It would be worse if we wanted to change the point of view of millions.

The collective unconscious mind is powerful. The apprenticeship is a mechanism that requires a relatively long time in our ST because the global wave function of matter prevails and influences our reflexes. The nature of proof or of an illusion (for witnesses from the past and the present) is determined only by the time period that we traverse. In fact, the truth is available only to those who look for it, especially in a world where every different possible reality is heard. "How much truth can we take?" I often ask myself.

Therefore, going back into the past of the material world changes the course of history only very little, because the person who goes back exercises only a local influence. The great events of our time are not important in their form, but rather in their profound causes. Collective causality thus has meaning. The inertia of our ST is a good reason for not using transformation energy unnecessarily when it comes to the need for experiences. The paradoxes of the grandfather and of knowledge are therefore inconsequential.

Note that the considerable number of worrisome occurrences in the world marks an intrusion of higher STs. This outbreak is caused by the whole of paranormal abilities and occurrences.

Creating multiple universes to explain each possible historic trajectory is pointless. To paraphrase the famous scientist Paul Davies, it provides but very few explanations, but is an event in a universe of profligate overprovision. Rather than imagining history as a linear route that we choose among so many others, I prefer seeing it as a bubble bath where all the soap bubbles are connected by a surface contact. If we make one bubble disappear, or even several, the foam keeps its coherent structure, because the adjacent bubbles take the place of the ones that have disappeared. It is important to understand that it is not the future that goes to the past and conversely, but higher STs that "inform" other lower STs. This has happened since the dawn of time!

As for the argument suggesting that a past occurrence could have taken place differently if a time traveler had intervened, please remember that the synchronicity of the high time densities generates the occurrences. The time traveler is thus confronted with an incompatibility: the

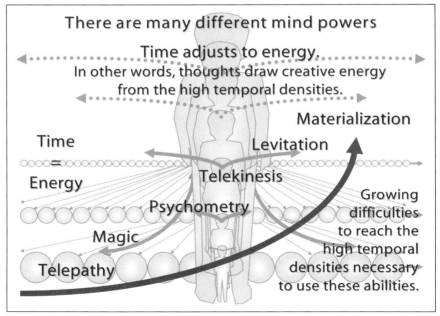

Figure 135

place of chance is already occupied by human intent. In a way, the place of choice is already taken.

The soap bubbles form, un-form and transform into freely moving gas (in particular after death). UFO and paranormal phenomena are these temporal intrusions. Therefore, time travel consists of switching to another ST where time passes more or less quickly because a given temporal flow is always either faster (future), or slower (past) than another. High temporal densities allow us to experience the future of lower densities. The entire history can thus be recorded. This is the role of the Akashic chronicles. From a high temporal density, we travel into the past of another because we systematically anticipate all the occurrences of our present. Since dates have only an intrinsic relevance to a specific ST, projecting ourselves to a specific date is a priori of no consequence whatsoever! Unless we are asked to make a choice...

CHAPTER 52

The causal function: the future of science

SCIENCE IS FOUNDED on the research of laws that link causes and effects. We can explain the mechanisms of the universe by studying these laws as closely as possible. We can control our environment by steering clear of or applying these processes. Science has successfully and exhaustively researched causal relations. The repeated experience of a cause-effect relation demonstrates and therefore determines the power of a lab test on which rests the conviction that this is the reality of the world.

We have seen that this relation is not as clear-cut as we would like, because we add a temporal asymmetry to the description. Therefore, reality leaves us perplexed. This confusion brings about a certain uneasiness, for we make a distinction between what can and cannot be explained. The boundary is fuzzy and we need to look at the universe from another perspective that I am calling the causal function.

This point of view clearly shows time is expressed as an intrinsic part of phenomena and cannot be seen as a separate phenomenon. Nature is not just made of structures that have their own internal interference mechanism (intrinsic causal links). These structures interact and add complexity to the causal network. The structure of our body, for example, absorbs the structure called "water." They become interlinked. The permanence of the links creates a constant need for interaction.

Nevertheless, in some cases these ties are loosened. Two structures can interact with each other without producing significant interactions. Water is composed of molecules from which gas can be extracted. The chemical connections of this gas are ensured by electrons. However, these electrons cannot establish a link between two molecules. This is why gas is liquid. All objects in nature have properties that represent the solidity of cause-effect relations.

Likewise, we can artificially create structures, material and otherwise, of which the properties can be deliberately chosen depending on our goal. That is particularly the object of nanotechnology.

Experimental sciences verify the attributes of a phenomenon. You will increasingly understand that regardless of whether we are talking about material technologies (in all sciences of matter, varying from inert to complex living structures) or about interpersonal relations, any progress could be rejected by the mere causal functions that we control (or almost), personally and/or collectively. The debate about the legitimacy of the soft sciences (human sciences, for example) as opposed to the hard sciences (sciences of matter) is unfounded. Science is all about knowing the causal function of any phenomenon that we observe or try to produce.

The complexity of the whole of cause-effect relations is so high that we substitute what we cannot explain for words such as "coincidence" or "synchronicity."

In reality, we should look for the origin of unexplained links or events, i.e., the causal function, in the ST fractals. This requires understanding and accepting the vital role of the mind. Behind this term numerous ideas are hidden, such as the desire, will, intelligence, emotion, habits, fears, strengths and weaknesses of every visible and invisible being. Whereas we can easily picture our physical body as being composed of a myriad of independent interacting cells constituting one single being, it is more difficult to admit that we are the cells of a larger body. This body is the planetoid called Earth!

Everything that applies to the physical aspect also applies to the more subtle aspects, such as the etheric, astral, mental or spiritual planes. We are all one single being without being aware of it. Do cells know that they are embedded in our brain? Do we know that we are part of this Earth? Will we prove to be the tumor or the genius of our planet? Are we being watched by an invisible neurosurgeon? The causal function, which is fractal in nature, is not just a mathematical toy but the quintessence of knowledge.

We know that the two most important philosophical paths of mankind complement each other, with the East and its passive and contemplative vision on the one hand and, on the other, the West and its active and positivist vision. The first path allows everything to take place in accordance with divine will and respects the cyclicity of nature. The second feels free to pursue any form of progress that serves its purposes. Wisdom dictates that we merge the two approaches by observing the intelligence of the principle of least action (God) and exercising free will uninfluenced by the possibilities of creation. True intelligence therefore consists of respecting and understanding the balance of life (material and spiritual), while developing the personal will to create and cooperate, as most ETs do.

Each event (also called action) is either a cause or an effect. It is also the potential cause-effect of another, different event. In that case, it will be part of a fractal level that is higher than this other event. This chain is called the causal function.

Quarks assemble into protons and neutrons to form nuclei. The nuclei, surrounded by electrons, join together and form molecules. The molecules connect with other molecules and form compounds. The compounds join together and form cells. The cells join together and form organs. The organs join together and form bodies. The bodies join together and form a community. The communities join together and form a race. The races join together and form a planetoid…

Let us stop there, for we should focus on the origin of these assemblies, which is where the laws of the mind reside. Interactions between the psychism of a being (an ET, for example) and a material "dematerializable" structure (a crystalline oscillator, for example) constitute the most efficient result of the causal path possible and unleash great creative powers. Every causal structure is expressed in several fractals. Knowledge therefore means being able to identify in every object or system the causal network of which they are part. The placebo effect[124] is a very good example. Its effect is indicative of our shame to consciously use the powers of the mind, which we call marginal. The cause is even taboo. In some situations, the opposite is true (we create a cause without knowing all the effects).

The placebo effect, which is well known in medical and pharmaceutical circles for its everyday use on millions of patients, is like involuntary telekinesis: the mind influences matter. In fact, the cause of this surprising effect is a given subconscious affirmation: "I will be healed." A sufficiently strong affirmation or suggestion produces spectacular effects. An affirmation does not necessarily need words. This is where symbols come in conveyed by emotional energy. Symbols are a conceptual summary full of images that favor the manifestation of guided thoughts. These can be positive, neutral — but what does neutrality really mean? — or negative. This is the purpose of propaganda used in commercials, sometimes disguised as news.

The fourth estate — the media — owes its great power and many investments to this highly suggestive effect. This genuine form of hypnosis, though subject to certain ethics, remains a strong inhibitor of personal will. A broadcasting company CEO once said that he sold his viewers' brain availability to advertisers.

We have not become total robots, because those who exercise their individual will are sufficiently vigilant to wake up their fellow citizens. They analyze the symbols and make sure that everyone willingly accepts or rejects the associated thought forms. That is the principle of discernment.

Our will is a primordial causal source. We often do not know its nature. Our consumption society creates the illusion of free will, for we choose what we want to do or buy. The more we consume, the less we exercise our will, for there is simply too much choice. We completely forget how to mentally want and ask for something. The answers come to us before we have even expressed the desire. The only thing we express is therefore the system itself.

Everything we mentally send out into the universe comes back to us. The universe is very obedient. If we do not express anything precisely or if we constantly change our request, we will experience the chaos of our ephemeral desires. However, if we are focused on a clear objective (in a group, if possible), the occurrences will be in line with this intention. We do not perceive the tangible reality of the causal power of will for two important reasons:

1. When we give in to the powerful stimuli we receive, we lose the ability to ask for something.
2. We do not know how to ask.

Saying "I want" means informing the universe of what we want. That is all. "Someone" knows that we want it. Then what? We pray (there are countless forms of prayer) that some invisible entity intercedes on our behalf, which it sometimes does. Then what? Do we constantly want to rely on the will of others? Proper interaction is not submission, but cooperation! The one who hears our prayers, if he is spiritually evolved, is faced with a dilemma. He either weakens us by always acting in our stead, in which case we lose our status of conscious beings, but his compassion urges him to help us. He also hopes that we follow in his footsteps. Or he does not respond to our request so that we understand our own co-creative powers.

This second solution is probably the highest form of love, because it allows us to access the same state of "conscious will" as the one from whom we expect to receive something.

At the same time, the second option provides new fields of research, sometimes solutions, into gaining more freedom. Authentic love consists of building one another up and seeing everyone as equal. The question "If God exists, then why does not He help our world?" can be answered by saying: "He loves us so much that He chose to share His powers with us." Divine will is one of them.

However, how then should we ask for something we want? The secret lies in the power of affirmation and the absence of doubt. This means making your own active affirmation this time, rather than repeating one that was imposed! The Holy Scripture has shown us the power of The Word. Let there be Light! And there was Light! Thy Will be done…through Us! Why else would we be here?

Newton's conception of inertia — reference frame without acceleration — is three hundred years old! Einstein's relativity is one hundred years old! The quantum mechanics laid down by Planck, de Broglie, Schrödinger and Heisenberg is almost sixty years old. The world is presently on the brink of a new era: 3D time and absolute relativity! To all those who claim that ET civilizations are way ahead of us because they sometimes have millions of years of evolution to fall back on and we do not and that, as a consequence, we will never catch up with them, I would like to say that time is a fantastic springboard. The concept of temporal density can make millions of years disappear. A few years of research could thus easily eliminate this "head start" and allow us to take a technological leap and bridge the widened gap. Just look at the mobile telephone industry. It has efficiently dealt with bad communication networks allowing the emerging nations to reach the same communication level as developed nations almost overnight. Is not humanity rising to the space dream challenge?

We have just agreed to a scientific paradigm shift! Is not that reason enough for ETs to verify our motivations? Is that perhaps why we are so often visited, in particular since the discoveries made by fundamental physics? Since the discovery of nuclear energy?

Mankind is getting ready for a spectacular leap into the unknown!

CHAPTER 53

The source of disinformation

ALTHOUGH IT IS A SOMEWHAT limited approach, wary ufologists have the habit of distinguishing between two ethical groups of ETs depending on their conduct towards man (abductions) and animal (mutilations): "benevolent" and "hostile" ETs.

The so-called hostile ETs are motivated by reasons that need to be understood. Much has been said about a hypothetical conspiracy of the Illuminati, of a world government and in particular of the American authorities. There are numerous versions out there. No one understands exactly why such a conspiracy would come into existence unless it implies a hypothetical agreement: abductions against technology.

Considering their mental abilities, I wonder why aliens would ask permission from a government for something it has no control over! Especially when we take into account that the abductions (in fact an incorrect term) are often positive. An association between evil ETs and humans in positions of power is often mentioned in this respect. However, very few know why and what this association consists of, who it concerns and what the underlying reasons are. What follows is a perfect explanation of the present situation.

The current reality may seem complicated because numerous smoke screens have been put up, but this can be easily explained. Representatives of the conservative fringe of the American authorities, very few and assisted by certain foreign allies, broke a nuclear disarmament treaty with ETs that were non-aggressive at the time of the original agreement. Nuclear weapons are detrimental to ETs because the nuclear reactions produce catastrophic temporal collapses (earthquakes in their ST). When such nuclear explosions take place inside the sun they meet three criteria: they are permanent, controlled (degenerate energy levels) and mapped by billions of ETs, in the same way as all the stars. On Earth we take the necessary precautions to predict the occurrence of seismic activity as best we can. The Japanese are particularly famous for their skills. However, nuclear weapons can be used underground (causing genuine earthquakes), on Earth and in space, at any location. Once a bomb is no longer affected by Earth's gravity, it can travel very far into the cosmos. Therefore, they see us as an imminent potential threat.

In exchange for exotic technologies, these ETs, currently called hostile, ordered the authorities to disarm. Some are particularly vulnerable to nuclear arms as these affect very specific temporal fractals, the ones of these species. These men in authority pretended they would honor the treaty to obtain the alien technologies they indeed obtained, but only in part. Shadow men have been working in retro-engineering to understand how these technologies work ever since. In reality, the essence of this technological breakthrough is of a genetic nature. The military did not notice that the essence of this new kind of technology was missing in the transfer until it was too late.

To make a useful distinction, the UFO crash near Roswell in 1947 (a little more than two years after Hiroshima) was probably the result of an unfortunate maneuver. Perhaps a low number of fissile[125] cores caused the fission to stop. Unless the cause is Los Alamos (in the north of New Mexico), the first historic integration site of the bomb, a few kilometers away. Perhaps it was simply the first test of a subterranean nuclear explosion in the Nevada desert or a neighboring state. Considering the speed of these vessels, a few hundred kilometers will not make much of a difference. The UFO came to inspect the first human military base in possession of nuclear weapons. Indeed: Roswell! It happened to be American. A temporal collapse (excessive temporal pumping of the void towards the macroscopic scale) caused the vessel to lose mental helm control and to materialize.

In 1954 benevolent ETs officially warned Eisenhower to discontinue all nuclear programs to avoid a confrontation with those who were most affected and with whom it was preferable not to reach an agreement. They strongly urged him to follow their advice.[126] The choice for this Earth representative (the American president) is quite logical. He was the leader of the first nation to manufacture nuclear weapons. It had nothing to do with cultural preferences.[127] These ET allies did not offer anything in exchange except for spiritual cooperation. The president of the U.S. probably reflected upon this agreement. However, his conservative lieutenants would not hear of it.

Despite the situation, these men pursued their nuclear armament program, developed nuclear plants for civil purposes and antimatter experiments. After the terms of the "contract" had been breached, the hostile ETs initiated a lengthy abduction program, of which the U.S. was not surprisingly the main target. It became important for the hostile ETs to change this immoral and mentally immature human race. They felt they had the right to defend themselves on behalf of all ETs. In their own way, which does not necessarily correspond to our ethics, they therefore tried to render our race less belligerent on a cosmic scale by means of genetic modification. Recent human experiments have shown that we are already capable of doing so via the D2 genome. In a way, they have a well-developed sense of responsibility. Billions of ETs are affected by the nuclear dilemma. They feel entitled to deal with humans as they seem fit, because we proved unworthy of a treaty. ETs apply a strict logic. We should not forget that they represent the discipline of the incarnated mind. However, their spiritual level chains them to the paradigm of survival; in their case, the survival of their mental identity. Originally, they did not have the desire to distinguish between the humans and regarded us as equals on the galactic scale. Nevertheless, the parameters evolved.

The problem is that the people affected by this breach of agreement, currently the world's largest military-industrial complex, were out of line and are unwilling to acknowledge the danger they themselves created. They started applying the logic of outbidding and ended up in a suicidal vicious circle. Why have we accumulated such an astronomical number of nuclear weapons — thousands worldwide? Why have we acquired an arsenal capable of obliterating the Earth several times over when two bombs were enough to end a global conflict? For the simple reason that this arsenal is not entirely destined for us! Even today, if a new state produces but a single nuclear weapon, it upsets the world. By objectively evaluating the history of overarmament, reduction and nuclear disarmament, we take a step towards a better understanding of the situation. The human conspiracy thus consists of a double strategy:

1. Denying the existence of ETs to avoid having to answer the inevitable questions if their existence was admitted. This escape forward has resulted in our present defensive and offensive technologies, including the HAARP program (anti-UFO radar and ionic field emitter), the Star Wars program (powerful lasers

in space) and the Stargate program (remote viewing), of which the ET enemy can be the only possible and serious target.

2. Unconsciously convincing ourselves via one-sided science fiction series or films that ETs are our adversaries. This already started a long time ago. Their enemy should be our enemy. Consider series such as *The Invaders, V, The X Files, Stargate SG-1,* etc. Where do these series come from?

Conspiracies come knocking at our door by amplifying disinformation.[128] A technique called "spoon feeding" uses people who lack all credibility to see conspiracies and cry out against everything. This amalgamation of fact and fiction is nurtured to convince us that "those who speak of conspiracies are bizarre."

It is interesting to observe that the former U.S.S.R. — in possession of nuclear weapons and having developed research on the paranormal earlier and more extensively than the U.S. — also applies a specific strategy. The Ummo or Ummite letters, well known to ufologists because of their longevity, bear a striking resemblance to a large information-disinformation operation. Let us not forget that the Ummites claim to have made their first appearance in the 1950s, also to the Americans. The Soviets probably understood the importance of telepathic communication with ETs before the Americans did. I assume that the Ummites do exist and are in contact with the KGB. However, their letters are human creations as they are too academic in style and tainted by rhetoric in line with the ruling communism and technological state (Soviet science) of those days. The importance of such an operation is to let the CIA know that the KGB has its own ETs, and maybe their technology, and — more importantly — it has the ability to communicate with the public via letters conveyed in such a way that the true information is concealed behind presumed deliberate errors while hinting at the reality of this contact. The Ummites (I am certain that is not their real name) are ETs, but their letters are of human origin. I assume that the Soviets (currently the Russians) were and are far from knowing everything about their ET pen pals. That is also one of the objectives of these letters: to hear from those who also have contact and might know a little more about them. The freedom of expression in the West allows such a strategy to exist. Hence their appearance in Spain. Informed readers may remember that the Spanish community is known for its inclination towards the occult sciences, in particular in South America where the Ummites are actually very well known. Jordan Peña, who refuted the authenticity of the

Ummites after having promoted them for a long time, was also quite interested in esotericism.

In general, man is supposed to interpret ET communication attempts as more or less skilled threats of domination. This was the objective of a pseudo-project called Blue Beam[129] conducted in the 1960s and 1970s to anticipate a possible and authentic contact scenario, with the help of a misguided description, selling it off as an effective conquest strategy. That would take care of our judgment! Thus, the ultimate goal is to make us want the destruction of ETs ourselves, disguised as a constant fear. We must disregard the huge responsibility of the military-industrial complex that creates the excuses, needs and conditions of future armament markets itself. Is there any better publicity than a worldwide operating theatre? Still, it is generally known that ETs have never been openly aggressive. It requires a publicity campaign to invent a war, which is undoubtedly the most profitable industry of all times. The growing expertise it requires is synonymous with added value, i.e., substantial benefits. What do people with money want? Even more money! What do people with power want? More power!

Just a "minor detail." What they fail to tell us is that ETs are... ExtraTemporals, in other words immortals! They are like the human soul but at a much more advanced level because they embody at will! They have cast out death. In this respect, the film of the autopsy performed on an alien at Roswell approximately ten years ago — hundreds of millions of viewers around the world[130] were glued to the television screen — was one of the most prestigious and yet stunningly misinformative episodes. It killed three birds with one stone.

The film was sufficiently modified to resemble an authentic documentary while leaving behind visible breadcrumbs for professionals to reveal it as a hoax. The operation was meant to sow doubt to shatter the dream of extraterrestrial life more efficiently. Curiously, it was broadcast a few weeks before the American Congress issued a shattering report on ufological activities on U.S. territory and more in particular on the Roswell affair. This report sank into total oblivion, because the propaganda film filled with conjured up information on which everyone focused made it lose all credibility.

The second "bird" is much more subtle but most efficient. The promoters who thought up the "prank" used the images of an autopsy, even if it was fake, to send a subliminal message that no one has ever even considered denying: ETs can die! If they can die — a conclusion based on unconscious images installed in our minds for decades — we can fight them…and justify war somehow! You do not attack an invincible enemy.[131] That would be to deny the very essence of the war industry. People must therefore see dead ETs!

The third "bird" is of an even larger scope. The subliminal message conveyed was: "even extraterrestrials have not overcome death in spite of their extraordinarily superior intelligence and technology. In other words, you my dear Earthlings should not envision the survival of the soul or even less having long-term projects that could threaten ours. So do as you are told: consume!".

What do you think we could do against immortals? Another similar amplifying disinformation was thus implied: the Greys would be ill and in search of a genetic solution amongst humans. Hence the abductions. If we see them as mortals they remain vulnerable to canons. Who manufactures the canons? Who finances them via the so-called Black Budgets?[132] You, directly or indirectly! Don't you think that ETs mastered genetics a long time ago, or at the very least their own? They certainly would not need to perform so many abductions[133] to find a hypothetical genetic remedy. In fact, very resourceful disinformation agents pass on information to them about all human activities.

The combined practice of abductions of and genetic research on captured EBEs[134] is particularly unclear. Experts disregard that the genetic mutation of mankind is necessary to use alien technology by virtue of 3D time. The dematerialization and materialization of a vessel at will requires the body of its pilot to adapt to higher temporal densities in order to control the craft. The only solution is to have a much more complex DNA — larger number of helicoids and a different hydrogen link — able to manage the information flow once the physical body has dematerialized. The process equals that of the brain, the complexity of neural links of which allows us to tune into high time densities. An ET body is in itself a brain in terms of connectivity. We should note that the size of the encephalon in most ETs is exactly right for a perfect control of the mental information flow.

Our death is essentially caused by our body's inability to receive the higher cellular regeneration energies only an altered DNA could process. Research in this area is underway. This is the very essence of the American secret: controlling the essence of genetic engineering before any true spatio-temporal inclinations. That is the object of research on EBEs. We have seen that it is motivated by reasons that have little to do with the information available to us. This explains why the Americans do not use extraterrestrial technology on a large scale yet. It also explains why these secrets are protected by spreading rumors of the most extravagant revelations via trustworthy witnesses. When it comes to testimonies, we must first read between the lines. What is the message we are overlooking?

Immortality frightens the military industry. It marks the end of battle and domination. It is a paradigm of an unprecedented psychological power. Curiously, man wages war to avert death, to feel he has surpassed it. What would happen if we were immortal? Our perspective would shift 180 degrees. We would live and define life in a totally different way. What would we have to fight other than suffering or our inner selves? We would have the time to do and get everything we currently run after. However, we would also do our utmost to establish peace so that immortality does not prove a living hell. In essence, ETs are pacifist beings. Is it not true that physical incarnation, and even more reincarnation, should lead to inner peace and eventually immortality, whether it is physical or not?

In summary, the UFO concept is the joining of three aspects: materialization technique + ad hoc genetic structure + mind powers. These three elements come together in one single package: absolute relativity, of which 3D time is the main instrument. I cannot stress the meaning of these words enough.

Negative creatures tend to control beings in inferior realms — our approach towards animals, for instance. They are negative because they go against evolution. This is an outward movement (like the current sciences). Positive creatures constantly adapt and focus on superior realms. They respect the integrity of every life form. This happens when we apply personal development techniques to reach states of greater harmony with our surroundings. This is an inward movement (such as millennial mysticism). Superior realm beings (benevolent ETs and even highly spiritual humans that have passed on) can help us with this process if we prove ready. No one can learn if the desire is not already part of the soul. No one can help us if we do not ask. Neither evolved humans, nor even benevolent ETs. That is a universal law. It is futile to blame the ETs for the hardships that plague humanity. The trials and tribulations we bring about may become increasingly frequent and intense in nature if it is true that humanity refuses to accept, hopefully temporarily, a pacifist and well-known ET message: "Do you want us to appear?".

Intent is what makes a creature negative or positive. The words "negative" and "positive" do not have a moral connotation in this case, but mark the battle between interest (survival) and gratitude (cooperation).

Certain hostile ETs follow in the footsteps of mankind. If we show them the goodness of our hearts and abandon all thoughts of interest they will do the same, since they will be touched by our inner strength, they who search a means to free themselves from the logic of enslavement that weighs them down. In a way, mankind must grant them absolution for their actions by radically breaking free from the vicious circle of war kept intact by belligerent conservatives. Forgiving them gives us the chance to live in harmony, because they will see in us a model for liberation. If we can muster up the courage to do so, they will also dare to take that step towards self-realization.

However, if mankind does not break free from its war intoxication, the hostile ETs will be able to complete their program and may trigger, even in part, the self-destruction of humanity. After all, hostile ETs merely anticipate the destructive path that we take. After the conflicts and the planetary convulsions they will bring the future human civilization to Earth. Unless a miracle happens...

Conclusion

WE HAVE REACHED THE END of this book, but we have not even begun exploring the depths of the laws of the cosmos. We now know that nothing, absolutely nothing can top personal experience, not even academic arrogance. My hope is that the explanations I have proposed help you keep an open mind, become more understanding and even enlightened in our evolution towards something larger than ourselves. The stars are within reach, but will we answer the door?

We are going through a spectacular transition. Mankind is shifting from being stuck in old mental structures towards embracing a truly new paradigm. This "era of transfer" encompasses the following aspects:

1. technology transfer (matter)
2. transfer of concepts (mind)
3. transfer of individuals (soul).

Although this information is based on meetings with so-called extraterrestrial beings, it cannot only be characterized as ufological. 3D Time and absolute relativity, though still diamonds in the rough, could influence the scientific community. However, the acceptance of the general public is even more important. When UFOs are no longer associated with ufology, ETs will make sure the world is rocked to the core.

Endnotes

1. The study of UFOs (Unidentified Flying Objects).
2. The Trinity Site was located 150 kilometers from Alamogordo in a region called Jornada del Muerto (The Journey of Death).
3. Under the leadership of Leo Szilard, the same man who convinced Albert Einstein to write a letter to President Roosevelt expressing his support for the development of nuclear weapons.
4. *Pour la Science* magazine, the French edition of *Scientific American,* special edition on scientific geniuses centered on Richard Feynman.
5. The lunatic fringe of ufology is interested in extraterrestrial races. Unfortunately, there are many subdivisions.
6. Fabrice Bonvin at www.ovni.ch.
7. Kenneth Arnold pointed out that the vessels looked like "saucers bouncing off the water." Based on this expression, a journalist later invented the term "flying saucers." The term UFO was introduced later.
8. This is increasingly contradicted by relativist quantum mechanics.
9. *Pour la Science,* edition on scientific geniuses, Richard Feynman, page 13.
10. In Cartesian coordinates.
11. $1.62,10^{-35}$ meters.
12. Value of Planck time: $5.4,10^{-44}$ seconds.
13. The universe is only 0.135 billion centuries old.
14. $6.626,10^{-34}$ joules/second. This value is the smallest amount of energy possible or the smallest mechanical action possible.
15. Often used as a reference to the famous parapsychologist Charles Fort.
16. Mars is just the first planet to be explored.
17. "Enquête sur les ovni, voyage aux frontières de la science," Jean-Pierre Petit, éditions Albin Michel, 1992. J. P. Petit is the former Research Director of CNRS.
18. *La Recherche,* nr. 102, July/August 1979.

19. See the research conducted by the Institute of Noetic Sciences in the U.S. and Princeton University on random generators. Apparently, they are not so random.

20. It seems that parapsychology is a misleading term. Many (para) psychologists (who essentially study the so-called human sciences) do not have any significant background in fundamental physics. Therefore, they fail to recognize the most important aspects necessary to solve enigmas.

21. Science & Avenir, January 2004. Several extracts.

22. La Recherche, nr. 372, February 2004.

23. Definition provided by Chambers Dictionary: use of words, especially as an error in style, that repeat something already implied in the same statement. In other words, something is true, because it is true.

24. www.obs-besancon.fr/www/tf/equipes/vernotte/echelles/ech_intro.html.

25. Physician, Vice-Director of the department for matter sciences at the Atomic Energy Authority, Professor at a Polytechnic.

26. Science & Avenir (special issue), "les grands paradoxes de la science," June/July 2001.

27. La Recherche, nr. 8 (special issue), 2002.

28. Jean-Jacques Velasco, former Director of the Research Department of Rare Aerospace Phenomena, which is part of the National Centre for Space Research, estimates it is 13.5%. According to American research, the percentage is somewhat higher.

29. La Recherche, nr. 8 (special issue), 2002.

30. The inflation theory was introduced by Alan Guth.

31. Incorporated in the hypothetical M-theory.

32. Le cantique des quantiques, Jean-Pierre Pharabod, Sven Ortoli.

33. Independent scientists provide a technical assessment of an article prior to publication. The problem is that everyone knows each other in the small scientific world, in other words, mutual back-scratching.

34. Pour la Science, March 2000.

35. Atomic Energy Authority.

36. CNRS meetings, Sciences & Citoyens.

37. National Scientific Research Center.

38. Path integrals are to quantum mechanics what the principle of least action is to classical physics. When the value of action S approaches h (Planck's constant), all possible paths of a particle going from point a to point b contribute to the sum of probability amplitudes. In other words, there is no solution in which probability P (a,b) of the trajectory that minimizes action S can approach 1.

39. There are even imaginary numbers such as $\sqrt{-1}$.

40. "On the electrodynamics of moving bodies," Original published in Annalen der Physik, 17, 891–921, 1905.

41. He worked at the Federal Patent Office in Bern that received numerous patent requests for the electromagnetic systems of clocks.

42. La Recherche, edition on time (special issue).

43. There are two types of transformation of system variables (that keep the formulation of laws intact): global symmetries and local symmetries (e.g., Lorentz.)

44. This is a personal equation.
45. However, for J. Wheeler, the world-line of an electron allows it to go back in time. He called it the positron. Please note that Wheeler and Feynman proposed "retarded" and "advanced" solutions for Maxwell's equations in interactions between distant electrons that, in the traditional solution, use fields to travel. The advanced solution foresees that the effect precedes the cause, responding to the need to eliminate the resistance to the radiation that predicts the electron's self-interaction.
46. Neil Armstrong, who was the first man to land on the moon, spoke the famous words: "One small step for a man, a giant leap for mankind."
47. See "Time for explanations." It is said that chronons are time particles.
48. Do not forget that they are in fact wave functions.
49. The modern theory speaks of gauge fields that have designated carrier waves. Photons, for example, carry the gauge field of the electromagnetic force.
50. Where each fractal has a specific number of chronons, which increases in inverse proportion to space.
51. Classical hypothesis of an experiment at sea level at 1013.25 hectopascals.
52. In Hamiltonian H, this is impulse p.
53. Like so many others, such as the meson that represents the transformation from proton into neutron, and vice versa.
54. *La Recherche,* edition on time (special issue), 2001.
55. It is only unsurpassable because he believed in the concept of causality. Hence the idea of "superluminic tachyons."
56. Coherent Raman Effect of Incoherent Light (CREIL).
57. *La Recherche,* edition on time (special issue), 2003.
58. 10^{36} times weaker than strong interaction.
59. By distinguishing between a material and a spiritual world, the description is simplified on purpose. In reality there are many others.
60. *Science & Vie,* November 2003.
61. Legendary Star Wars character.
62. Original title: "O vozmozhnosti eksperimzental'ngo issledovaniya svoystv vremeni."
63. "What can be obtained from the substantial conception of time?" L.S. Shikhobalov, *World Scientific,* 1996, p. 174–221. See also www.chronos.msu.ru in "Library of electronic publications."
64. "Experiments on the change of the direction and rate of time motion," Vadim A. Chernobrov, in Proceedings of International Scientific Conference, *New Ideas in Natural Sciences,* 1996, St. Petersburg.
65. Vadim Chernobrov said he obtained a time flow rate change of 0.99 (T/Te).
66. www.chronos.msu.ru.
67. William Tifft is president of the Scientific Association for the study of time in physics and cosmology, which conducts time research.
68. "Three-dimensional quantized time in cosmology," W. Tifft, conference on time in physics and cosmology, Tucson, April 1996.
69. "Periodic time and the stationary properties of matter," A. Lehto, Chin., J. *Phys.* 28 (1990), 215–236.

70. The doubling theory was addressed in four subsequent scientific publications in the following international journal: "The Doubling Theory" by J. P. Garnier Malet, *International Journal of Computing Anticipatory System*. Published by the Centre for Hyperincursion and Anticipation in Ordered Systems. Ed. By D.M. Dubois, Institut de Mathématques, Liège University, Belgium, 1998 — Vol. 2, p. 132–15. 1999 — Vol. 3, p. 143–160. 2000 — Vol. 5, p. 39–61. 2001 — Vol. 10, p. 311–321.

71. "Changez votre futur par les ouvertures du temps," Lucile and Jean-Pierre Garnier Malet, JMG Editions.

72. www.garnier-malet.com.

73. www.garnier-malet.com.

74. Roger Penrose distinguished the following mathematical theories: the most efficient (superb: quantum mechanics, relativity, electromagnetism, quantum electrodynamics), those that have less predictive power and internal coherence (useful: electroweak theory, quantum chromodynamics, standard model of cosmology) and those that are elegant but yet to be validated against experimental data (tentative: string theory, noncommutative geometry for quantum cosmology).

75. "Epistémologie," Hervé Barreau, Que sais-je?

76. Does not Lagrangian or Hamiltonian mechanics ultimately express a relation between the ST used by an object and the one it could use?

77. "The character of Physical Law," BBC, 1965.

78. *Science & Avenir*, "Les grands paradoxes de la science" (special issue), June/July 2003.

79. The example of Achilles' race was used by Zeno.

80. Maslow defined a hierarchy of five needs and knew that humans seek to satisfy successfully higher needs: physiological, safety, love/belonging, esteem and actualization.

81. Countless war pilots reported small lights moving very fast that followed them closely during flights; hence the name foo fighter.

82. Very fast light particles as small as cherries or as big as a basketball have already been filmed flying above crop circles that are being formed.

83. Permanent temporal line of the fractal universe.

84. There are more potential connections in the brain than there are atoms in the universe.

85. "I believe only what I can see" then means "who I think I am is equivalent to what I have, for what I have must be separate from who I am." Materialism is based on this confusion between being and having.

86. *Pour la Science* (French edition of the *Scientific American*), February 2004.

87. Loop after loop in the ST.

88. Dunod Editions, Quai des sciences collection, October 2003.

89. It is interesting to note that Planck time (10^{-43} seconds) has been defined as Planck length (10^{-35} meters) divided by the speed of light. The fact that light speed is variable, as João Magueijo pointed out, simply means that Planck time is not the smallest time unit and, as a consequence, neither is Planck length.

90. "Enquête sur de mystérieux éclairs cosmiques," quote of Jacques Paul, p. 30, *Ciel & Espace*, nr. 413, October 2004.

91. In other words, descriptive differences.

92. I should say in his defense that Benoît Mandelbrot's fractals appeared in the 1960s, after the genius died.
93. God is always extratemporal. He is all the time at the same time!
94. Absolute value of an algebraic sum of a conjugation of spins that are lower than or equal to 2.
95. This is similar to the principle of gravitational lensing, because a galaxy located between the source and the Earth is also a spatio-temporal prism. Gravity alone does not explain the existence of twin quasars.
96. Bose-Einstein condensate.
97. It is a journey into a time density that cannot be accessed by our senses and measuring instruments.
98. *Science & Vie*, November 2003.
99. Artificial form of carbon C60.
100. The Lorentz transformation (if $x' = (x-vt) / (\sqrt{1-\beta^2})$, $y' = y$ and $z' = z$, then $t' = (t-(vx/c^2) / (\sqrt{1-\beta^2})$, where $\beta = v/c$ and c = the speed of light) is reduced to the Galilean transformation (if $x' = x-vt$, $y' = y$ and $z' = z$, then $t' = t$) for very small velocities v compared to light speed c, or by ensuring that the latter tends towards zero.
101. Neutrons were discovered by Chadwick in 1932. In fact they are protons due to a transformation of SU(3).
102. See www.ap.univie.ac.at/users/Klaus.Hor...ch/décohérence/
103. E=hv, where h is Planck's constant and v is the frequency. Energy E diminishes as the frequency is lowered.
104. The Compton wavelength is $\gamma c = h/mc$, where h is Planck's constant, c is the speed of light and m is mass.
105. See: "On a perdu la moitié de l'univers," Jean-Pierre Petit, former research director at CNRS, Albin Michel, 1997.
106. $S = k.\ln.\Omega$.
107. La Recherche, 2003.
108. Professor of theoretical physics at the University of Jerusalem.
109. Jacob Bekenstein called it level X.
110. The existence of micro black holes was suggested by the Englishman Stephen Hawking.
111. Large Hadron Collider.
112. The European Organization for Nuclear Research just celebrated its fiftieth anniversary. It is remarkable that its establishment coincided with the first sightings of modern UFOs.
113. *Science & Avenir*, June 2002.
114. Gra for gravitational, Va for vacuum, Star for star.
115. Countless eyewitnesses have confirmed that the interior volume of ET vessels is much larger than their size suggests. High temporal densities cause the perceived volume to increase. This also happens to the astral body!
116. The "nuts and bolts" vision of ufology.
117. The degree of paralysis depends on the intensity of the temporal field affecting the eyewitness. The same applies to physical phenomena that vary depending on distance and temporal dilation. Therefore, there are many possible situations.

118. Appearing in general before the harvest.
119. Original French term for crop circles.
120. Lab tests have shown that electric fields higher than 30 kilovolts/meter cause plants to stand vertically upwards (ref. Paul-Sabatier University of Toulouse).
121. Apparitions of the Virgin Mary through a medium are definitely fake. She appears as an entity only to psychically qualified eyewitnesses (innocent children, for instance).
122. High Frequency Active Auroral Research Program.
123. Of which the nerve fibers send a considerable amount of information.
124. In a hypnosislike state, patients are told that a certain type of medication will restore their health. This goal can be achieved partially or totally as the patient is more or less convinced of the suggestion. The different results depend, of course, on the physical problem, but also on the power of suggestion. Some argue that up to ninety percent of all medications administered in hospitals are placebos.
125. Definitely below the critical mass of uranium 235.
126. Thanks to the possibilities of time travel, ETs should have known that the Americans would probably land on the moon and have the possibility to send a nuclear warhead into space.
127. Please note that every state in possession of nuclear weapons has been visited by ETs on numerous occasions. Sightings were recently reported in Iran, China and India.
128. Expression used in the COMETA report, written in France by former auditors of the French National Defense Research Institute. It describes the national security threat posed by UFOs.
129. Four-phased high-tech hoaxes suggesting the existence of a conspiracy, practiced by fundamentalist Christian movements. Essentially based on illusions and hallucinations produced by very elaborate techniques aimed at establishing a new world order.
130. In France, this film was discovered during the broadcast of *Mystères* presented by Jacques Pradel. It cost him his television career; a very high price to pay. As a consequence, other journalists were scapegoated for conveying positive messages about UFOs. UFOs subsequently disappeared completely from French television, except for some mockery of the UFO mystery.
131. A remarkable story emerged in the U.S. On 21 August 1955, in Kelly, Kentucky, the Sutton family (eleven people) tried to shoot humanoids that had entered their farm. However, none of them died. The bullets could not hurt them. The description of these ETs is similar to that of the Grey (the ETs featured in the autopsy of the Roswell alien).
132. National budgets that often run into millions of dollars without any supervision by democratic institutions.
133. According to estimates, between several thousands and hundreds of thousands.
134. Extraterrestrial Biological Entities. From a biological perspective, a dead EBE is of no interest. Everything a body contains can be discovered by applying the proper technical means to a living creature. In research, a good EBE is therefore a living EBE!

Notes

Notes

Notes

Notes

Notes

Notes

Notes

Notes

Notes

Notes